OLD TIMES THERE
SHOULD NOT BE FORGOTTEN

OLD TIMES THERE
SHOULD NOT BE FORGOTTEN
CULTURAL GENOCIDE IN DIXIE

LESLIE R. TUCKER, PH.D.

SHOTWELL PUBLISHING

COLUMBIA, SOUTH CAROLINA

Old Times There Should Not Be Forgotten: Cultural Genocide in Dixie -
Copyright © 2020 by Les Tucker

Produced in the REPUBLIC OF SOUTH CAROLINA by

SHOTWELL PUBLISHING, LLC

Post Office Box 2592

Columbia, South Carolina 29202

www.ShotwellPublishing.com

Cover Image: Members of the Egbert J. Jones Camp of the United Confederate Veterans in Huntsville, Alabama (1928) Retrieved from the Alabama Department of Archives and History

Cover Design: Hazel's Dream / Boo Jackson

ISBN: 978-1-947660-27-4

10 9 8 7 6 5 4 3 2 1

CONTENTS

PREFACE

MERRIAM-WEBSTER DEFINES ETHNOCIDE as "the deliberate destruction of an ethnic culture." Encyclopedia.com defines it as ". . . acts that contribute to the disappearance of a culture, even though its bearers are not physically destroyed. Acts of ethnocide include denying a group the right to speak its language, practice its religion, teach its traditions and customs, create art, maintain social institutions, or preserve its memories and histories." The term is most often used in the discussion of indigenous peoples, but the above definitions do not limit it to such. The root of the word suggests that it includes all ethnic groups.

The question as to whether the South qualifies as an ethnic group is another subject of debate which could fill a book. I present a quote by Dr. Clyde Wilson, in a statement he made in a court case in South Carolina, "Speech, religion, music, manners, and cuisine are the universal markers of ethnic distinction." Max Weber maintained that ethnic groups were künstlich (artificial, i.e., a social construct) because they were based on a subjective belief in shared Gemeinschaft (community). Secondly, this belief in shared Gemeinschaft did not create the group; the group created the belief.

Even though UNESCO's target for discussions in the Declaration of San Jose in 1981 was indigenous peoples, I see it as applying to all ethnic groups. In this document they said, "Ethnocide means that an ethnic group is denied the right to enjoy, develop and transmit its own culture and its own language." They then state, "This involves an extreme form of massive violation of human rights and, in particular, the right to ethnic groups to respect for their cultural identity." The French ethnologist Robert Jaulin stated ". . . ethnocide would be the systematic destruction of the thought and the way of life of people different from those who carry out this enterprise of destruction. Whereas the genocide assassinates the people in their body, the ethnocide kills them in their spirit."

My primary objective in writing this book is that I hope to correct a great injustice which is being committed against those of us who are proud of our Southern heritage. Our Southern history is being erased at an unbelievable pace. This is being done because of the mistaken belief that Confederate history stands for nothing but slavery and racism. There are tens of millions of Americans descended from Confederate veterans. What is happening now is a wrong being committed against the dead, as well as those of us who are descended from Confederates. Those honoured dead are part of our history, and thus part of our heritage, and thus part of our identity. Those responsible believe that they are striking a blow against racism. They claim to be concerned about the sensitivity of African-Americans. It appears that they have no sensitivity toward those Southerners who came before us, nor for those of us who are proud to be their descendants.

I do not condone slavery or racism. The only crime I am guilty of is that I am proud of my ancestors. Those who like to bring up slavery are careful to blame the South for all the ills of slavery, while ignoring the part Africans, Yankees, and other foreign powers played in the system of slavery. Racism is a relatively recent term, usually reserved for disparaging political opponents. Using our cultural values to criticize people from a different era is called presentism, and is not considered a valid historical perspective. It is much more accurate to see people in the past as a product of their times. If we use today's values concerning race, we would find the vast majority of the citizens of the 19th Century would be seen as "racists."

> I will say then that I am not, nor ever have been, in favor of bringing about in any way the social and political equality of the white and black races, that I am not nor ever have been in favor of making voters or jurors of negroes, nor of qualifying them to hold office, nor to intermarry with white people; and I will say in addition to this that there is a physical difference between the white and black races which I believe will forever forbid the two races living together on terms of social and political equality. And inasmuch as they cannot so live, while they do remain together there must be the position of superior and inferior, and I as much as any other man am in favor of having the superior position assigned to the white race. [1] — Abraham Lincoln

Those responsible for destroying Confederate symbols and monuments seem to think that they are striking a blow against racism. They want to erase history rather than study and learn from it. It is becoming apparent that they seek to destroy all Western, Christian culture and history. They now seek the removal of monuments ranging from Christopher Columbus to Thomas Jefferson to Father Junipero Serra. It is a great injustice to condemn people from a different era because they do not meet today's cultural standards. To

---

1 Walter D. Kennedy, *Myths of American Slavery* (Gretna:Pelican,2003), 164

erase history accomplishes nothing. Those who came before us deserve respect, they are part of what we are today. To condemn those of our past is to condemn our cultural identity, and thus our ethnicity.

Those who are erasing our past are trying to control the way we view history, and thus the way we view the world. This is not only for today but for future generations. They are creating a world very much like the one described by George Orwell in his novel *1984*:

> The past is whatever the records and memories agree upon. And since the Party is in full control of all records, and equally in full control of the minds of its members, it follows that the past is whatever the Party chooses to make it. It also follows that though the past is alterable, it never has been altered in any specific instance. For when it has been recreated in whatever shape is needed at the moment, then this new version is the past, and no different past can ever have existed.[2]

Those attacking symbols of the Old South claim they are offended. Many Southerners have surrendered to this notion for the sake of harmony. I am not one of them. I am offended by their attitude. These are the symbols of my ancestors and my heritage, and I feel they are saying my ancestors do not deserve to be remembered and honored. I am not only offended by this anti-Southern bigotry, but I believe that the North was wrong. The North waged an unconstitutional and barbaric war of invasion. Their armies raped, pillaged and plundered indiscriminately. The victims were white, black, red, and brown, and they all suffered from the brutal invasion. Most Confederate soldiers did not own slaves. They were fighting to defend their homes, and for the right to live under a government of their own choosing. Just like the patriots of 1776, those of 1861 fought for the principle of self-government. I am an unreconstructed Southerner. We may have lost the war, but that does not mean that we were wrong.

The guardians of American culture tell us we are a diverse people. We celebrate Cinco de Mayo, Saint Patrick's Day, or Kwanza. African-American, Irish-American, and Native-American are all acceptable heritages to celebrate. Southern heritage, however, is deemed evil and we are expected to be ashamed of it. African-American should include the many, slave and free, who fought and aided the Confederate cause. Those who were tortured and died defending their homes and supporting the war effort are heroes the same as those of any skin color. We see a different story, as they are an embarrassment to the keepers of cultural diversity and must be marginalized or explained away. Their dignity is what really suffers in the attempt to demonize everything Confederate.

---

2 George Orwell, *1984* (New York: Harcourt, Brace, Jovanovich, Inc.,1949), 176

This course of cultural genocide, or ethnocide, is wrong. Their distortion of history began with propaganda efforts during the war as the North tried to justify its war of invasion. Today this effort continues, and the pace is increasing. My intent here is to write an outline of Southern history, which will put this all in perspective. There are those who will disagree, which is often the case with history. I will show that there is an alternative view to that being espoused by the destroyers. I believe their view of history is distorted and thus it is wrong to act on their interpretation. The War to Prevent Southern Independence, usually called the American Civil War, has thus been the most controversial topic in American history, generating much debate.

The war was a contest over the nature of our federal government. Southern defeat meant a change in our government, and Reconstruction was a dark time in our history. Eventually the wounds began to heal and the states once more became a union. Not all was forgotten or forgiven, but those in the North put their energies elsewhere, and those in the South learned to accept defeat and began rebuilding. The surviving veterans organized the United Confederate Veterans and the Sons of Confederate Veterans, and the ladies of the South created the United Daughters of the Confederacy. Together they dedicated themselves to the memory of those who sacrificed so much for their homeland and their people. They built monuments, published memoirs, and worked together to see that the true history of the South would be preserved for future generations. They often stated that they were aware that history is written by the victors. They wanted to make sure that their point of view was preserved for future generations. Some still spoke of "damn Yankees" and others looked down on Southern "hillbillies." Yet, on both sides of the Mason-Dixon Line they learned to accept each other. United once again, they fought together in the Spanish-American War, two World Wars, as well and Korea and Vietnam.

This spirit of unity allowed the South to honour its past. Figures as diverse as FDR, Dwight Eisenhower, and Winston Churchill praised Confederates. JFK praised John C. Calhoun. Even during the time of Martin Luther King, Jr., honouring Confederates was accepted. One reason this changed was the misuse of Confederate images, especially the Battle Flag, by many white Southerners in response to the Civil Rights Movement. Though African-Americans had made strides toward equality, they still were often denied basic rights such as voting, educational opportunities, and access to some public facilities. The successes of the Civil Rights Movement led to changing attitudes among most white Southerners. Those who still misused the Battle Flag for racist motives were reduced to a small number of people rarely seen.

Fortunately, it is hard to find social injustice today, and the Civil Rights Movement had to find a reason to continue its existence. A host of pathologies have followed on the heels of the movement's successes. Drugs, gang violence, lack of educational opportunities, and single parent families are found in many inner city areas where African-Americans live. Most government solutions have failed, or worse exacerbated the problems, making them difficult to address. Thus we have the 1991 resolution from the National Association for the Advancement of Colored People claiming that the "tyrannical evil symbolized in the Confederate Battle Flag is an abhorrence to all Americans and decent people of this country, and indeed, the world and is an odious blight upon the universe."[3] It is much easier to condemn an inanimate object than to solve pressing problems.

Booker T. Washington, the great African-American educator, said:

> There is another class of coloured people who make a business of keeping the troubles, the wrongs, and the hardships of the Negro race before the public. Having learned that they are able to make a living out of their troubles, they have grown into the settled habit of advertising their wrongs — partly because they want sympathy and partly because it pays. Some of these people do not want the Negro to lose his grievances, because they do not want to lose their jobs.

It seems things have not changed. Thus, we have increasing attacks on Confederate symbols and monuments. These symbols cannot hurt anyone. Such things did not have any impact on the Civil Rights Movement in the past. The only complaint against these objects today is the claim that such things are offensive. Being offended is not a good reason to deny others their heritage. Claiming to be offended is often no more than an excuse to hate.

I can recall the 1988 reenactment of the Battle of Honey Springs. This was the largest battle fought in Indian Territory during the war. It was the battle where the First Kansas Colored fought, before the battle at Fort Wagner which was made famous in the movie *Glory*. It took place near the present location of the all black town of Rentiesville, Oklahoma, the home of the famous African-American historian John Hope Franklin. I can remember how some of the blacks who lived in the area approached not only those in the blue, but also those of us wearing grey Confederate uniforms and carrying Confederate flags. They did not act offended, but only talked to us about history. There was no animosity from any of those present. They spoke with pride about how the battle took place on land that they owned, or land that they grew up on. I can remember how we sometimes spent the evenings at the Down Home Blues club in Rentiesville, and how we enjoyed the music of DC Miner who also came from that town. We all enjoyed the hospitality of the community and I do not recall any disapproval of the flag that we carried. I saw no conflicts between the blacks who lived in the community and the Confederate reenactors. This seemed typical before 1990.

---

3 NAACP Resolutions, 1991.

The attack on innocent worshippers at Emanuel African Methodist Episcopal Church in Charleston, South Carolina, escalated attacks on the Battle Flag in recent years. Wal-mart, Amazon, and ebay were among the retailers to decide not to sell merchandise which displayed the flag. Perhaps the most symbolic blow came from the Southern Baptists. They passed resolution 7 in 2016, which stated,

> That we acknowledge both the importance of remembering family heritage and sacrifice, as well as the urgency of pursuing a unified Body of Christ and racial healing in America.

They then concluded,

> RESOLVED, That we call our brothers and sisters in Christ to discontinue the display of the Confederate battle flag as a sign of solidarity of the whole Body of Christ, including our African-American brothers and sisters.

The Civil Rights Movement has morphed into identity politics. If one can be shown to be a victim, political benefit can come to a politician or party addressing the worries of the victim. Identity politics starts from analyses of oppression to recommend a restructuring of the existing society. As stated in the *Stanford Encyclopedia of Philosophy* relating to identity politics, "The second half of the twentieth century saw the emergence of large-scale political movements—second wave feminism, Black Civil Rights in the U.S., gay and lesbian liberation, and the American Indian movements, for example—based in claims about the injustices done to particular social groups." There are those who criticize Identity Politics for being destructive to a unified country, but it does appear to have played a major role in the 2016 election.

The Southern Poverty Law Center, SPLC, had assumed a leadership role in attacks against the Confederate aspects of our Southern heritage before those events in 2015, but they have escalated their attacks since then. They produced a publication titled *Whose Heritage?: Public Symbols of the Confederacy*. In it they listed 1,503 symbols of Confederate heritage which should be eliminated. This included 718 monuments and statues, 109 public schools named for Confederate icons, 80 counties named for Confederates, 9 official Confederate holidays in six states, and 10 U.S. military bases. They assume, in their ignorance, that a majority of Americans view Confederate symbols as offensive. Yet in poll after poll, a majority of Americans in the South do not have a negative view of Confederate symbols. A national poll by liberal news outlet CNN found a majority viewed the Confederate Battle flag as a symbol of Southern pride. A poll on Mississippi's state flag, which incorporates the Confederate Battle Flag in its design, found not only a majority in favour of the current flag, but 30% of African-Americans favoured it. Apparently, only the opinions of African-Americans who toe the party line are of value.

This view is typical of those who wish to destroy our heritage, and then our civilization. Facts do not matter to these people, only the promotion of the narrative. Attacks on Confederate symbols serve to marginalize a significant portion of the Southern white population. There is a growing percentage of Southern whites willing to abandon defense of Confederate symbols. Those who do not deny their heritage become targets for the SPLC and other Liberal Revisionist who label them "neo-Confederates," or those who are believers of the "Lost Cause myth."

Anti-Confederate thinking has become part of identity politics. The SPLC publication is titled *Whose Heritage?*, with the idea that Confederate symbols are only for white Southerners. They stated,

> The effort to remove them is about more than symbolism. It's about starting a conversation about the values and beliefs shared by a community. It's about understanding our history as a nation.

The conclusion is that they are saying the symbols are not "shared by a community," and that they are interested only in "our history as a nation." They express no objection to African-American symbols which are not shared by all. The SPLC seems to have no problem with Black History Month, Miss Black America, or the Black Caucus in Congress.

It is unfortunate that they choose what constitutes African-American history. Blacks served honourably in many Confederate Army units, most as slaves, but many as free men. Those who remained loyal, helped keep the home front safe and worked at their jobs were essential to the maintenance of the Confederate Armies. They also suffered, were raped, tortured, and starved along with all in the Confederacy. This is part of African-American history, too. In conclusion I will share a speech, given by an ex-Confederate general, which illustrates how the truths of history can contradict the revisionists' tale. Nathan Bedford Forrest was invited to speak to the Independent Order of the Pole-Bearers in Memphis. This was a civic organization, and the invitation was to help foster peace between the races in Memphis. Miss Lou Lewis, daughter of one of the officers of the organization, presented flowers to Gen. Forrest, who made a short speech:

> Ladies and Gentlemen I accept the flowers as a memento of reconciliation between the white and colored races of the southern states. I accept it more particularly as it comes from a colored lady, for if there is any one on God's earth who loves the ladies I believe it is myself. (Immense applause and laughter.) I came here with the

jeers of some white people, who think that I am doing wrong. I believe I can exert some influence, and do much to assist the people in strengthening fraternal relations, and shall do all in my power to elevate every man to depress none. (Applause.) I want to elevate you to take positions in law offices, in stores, on farms, and wherever you are capable of going. I have not said anything about politics today. I don't propose to say anything about politics.

You have a right to elect whom you please; vote for the man you think best, and I think, when that is done, you and I are freemen. Do as you consider right and honest in electing men for office. I did not come here to make you a long speech, although invited to do so by you. I am not much of a speaker, and my business prevented me from preparing myself. I came to meet you as friends, and welcome you to the white people. I want you to come nearer to us. When I can serve you I will do so. We have but one flag, one country; let us stand together. We may differ in color, but not in sentiment Many things have been said about me which are wrong, and which white and black persons here, who stood by me through the war, can contradict. Go to work, be industrious, live honestly and act truly, and when you are oppressed I'll come to your relief. I thank you, ladies and gentlemen, for this opportunity you have afforded me to be with you, and to assure you that I am with you in heart and in hand. (Prolonged applause.)

Gen. Forrest again thanked Miss Lewis and gave her a kiss on the cheek. This was an unheard of act in 1875, and his appearance went a long way to improving relations between the races in Memphis. These African-Americans, along with others across the South, wanted to keep the good relations they had with their neighbors. They helped fund and dedicate monuments, they marched in Gen, Forrest's funeral by the hundreds, and they helped rebuild the South. Their descendants and the revisionists dishonour them when they trivialize their contributions and insult their motives. The hate of the social justice warriors stands in stark contrast to those who went to work rebuilding the South.

INTRODUCTION

WHILE OTHERS ARE HONOURED with various holidays and festivals, Southerners are supposed to stand by as all signs of our Confederate heritage are erased from the pages of American history. In 1996, I visited the California high school from which I graduated. As we entered the auditorium, the principal, a former classmate of mine, pointed out a display of more than one hundred flags and boasted that they represented the diversity of his student body. I did not see a Confederate flag, nor would I ever expect to see one. It is not just that our heritage and ancestors are ignored, but that they are often vilified. There is an obvious limit to the embrace of diversity

My main goal is to help people see how wrong this is. What those who attack us are doing goes beyond just a difference of opinion; they are participating in cultural genocide. Tens of millions of Americans are descended from Confederate Veterans and others who supported the cause, and helped to construct the memorials to their loved ones. These Southern families were among the same families who established the United States of America. No better example of this is a man who has become a target of attacks himself, Robert E. Lee. His father, Lighthorse Harry Lee, was an officer in the Revolutionary War. Two members of the Lee family signed the Declaration of Independence, and several others served in the early governments of Virginia and the United States. The main topic which taints all of Southern history is the war. Therefore, the reasons for the war will be the focus of this work. Southern heritage is about the Southern experience, both cultural and political.

Those who attack Confederate heritage are not just one group. While many African-Americans are involved in the attacks, the largest group is liberal whites, suffering from white guilt. Wikipedia defines white guilt as "the individual or collective guilt felt by some white people for harm resulting from racist treatment of ethnic minorities by other white people both historically and currently." Their empathy for victims of racism causes them to say Confederate symbols, especially the Battle Flag, are offensive. They do not care that we find their attacks on our heritage offensive. Neither are they deterred by numerous polls showing that many black people do not find Confederate monuments and symbols offensive, but merely a part of history.

My first objective is to outline Southern history and to show it in its true diversity. Many revisionists historians reject much traditional   interpretation of Southern history as simply a defense of slavery. Many who attack Confederate heritage have endeavored to make the Confederacy the scapegoat for many ills. I believe that an accurate history will go far in understanding why this is a continuation of a myth born of Northern attempts to justify a brutal war.

My second objective is to inventory the relevant interpretations of the Liberal Revisionist historians. These historians, whom I refer to as *Librevs*, contribute to the mistaken idea that Confederate history is all about slavery and oppression. They function as the old royal court historians, serving the interests of their masters. Historians can agree on a given set of facts, yet come to different conclusions on what those facts represent. Many *Librevs* are not always the objective intellectuals that they would like us to believe they are. They may insist on one interpretation of history, to the exclusion of any others, and often to the exclusion of basic facts. They play an active role in the destruction of Confederate heritage.

My third objective is to correct some of the common myths which some defenders of the South have in their understanding of American history. Inaccurate rhetoric will not counter the Librev's arguments. We must respond with factual history, both Southern and American history in general. We can concede they are right when they correctly present facts, but we should challenge them when they are wrong.

My fourth objective is to show that we should not deny historical facts, such as the existence of slavery. We must strive to present a true history, however, which they often fail to do. Slavery was practiced in many parts of the world at the time of the founding of the United States. Africans enslaved other Africans, selling them to Arab, European and American slave traders. Most ships in the American slave trade were from New England ports. Slave labour was used in the construction of many of the cities on the East coast of the United States. Few slaves in the North were ever freed, but mostly sold South. Yet despite these facts, the South is tarred with the broad brush of slavery.

We should not disown our ancestors because they lived in a different culture than we do. It is wrong to judge the past through the prism of the present. We may not like some actions of those in the past, but it is wrong to erase a heritage because of that. What will future generations think of our actions today? We can only hope that they will respect the good that we accomplish and understand that we are the product of the times in which we live. It is interesting that those who today preach diversity and acceptance of people of different cultures do not extend these feelings of acceptance to those who lived in the past.

My fifth objective is to include the history of black Southerners.   A major excuse used for erasing our past is to assert that Confederate history excludes black Southerners and should be banned in public areas. The name of the Southern Poverty Law Center (SPLC) publication that advocates the removal of our history is Whose Heritage? They believe that Confederate heritage is not for all

Southerners. This reasoning is invalid. Memorials to Martin Luther King, Jr. may be more meaningful to black Southerners than to whites, but that is no reason to ban them from public places. Neither should we remove those memorials which are more meaningful to white Southerners. We can have streets named after King as well as others named after Lee. In Montgomery there are memorials to MLK, and there is also the first White House of the Confederacy. Both are part of the history of that city, and both are part of the history of the South. One may be of greater significance to one segment of the population than the other, but both are part of the history of all of us.

My sixth objective is to explore why there is an apparent decline in the numbers of unreconstructed Southerners. Healing the wounds of war was slow, yet as those who suffered first-hand the results of the war passed from the scene, interest in the cause faded somewhat. Many who lament the attacks on our Southern heritage, and even have pride in their ancestors, still accept the destruction. If all those who share Confederate ancestors would stand up for the truth, our heritage would not be disappearing so rapidly.

LIBREVS

So, who are the *Librevs*? The short answer is that they are those professional historians who are liberal and engage in the revision of American history to confirm their liberal bias. They have made revisionism a bad word to many Americans. History is written by the winners, everyone realizes this. This is the main reason why those who fought for independence in 1776 look better in history books than those who remained loyal to England. Likewise, this is the main reason why those who fought for the North are portrayed more favorably than those who fought for the South.

Librevs also benefit from a major problem in America—the liberal bias in academia. The most influential scholars come from Harvard, Yale, and other prestigious Northern universities. This has created a Northern slant with a liberal bias. Academic liberalism has become a self-justifying system. Those who step too far over the line of liberalism can never hope to be accepted into one of these institutions, and therefore non-liberal views will never be incorporated into academia. The academic elite equate liberalism with intelligence and conservative views with ignorance. Unfortunately, this has spilled over to secondary and primary education, and to the general public, even in the South. Southern universities have surrendered to it. This liberal bias has been shaped by white guilt and has given us political correctness.

A historiography is quickly growing around the issue of Confederate heritage. Some books defending our heritage have been written, including a more traditional view of the South in Mike Grissom's *Southern by the Grace of God*, and more activist books such as James R. and Walter D. Kennedy's *The South Was Right!*, among many offerings. Liberal revisionists have also entered the fray. Though they claim objectivity, they all conclude it is time to furl the flag forever. This would include Tony Horwitz with *Confederates in the Attic*, David Goldfield's *Still Fighting the Civil War*, and K. Michael Prince with *Rally Round the Flag, Boys!: South Carolina and the Confederate Flag*. Anyone interested in preserving our heritage should read these books. Know the enemy.

A recent big seller whose main objective is discrediting our heritage is *The Confederate and Neo-Confederate Reader: The "Great Truth" about the "Lost Cause,"* edited by James W. Loewen and Edward H. Sebesta. This is not a history book, but a platform for the authors to promote their belief that "neo-Confederates" perpetuate racism in America. This book is nothing short of an addendum to an earlier publication, *Neo-Confederacy: A Critical Introduction*. This was a collection of essays by assorted SPLC authors. Both books attack "neo-Confederates," especially the Sons of Confederate Veterans (SCV), and to a lesser degree the United Daughters of the Confederacy (UDC). Loewen and Sebesta significantly influenced James McPherson, the Pulitzer Prize winning historian considered by many as *the* expert on Civil War history. Together, these three men are among the most important enemies of those proud of their Southern heritage.

This book has had an unjustifiable influence on the history profession. From academia it is spreading into secondary education and becoming part of the new American heritage. The book should be of concern to anyone who is proud of their Southern heritage and the Confederate soldiers and citizens who fought to protect their homeland. These books are being given more attention than they deserve because they confirm the prevailing bias against the South and its struggle for independence. The two books mentioned above identify a common enemy which is included in the title of each, "neo-Confederates." Just because we are proud of our Southern heritage does not mean that we should be diminished in the eyes of our fellow Americans.

Librevs have started using the term "Lost Cause Myth" to describe the belief of those who think the South was right. I find that term offensive when it is used to discredit those who do not accept their revisionist views. *Librevs* have identified Southern patriotic groups such as the Sons of Confederate Veterans and the United Daughters of the Confederacy as defenders of the "Lost Cause Myth." Just because the Southern people were defeated does not mean they were wrong.

The mothers, daughters, and widows of the Confederate soldiers sacrificed much when they literally collected their pennies to construct monuments to their sons, brothers, fathers, and sweethearts, who bravely defended their homes from foreign invaders. We should feel shame every time one of these memorials is destroyed in the name of political correctness. These people were our ancestors, our culture, and our heritage. They need not be sacrificed for the sake of historical accuracy or political correctness. I find it offensive when the pride we have in our heritage is dismissed as a myth. I also find it offensive to imply that those who believe in the nobility of the Confederate soldier are reduced to a lunatic fringe labeled "neo-Confederates." If the celebration of our heritage offends the *Librevs*, I want to point out to them that some of us find their views and actions offensive.

There are professional historians who do not fit into the *Librevs'* category. Among the published and well-known historians and scholars who have been attacked for having pro-Confederate views are Grady McWhiney and Thomas DiLorenzo. There are others such as Gary Gallagher, Marc Egnal, or the English historian Mary-Susan Grant, who have no Confederate ties and who do not accept the universal condemnation of all that is Confederate

The Abbeville Institute, an organization composed of professional scholars, rejects the hatred promoted in the books of Loewen and Sebesta. The Abbeville Institute's own explanation for why they were founded is that "in a healthy society, education is the thoughtful enjoyment of a cultural inheritance." They speak of a culture war in which "if Southern tradition is mentioned at all, it is usually vilified as little more than a mask for racism." If this is not the purpose of Loewen and Sebesta and others in the SPLC, then they are leaving the wrong impression with many of us. The well-known historian Eugene Genovese, who was "a northerner and a man of the left" for most of his career, said "Rarely these days, even on southern campuses, is it possible to acknowledge the achievements of the white people of the South . . . To speak positively about any part of this southern tradition is to invite charges of being a racist and an apologist for slavery and segregation." He continued speaking of the attempts of the "academic elite to strip young white southerners, and arguably black southerners as well, of their heritage, and, therefore, their identity." This is what I resent the most and the main reason I am writing this book. "They are being taught to forget their forebears or to remember them with shame."[4]

LIBREV ISSUES

There are five main topics that the *Librevs* take a position on which are relevant to the defense of our heritage. The *Librevs* are professional, educated, and skilled historians, but I take exception with them on these issues. These issues will be discussed in more detail throughout the book.

The first topic is the question of Southern distinctiveness, which *Librevs* see as related to the "Lost Cause Myth." They argue that the Confederate flag and other symbols are not part of our heritage since we did not have a heritage before the war. I do not agree with this idea. While the terms North and South did not mean the exact same thing before the war as they did after, there were still cultural differences between the two regions. Statesmen such as George Washington and Thomas Jefferson had commented on the difference between the populations of the two regions. Grady McWhiney wrote about what is called the Celtic Fringe theory. To simplify, he said that the difference between North and South existed in the British Isles before the American colonies were founded. It dates back to the conflict between the Celtic population that lived there before the Roman occupation and the Anglo-Saxon arrival.

4. The Abbeville Institute, http://www.abbevilleinstitute.org/about.php, 5/22/02

The second topic has been a big question in American history since 1861—the cause of the war. *Librevs* still argue that the Civil War was fought over slavery, and of course, this is the primary reason they view the flag as a symbol of slavery. The SPLC has gone so far as to say that is all that the Confederacy was about. I disagree with this simplistic cant.

The third topic is the attitude that North is morally, intellectually and culturally superior to the South. Since the first Puritans, to the days of the Northern abolitionists, to the present academic elite, there is a tendency to view the South as backward. Northern liberals seem to have developed an attitude of self-righteousness, and I suspect that they are not quite as open-minded as they claim to be. Southern morality is based on strong religious views. These are not generally accepted by liberal society as legitimate, and are often condemned for not being politically correct. The *Librevs* assume Northern secular humanist morality to be superior to Southern religious morality, but there are those who do not accept their assumption.

The fourth topic is the nature of Reconstruction. Since *Librevs* view the war as a moral crusade to end slavery, they naturally see the military occupation and carpetbag governments in the South after the war as agents of moral change. Though there were good people who came South after the war to ease the former slaves' transition to liberty, most of those coming South were simply after political power and money. The Republicans saw absolute control over the Southern state governments as their ticket to continued power in Washington. They went about the task of denying most whites the vote while enlisting the newly freed slaves into the ranks of Republican voters.

When it comes to the fifth topic of slavery, there are a number of subtopics the Librevs like to pursue. I do not defend or justify slavery, and do not know anyone today who does. There were those in the North and South who were for slavery, and there were those who were against it. The South particularly had many anti-slavery societies. One unfortunate aspect of slavery in America is that the movement for gradual and compensated emancipation suffered setbacks with the rise of militant abolitionism. The call for violence by some of these radicals served to force Southerners into a defensive position on slavery toward the middle of the 19th Century.

Slavery was part of the world throughout history, and the South did not invent it or enslave people. That was done in Africa, with many nations participating in the slave trade. The main point I am trying to make was best said by a former slave, Elizabeth Keckley, "I have kind, true hearted friends in the South as well as the North and I would not wound those Southern friends by sweeping condemnation, simply because I was once a slave." She explained, "They were not so much responsible for the curse under which I was born, as the God of nature and the fathers who framed the Constitution of the United States. The law was descended to them, and it was but natural that they recognize it, since it was manifestly their interest to do so." She did not defend slavery, but simply accepted reality. She added, "And yet a wrong was inflicted upon me..."[5] She did believe that slavery was wrong, but Southerners were not the only ones responsible for its existence.

One aspect of slavery which has been studied frequently is whether the system was harsh or benign. To call it benign can be taken as defending it. Many masters had a paternalistic attitude towards their slaves, and the majority of slaves did not hate their masters. Still, there were cases of cruelty, brutality and mistreatment. Laws designed to protect slaves from extreme abuse were not always enforced. Regardless of how many were treated harshly or kindly, the vast majority would have preferred freedom. Like Keckley above, many might not put the blame on their masters, but they still felt that a wrong had been done to them.

Another subtopic of slavery is the preservation of African families, religion, or culture. This is a topic I enjoy myself. I lived in Africa for a year, and not only do I believe that African-Americans have preserved many African ways, but also that their African culture has had a significant influence on the white population of the South. I will discuss this in greater detail later. I believe that those Africans were Southerners also, and that they contributed much to making the South what it is. I have a dream that they will began to see this and realize that Southern history and culture is theirs too, not something to be erased from the pages of history

There is one issue that is at the center of the condemnation of all things Confederate, and that is the role that slavery played in their war for independence. It is wrong to condemn all things Confederate on the grounds that it was all about slavery. I feel I must lay the foundation here for my later discussion of this critical aspect of slavery. Here I will focus more on the historiography of the subject.

The main reason that some, such as the SPLC, can overlook the fact the North had slavery at one time, and at the same time be so contemptuous toward the South, is that they say that the Confederacy was all about slavery. When the United States began, and they drafted and ratified the Constitution, they guaranteed the protection of slavery. Those who hate our heritage insist that the government and Constitution of the Confederacy was about nothing but slavery. It is critical for them to prove that the Confederate States of America and the war they fought for independence was about nothing but slavery. If not there would be no logic in singling out the Confederacy in the condemnation of that institution which most find so detestable today. It is probably true that most historians today believe that slavery was the main cause for the war, but there are many who do not agree. I am one of the latter.

The April 2011 edition of the *Magazine of History*, published by the Organization of American Historians, was dedicated to the origins of the Civil War. This magazine deserves our attention here not only because it reflects the latest trends among academic elite historians, but this publication is aimed at

---

5. Keckley, Elizabeth, *Behind the Scenes, or Thirty Years a Slave, and Four Years in the White House* (New York: G W Carlton and Company, 1867), 3.

secondary education. Therefore this is the view promoted by the profession to be passed on to the next generation of Americans, most of whom study no more than high school level history. As Matthew Pinsker says in the Foreword, "What follows are a series of historical claims and counter-claims - all grounded in evidence and argued with a high degree of professionalism - without any easy consensus emerging in standard textbook fashion." He then pointed out that "the question of what caused the war has provoked more arguments than almost any other in American history." He then said of the five articles presented "None are in full agreement about anything except perhaps the principle that good history is complicated and always requires careful attention to facts, evidence, and the ever-elusive mysteries of human behavior."

The articles in this issue all mention the importance of the role of slavery, but most do not agree that it was the main cause of the war. Jonathan Earle claimed that it was ultimately political in origins. Paul Finkelman did believe that the main cause was slavery. Loewen certainly did not come up with an original point of view. Elizabeth R. Varon looked to gender issues and claimed that they played a role. Marc Egnal wrote on my personal favorite, the economic origins, and insisted "Economics more than high moral concerns produced the Civil War." Nonetheless Loewen, in his essay, refers to the "flatly wrong 'answers.'" He claims that the documents reproduced in his book show that the "Confederate leaders themselves made it plain that slavery was the key issue sparking secession." Please note, he says "secession" but the title of his essay talks about the origins of the Civil War. Just as in his book, he does not seem to understand that these are two different questions.[6]

My Interpretation

If not slavery, then what is the main cause for the war? The reason that I want to cover this in the introduction is that it is my interpretation of what the war was about, and the slant with which I interpret Southern history. Now I will cover the general causes of the war. I will focus more on historical facts in the chapter on the war.

I believe the cause for the war was too complicated to be reduced to just one cause, but generally I do lean toward an economic interpretation. I believe that each one who supported the cause of Confederate independence had their own reasons, from the lowly private to the commanding officer, as well as those of the civilian population and even the slaves. If we could ask them we would find that there are many reasons for the war.

---

6. Elizabeth R. Varon, "Gender History and the Origins of the Civil War," *Magazine of History*, 25 (April 2011), 23; Marc Egnal, "The Economic Origins of the Civil War," *Magazine of History*, 25 (April 2011), 33; James W. Loewen, "Using Confederate Documents to Teach About Secession, Slavery, and the Origins of the Civil War." *Magazine of History*, 25 (April 2011), 35

Introduction

There is no doubt that the issue of slavery served as a catalyst to most other causes that may be argued. It is obvious that the question of slavery's extension into the territories was a factor which led to the organization of the Republican Party, which led to the election of Abraham Lincoln, which led to the secession of South Carolina followed shortly by six more states. What Loewen and Sebesta fail to understand, probably because they are not real historians, is the big picture and how slavery was related to other issues. We must attempt to understand how slavery influenced other topics such as modernization, nationalism, and economics. At the time the European colonies were established in the Western Hemisphere, few people considered slavery morally wrong. In the Middle Ages the Pope had ruled that Christians should not be held in slavery so that the institution was uncommon in Europe at the time the Age of Exploration began. The Church at that time concluded that pagans, such as Africans, could be slaves. The Europeans learned that certain crops were very profitable, but they were labor intensive. Slavery met the demand for cheap labor to grow tobacco, sugar cane, and later cotton.

Meanwhile the scientific revolution came, which led to the Enlightenment. The new philosophy began to question moral values and eventually this included slavery. The English led the way in abolishing the slave trade and then the abolition of slavery itself. The adoption of this new moral value system did not come to all Europeans at the same time. England itself had abolished slavery in her empire only a few decades before the United States. For others it would not come until a few decades after the United States. In some parts of the world it existed well into the twentieth century. The abolition of slavery was part of the modernization process.

The modernization process was intertwined with the rise of the merchant world market economy. The European powers competed for domination of the world market economy. Slavery was a way that they all found to compete. When England began the campaign against the slave trade, many merchants objected, mainly the ones who profited the most from the system. Thus slavery was very much a part of the economies in the modern world.

The economic competition meant that the merchants needed protection in the world markets. At first they turned to their monarchs as the first form of centralized government to protect their interest in the contest. This led to nationalism. Some merchants believed that they needed to give their monarchs, and later their republics, more power in order to protect their interest in the world market. In order to have a stronger central government, the smaller local communities often had to yield to the more populous communities which tended to control the more centralized governments. Some citizens resented the sacrifice of individual belief systems. A very major point of conflict which came with growing nationalism was between centralism and localism. In the United States this conflict took on the name of "states' rights."

One of the specialized fields of study in the history profession is the rise of nationalism. As many nationalism scholars have pointed out, "very few nationalisms can be described as instinctive." Mary-Susan Grant began her book, *North Over South*, with a discussion of the rise of nations since that was an important part of the regional conflict. Nationalism means to forge the identity of many subcultures into one nation. Benedict Anderson spoke of "an imagined political community," that would fulfill "psychological as well as economic imperatives." The creation of one nation "involves ceaseless re-interpretations, rediscoveries and reconstructions; each generation must re-fashion national institutions and stratification systems in the list of the myths, memories, values and symbols of the 'past.'"

Grant then pointed out that "myths of origins and descent, of liberation and migration, of the golden age and its heroes and sages, perhaps of the chosen people now to be reborn after its long sleep of decay and/or exile." This not only explains the attempt by Northerners and Southerners to determine what those myths would be, but it also gives us an idea of what is going on with historians since the 1960s, when many became a generation with a new interpretation. I have always said that Americans constantly rewrite their history in response to the changing face of the nation. This is nothing new. A lot of what was going on in the Civil War was a struggle between the North and the South to define what the United States is. A lot of what is going on today with the destruction of symbols of not only Confederate history, but also other American symbols of the past, is an attempt to redefine our national identity. Those who are destroying our culture are generally those endorsing the new global economy and multiculturalism.

A recent publication which helps us understand this is Colin Woodard's *American Nations: A History of The Eleven Rival Regional Cultures of North America*. He points out the current situation, the division of red states and blue states, is nothing new. "Americans have been deeply divided since the days of Jamestown and Plymouth." The North American colonies were settled by people from distinct regions of the British Isles, as well as other European countries, each with its own religious, political, and ethnographic characteristics. "Throughout the colonial period, they regarded one another as competitors - for land, settlers, and capital - and occasionally as enemies." He pointed out that the colonies were being established at the time of the English Civil War "when Royalist Virginia stood against Puritan Massachusetts."

Woodard sees a total of eleven nations in what is today the United States. "Divisions are not between red states and blue states, conservatives and liberals, capital and labor, blacks and whites, the faithful and the secular." He claims that "Rather, our divisions stem from this fact: the United States is a federation comprised of the whole or part of eleven regional nations, some of which truly do not see eye to eye with one another." Thus, instead of American Exceptionalism, we have competitive nations who believe that their set of values is what the whole nation is about. The North won the war, battling slavery, and thus the

North is good and the South is bad. As Woodard said, ". . . the related intra national struggle to control and define the federal government triggered the Civil War."

Woodard says it was not even a simple struggle between North and South, which he said are ". . . two regions that, culturally and politically, didn't actually exist." He said "The Civil War was ultimately a conflict between two coalitions. On one side was the Deep South and its satellite, Tidewater; on the other, Yankeedom. The other nations wanted to remain neutral, and considered breaking off to form their own confederations." If we can set aside ideas of American Exceptionalism and look at what is going on in the rest of the Western world at the same time then we can see that the Civil War was part of the universal struggle of centralism versus localism. Not everyone in the South wanted secession, and not everyone in the North supported a brutal invasion. "When the war was over those who had been on one side created the "Lost Cause Myth," while those who had been on the other side rallied around their new identity of the "Union.""[7]

Mary-Susan Grant wrote about the rise of Northern Nationalism in her book *North Over South*. In the first chapter she argues that "many of the current theories that prevail concerning European nationalism can be equally applied to the American case." In the second chapter she traces the development of the North between 1820 and 1860. "It uncovers the background of the northern critique of the South and shows that this, ironically, had its origins in a national outlook that, over time, became entrenched in a sectional ideology." She then points out that this ideology ". . . was not national at all but was predicated on opposition to the South."

It is after the Mexican War that the issue of slavery became more important in the struggle between the Deep South and Yankeedom in determining the future of the Union. By 1860 the concern about the "Slave Power" had increased. Kenneth Stampp observed that those in the other states, or what Woodard called nations, began to change after the Dred Scott case, and agreed with the view in the *Cincinnati Daily Commercial*, a non-abolitionist paper, that "There is such a thing as THE SLAVE POWER."

Grant offered a good bibliography on the development of northern nationalism and the hatred of the South. Grant also mentioned Eric Foner who "uncovered evidence that supported his contention that northerners - particularly Republicans - were overtly hostile toward the South." She spoke of Howard Floan in his study *The South in Northern Eyes*, and how "Most antebellum northerners . . . knew little about the South and cared less." New Englanders, or Yankeedom, ". . . succeeded in convincing many antebellum Northerners of the backwardness of life in the South; that image has had a pernicious influence ever since." Later Grant said, "...it is evident that northerners, no less than

---

7. Ibid., 230.

southerners, were engaged in a quest for self-definition that ultimately led to the development of an ideology predicated not on the American nation but on the northern one." I have always liked the quote from Major General Isaac Ridgeway Trimble, a man who was from a Quaker family, never owned a slave, and lived most of his adult life in Baltimore. Quoting from Trimble's diary, "Northerners hated the South, and that they drove the South from the Union by their bigotry & hatred of everything southern." Even the famous carpetbagger, Albion W. Tourgée, realized "That was our mistake. We tried to superimpose the civilization, the idea of the North, upon the South at a moment's warning. . . . It was a Fool's Errand."[8]

Slavery became an important issue in determining which nation would dominate and determine the future of the Union. Abolition was not the purpose of the war. As stated by Gary Gallagher, "Almost all Democrats and some Republicans initially expressed strong opposition to freeing slaves and arming black men, but military events changed their attitudes." Secession probably started over slavery, at least for the first seven states, but the war was over the nature of the Union- Was it to be national or federal?

Economics is very much a part of the contest over which nation would dominate and create the United States in their image. As expressed by Gallagher, "The citizens who labored to save the Union subscribed to a vision of their nation built on free labor, economic opportunity, and a broad political franchise they considered unique in the world." David Waldstreicher, in his book, *Slavery's Constitution*, pointed out that "livelihoods of the people in the North as well as the South depended on the products of slave labor." Even in 1860 there were still many in the North who depended on the slave economy of the South.[9]

Gallagher claims "Issues related to the institution of slavery precipitated secession and the outbreak of fighting, but the loyal citizenry initially gave little thought to emancipation in their quest to save the Union." He went on to explain "Students and adults interested in the Civil War are reluctant to believe that anyone would risk life or fortune for something as abstract as 'the Union.' A war to end slavery seems more compelling." He then noted how "Much Civil War scholarship over the past four decades has diminished the centrality of Union." Slavery has become connected to the revisionist desire to be more inclusive of African-Americans in our history.

---

8. Grant, *North Over South*, 2-4; Leslie R. Tucker, *Major General Isaac Ridgeway Trimble: Biography of a Baltimore Confederate* (Jefferson, North Carolina: McFarland, 2005), 115; Albion W. Tourgée, *A Fool's Errand* (reprint, New York: Harpers, 1961), 381.

9. Ibid, 6; Stampp, *Causes of the War*, 13; David Waldstreicher, *Slavery's Consitution: From Revolution to Ratification* (New York: Hill and Wang, 2009), 217.

I agree that slavery had much to do with the secession of the first seven states, but that does not negate to concept of states' rights. From 1776 to 1860 the question of the power of the central government had been a major point of conflict. This conflict too is part of the rise of nationalism previously discussed, which is the same thing as centralism versus localism. In the United States this became known as states' rights. If Lincoln and Congress were fighting for the Union then it is logical that the South was fighting for the rights of individual states.

The Constitution itself was primarily an attempt to increase the power of the central government. The main divisions between those who supported it and those who opposed it were economic and political. The Hamiltonians wanted to see a stronger central government to benefit businessmen. The Jeffersonians wanted to see the country remain a nation of farmers. Following the passage of the Alien and Sedition Acts, Jefferson and Madison drafted the Virginia and Kentucky Resolves in which they affirmed that a state had the right to nullify a federal law it believed to be unconstitutional. Following the Louisiana Purchase several New England states talked about secession in what is called the Essex Junto. Disagreement over the War of 1812 led to more talk of northern secession in the Hartford Convention. South Carolina cited the Virginia and Kentucky Resolves in their talk of nullification of the 1828 tariff. Since the beginning there have been disagreements as to how much power the central government should have over the states.

BLACK SOUTHERNERS

There is little doubt that when the SPLC titled their anti-Confederate publication *Whose Heritage?*, they meant to discredit any defenders who claim that Confederate symbols are heritage not hate. Their main objection is that they claim Confederate history is not the history of all Southerners, and therefore such displays should not be in public space. I have touched on this previously. I disagree and believe that Confederate history is the history of black, as well as white Southerners.

The painful legacy of slavery, second-class citizenship, and discrimination have led some backs to reject an identity with the South, though many have not. The famous African-American historian John Hope Franklin claimed, "The South, as a place, is as attractive to blacks as it is to whites." He added, "Blacks even when they left the South didn't stop having affection for it. They just couldn't make it there." He understood that living in the North did not solve all their problems and that in many ways the South was better. "It's more congenial, the pace is better, the races get along better. It's a sense of place. It's home. In rare moments, it's something that blacks and whites have shared."[10] Franklin's

---

10. Peter Applebome, *Dixie Rising: How the South is Shaping American Values, Politics, and Culture* (New York, 1996), 341.

opinion was supported by a recent survey in *Southern Cultures*. When asked if they had identification as a Southerner, blacks responded more positively than whites with 78 percent responding in the affirmative compared to 75 percent of the whites.[11] I hope to demonstrate that black Southerners are part of the South and that the Southern heritage is theirs too.

I assume that blacks were not reduced to slavery and second-class citizenship because they are inferior. I also assume that the actions of Southern whites were not due to inferior morality. It has been common throughout history for one culture to feel superior to another. It is not a matter of right or wrong, but just the way people are. Europeans have been in the process of global conquest since 1492. My hope is that white Southerners not only can better appreciate the black perspective, but that also blacks can better understand the white point of view.

I love the South. I love Southern culture. Blacks have contributed much to creating the culture I love. I am hoping that by knowing the truth, black and white Southerners will have a better understanding of each other and thus become more tolerant and respectful of each other. I have a dream that someday most blacks will understand that Confederate icons are just part of our past. I believe that most of the protest against Confederate icons has been led by the politically motivated, who have turned the destruction of our heritage into a racial issue for their own political gain.

The large black population is one of the main reasons that the South is so much different from the North. Blacks have influenced Southern language, lifestyle, food, music, storytelling, and even religion and philosophy. Whites need to recognize how much blacks have influenced and contributed to the Southern way of life, and I am hoping that blacks will realize how much the history of the South is their history too.

There are still some blacks who understand this feeling; I have met them at the Sons of Confederate Veterans reunions. H. K. Edgerton is one such man. He gained national attention by marching across the South carrying his Confederate Battle Flag. H. K. was at one time president of the NAACP chapter in Asheville, North Carolina. Today he works closely with the Southern Legal Resources Center, which defends Southerners who are discriminated against for displaying pride in their heritage. There are probably few blacks who feel as H.K. does about Confederate heritage, but I hope some will read my book and more will come to realize that H. K. was right when he said, "it is the flag of our Southern heritage." We need not deny the negative side of our shared past in order to focus on the positive and work for a better future.

---

11. Larry J. Griffin, "The American South and the Self," *Southern Cultures* (Fall 2006): 13.

THE PLAN

Chapter 1 will cover the colonial era up to the French and Indian War. Prior to 1763, there were many communities throughout the colonies. Unity did not begin until after the French and Indian War ended in 1763. By the time of independence, slavery was becoming less common in the North as the economy there became increasingly diverse. The South continued to depend on agriculture, and to a large extent, agriculture which was labour intensive. Thus slavery became more important in the Southern colonies for economic reasons, while in the North it was important as a source of trade. Most ships transporting slaves sailed from Northern ports.

Chapter 2 will be about the creation of the central government, between 1754 and 1789. The government we have today traces back to the ratification of the Constitution in 1789. The debate over the Constitution was heated, as supporters of a stronger central government collided with those who believed sovereignty resided in the states.

Chapter 3 will cover the early days of the United States. Between 1789 and 1848, the economic gap continued to widen, which manifested itself in economic issues. Much of the South continued to depend on slavery while the North cultivated alternative sources of cheap labor. The manufacturers of the North favored protective tariffs while the predominantly consumer South opposed tariffs. The North tended to support internal improvements, often funded by the federal government. The South generally did not support these improvements because they paid the majority of the taxes thus spent, and received few of the benefits.

Chapter 4 covers the period between the end of the Mexican War and the election of 1860. This is the time when the struggle over the spread of slavery into the new territories became a major dividing issue. It is also the time when more and more Northerners began to hate Southerners. The existing political parties divided between North and South as the general population did. This is also the time when radical abolitionism took hold in parts of the North, and the call by some for violence and slave uprisings alarmed the South. The *Librevs* are correct in identifying this period as crucial in determining the cause of the war.

Chapter 6 will be about Reconstruction, from the end of the war up to the Compromise of 1877. This has become a major battleground for the *Librevs* in their campaign against traditional interpretations of Southern history. They see this as an unfinished social revolution, rather than a dark period of corruption and violence.

Chapter 7 will cover a period of reconciliation. Between 1877 and the end of World War II, the South was left pretty much to itself. This is the era when many Confederate monuments were erected. Many saw this as a time to forgive and forget. As the Civil War veterans died, it became easier to do. By the end of the Second World War, Southerners were at least as patriotic about being American as those in the North.

Chapter 8 will cover the struggle for black equality and the rise of the civil rights movement since World War 2. Discrimination, race riots, school integration were all part of a time of national tragedy. Blacks sought true equality in American society and encountered much resistance. The struggle was intense in the South, as many who opposed equal rights invoked the term states' rights, and embraced the Confederate Battle Flag as a symbol of their resistance. Stereotypes of the South became more negative, as some characters portrayed in the movies *Deliverance* , *Smokey and the Bandit,* and the television shows *The Dukes of Hazzard* and *The Beverly Hillbillies* attest.

Chapter 9 will take us up to the present. Since about 1980, resistance to the rights of minorities does not seem to be any worse in the South than it is in the North. The invention of air-conditioning has made the Southern sun more appealing to Northerners. They had to change the name since it seemed easier to accept a move to the Sun Belt rather than a move to Dixie. For many Northerners, the Southern image is still negative but in a different way. The more recent image has been that of the Bush and Trump supporters and the American theocracy. These people are not the ones I am speaking to; they are more concerned with their political agenda and look to the Republican Party as their Messiah. They would willingly sacrifice their Confederate heritage to get the support of the Republican Party, seeing that as a small price to pay if we can stop flag burning, gay marriage or put Jesus back in the schools. Their compliance in our cultural genocide has made it much more difficult to preserve our heritage.

I: THE COLONIAL SOUTH

T HE COLONIAL PERIOD HAS become an important battleground for true Southern history. The *Librevs* claim that the South did not really have a regional identity until shortly before the war and, in fact, they claim that Southern identity was not really all that strong until Reconstruction. They call this the "Lost Cause myth." They consider the Sons of Confederate Veterans and United Daughters of the Confederacy to be defenders of this myth. I, like most unreconstructed Southerners, have no doubt that our people are different and that the difference is too deep-seated to be the result of the "Civil War."

Grady McWhiney has been the chief defender of a view that has become popular among the unreconstructed. McWhiney said that not only were Southerners different, but that the difference dates back to the British Isles. It is part of the Celtic fringe theory. The idea is that the colonists of New England were Anglo-Saxons who came from the Southeast of England. The dominant culture in the South was Scottish, Irish, Welsh, and those from the west and north of England. Most of the liberal revisionists do not like his thesis and they do not accept it, but they have not proven him wrong.

I believe McWhiney's idea that the Celtic population was different from the Anglo-Saxon, and that this culture has had more influence on the South. I do realize that not everyone in the South is Celtic, but they are numerous enough that they have had a significant influence on the Southern way of life. Even the *Librevs* do not dispute the homogeneity and Anglo-Saxon ancestry of the New England colonies, nor the large number of Scots in the South. For me, the main point is that they were different from the beginning, and became more so once in America.

The "Lost Cause Myth," widely accepted among the liberal academic historians, does not accept this view. They imply that it is a false view of history because the division between the regions did not exist before the war. I can accept that the division between North and South was greater after the war, but nevertheless has always existed. Woodard called this division an alliance between the eleven nations, some with the North and others with the South. With the war between the United States and the Confederate States, the other

1

divisions were reduced to two, the North and the South The *Librev* view cannot be considered proven, and thus opposing views cannot be called a myth. George Washington seemed to believe a difference existed; he made an effort to see that the two regions were equally represented in his cabinet.

McWhiney was not the only one to see the difference. Another view which has been popular with the unreconstructed was presented in a book published in 1989, by David Hackett Fischer, titled *Albion's Seed: Four Folkways in America*. Fisher also believes that the American British colonies were different since the earliest days, but he identifies four distinct cultures. East Anglia went to Massachusetts, and from there the rest of New England. The Cavaliers and indentured servants populated Virginia, coming mainly from the southern part of England. The Midlands populated the north Middle colonies to the Delaware Valley, and from there the Midwest. The main group in that region was the Quakers. The Celtic population is identified by Fisher as the borderlands people who influenced the west.

This is similar to Woodard's *American Nations,* though Woodard expanded on Fischer in that he sees eleven distinct cultures in what is today the United States. Woodard recognizes that the colonies had different origins. He also sees that some of the differences in the various colonies came from the diversity which was the British Nation. Thus, there were not only differences between the North and South, but there was more than one culture in the North as well as the South.

The most important point is that in all three of these interpretations the differences between North and South existed before the War for Southern Independence. It is not a myth, as the *Librevs* like to believe. I believe there is a bias which exists with some historians who find it important to deny a Southern culture. This means that there is no Southern heritage, and therefore the defense of Confederate icons as symbols of that heritage is invalid.

EUROPEAN BACKGROUND

There is some background information that we need if we are going to understand the English colonies in America. I do not believe that the conflict between North and South was over any morality issue such as slavery. I believe that the war was the result of economic and political competition. For this reason, it is important to understand the development of economic interest in America. The age of exploration and resulting colonization in the Americas came about because of the development of world markets. The world markets came about because of the transition from the agricultural feudal economy to the merchant economy of the modern age. This change did not occur overnight. The foundations were laid a long time before 1500. The transition was not complete by the founding of the colonies.

Perhaps the greatest influence of feudalism on America was the lust for land. Though the modern Englishman has generally led the way in the development of capitalism, they still attached a great deal of status to the ownership of land. Most of those who came to the colonies came in search of land. Some were the younger sons of the aristocracy, but most were the rising "middling sort." There were also those of the lower classes who would have had little chance of obtaining land of their own back in the old world. This passion for land included most who settled America, but the love of land is greatest in the South. Even today, the man who strikes it rich in the North looks for a penthouse in Manhattan, the Southerner still wants acreage with a big house, white rail fences, and grazing horses.

The lust for land caused Southerners to be more expansionist in the years before the Civil War. They needed the land for their plantations, or range and farm land for those described as the "plain folk" by Frank Owsley. Many ignored crop rotation, growing one crop year after year for profit, wearing out the land. They would then move West to cheaper land. Americans later paid a price for the abuse of land with erosion problems including the infamous Dust Bowl.

THE GROWTH OF THE WORLD MARKETS

The growth of the market economy accompanied the growth of cities. During the Middle Ages, the city of London never had more than ten thousand people. By the seventeenth century, it had hundreds of thousands. Merchants prospered and culture grew. Spain 'discovered' the New World and became a world power. The center of world commerce passed to Amsterdam after their conflict with Spain. By the eighteenth century, England captured the title and retained it until the twentieth century. The colonists who went to America were part of the British Empire and thus key players in the world-market economy.

NATIONALISM

Nationalism came with the rise of the world markets. Whereas the feudal peasant could turn to the local lord for protection, the globe-trotting merchant needed something more all encompassing. Thus, the monarch grew in power and authority, eventually to 'absolute' power as reflected in riches and palaces, such as Versailles. When the English achieved domination of the world markets, they did so with the rise of the English navy. When the English and the French established their colonies in America, they were struggling for their share of the world-market economy.

This struggle for national identity was as much a part of what was happening in the nineteenth century as anything. Though the Great Britain that we all know and love today was established with the unification Act of 1707, it took several more generations before the average Englishman achieved the level of national patriotism that we see today. There was still no unified Germany until the mid-nineteenth century. Neither was there a unified Italy. When we speak of Robert E. Lee as a man who was a Virginian first and an American second, we are not talking about someone clinging to the vestiges of feudalism. We are talking about a man going through the same experience that many other Europeans went through. The struggle for national identity was neither unique to the United States nor an example of Southern backwardness. Some people are still reluctant to surrender their local identity for the sake of the nation. This is at the bottom of many of the problems they have had in the European Union. This is why the Scots voted on the split from the United Kingdom. This is why the United Kingdom voted on a split from the European Union. Southerners should understand this better than other Americans.

THE DEVELOPMENT OF IDEAS

Increased literacy came with the rise of the merchant economy. The merchants and their families had a need to keep records of their business transactions, and thus, they had to learn to read and write. As more people became literate, they read the Bible, which of course led to the Reformation. Soon after came the scientific revolution, and people began to turn to the laws of nature as an explanation for the events around them. After defining the laws of nature, we next learned to harness them. This led to many technological advances that climaxed with the Industrial Revolution.

As the foundations of feudal society crumbled to the advances in literacy and learning, men began to question the nature and order of their societies. This is called the Enlightenment. This period gave us many things that we associate with the modern age, such as novels, encyclopedias, dictionaries, newspapers, and coffee houses for debating intellectuals. It also gave us economics, democracy, and the notion of government by contract. It is also at this time that we find a significant number of people questioning the institution of slavery.

The rise of new ideas does not occur everywhere at the same time. Some become convinced before others. This is also true regarding the abolition of slavery. In the early modern period, slavery existed in many parts of the world. Today few people would condone it. Though by 1860 more people were becoming opposed to slavery, most people were not affected by it and gave it little thought. The people who most profited from slavery, Northern slave traders and Southern plantation owners, were the strongest supporters of slavery. Much industry in the North also was dependent on Southern agricultural products such as cotton. This does not mean that those who profited from slavery lacked morality or that they were inferior to the ones who could find profits without slavery.

4

THE CONCEPT OF CLASS

I believe that the moves for independence in 1776 and 1861 were primarily about economic competition. I also believe that the economic interest varied by class. Therefore, it is important to reject the belief so many Americans have that ours is a classless society. The concept of class is considerably more complicated in the modern world. Feudal society had commoners, clergy, and aristocracy. Each of those had their well-defined layers. Everyone knew where they fit and what their roles were. Class in the modern world has often been ignored as the old aristocracy declined and the rising merchants ascended. Some of the old aristocratic families are still wealthy today, largely because of the lands they have controlled since the Middle Ages. However, most of the wealthiest and most powerful of the modern age have come from below and were catapulted to new social and class levels by their business enterprises.

America has stood for capitalism since its founding. Rejection of aristocratic titles has led many to deny that class distinctions are as great here as in Europe. We have all heard it claimed many times that America is a classless society. I have always tried to understand which part is classless—Beverly Hills or Watts? Since the first colonies there has been a demand for cheap labor, and those who did the labor have been looked down on by those who used their labor.

Capitalism, like feudalism before it, continued to have people who labored for others. After the merchant class turned to manufacturing they found a greater need for labor. The cheaper the labor, the greater the profits. In the colonial days of America, manufacturing was limited. Those who did this kind of business could meet their labor needs with family and friends. Many were cottage industries. The few that expanded their business first used the labor of young ladies between adolescence and marriage. This source for labor shifted to immigrants. At first it was the Irish, then later it would include other immigrant groups, all the way up to the illegal aliens of today.

The greatest profits accrued to those who exploited the labor of others. In the South, they turned to slavery. I will discuss the reasons for this in greater depth later. John C. Calhoun made a defense of slavery on the grounds that the Southern slave was better off than the Northern working class. In the days of Calhoun, there was a lot of truth in this. Of course, we cannot ignore the value of freedom. The reality is that workers depended on their meager incomes, and it was not always easy to quit a job. The main point I want to make at this time is that in both cases, there were those who profited off the labor of others. The Southern planter inherited a system that had been around since the first American colonies; the Northern manufacturer adopted a system that came into being after the Enlightenment. If a man exploits the labor of another, is one system really morally superior to another? In slavery, one does not have the freedom to choose. In the early nineteenth century, how much freedom did the working classes really have? Even today how many working people toil at a job they hate because they have a family to feed. They would often end up maimed or crippled by the machines they worked with. The planter was motivated to care for his workers since he had capital tied up in them. Was the early industrialist morally superior to the planter?

The Northern preference for immigrant labor may have been nothing more than an economic decision. They did not need a capital outlay that one needs when buying a slave. They did not have to feed or shelter the immigrant when production was down. Enlightenment thinking was leading the Europeans away from slave labor, but those who followed also found economic advantages. My purpose is not to defend slavery but rather to point out that the Northern choice of immigrant labor was not necessarily the product of moral superiority.

GROWTH OF DEMOCRACY

We quite often equate democracy with the concept of equality. American exceptionalism revolves around the notion that our nation produced modern democracy and thus has been the leader in a world campaign to show that "all men are created equal." For this reason, we have often thought of ourselves as morally superior to other nations. Northerners have seen themselves as the leaders in this. Intellectually they realize that men such as George Washington, Thomas Jefferson, and Patrick Henry came from the South, but they seem to think this fact has been negated by slavery. If we realize that democracy and related ideas did not come from America, then we must reject the notion that Northerners are leaders of the American crusade for equality. If we understand this, then it is more difficult to accept the Northern assumption that their invasion and conquest of the South was part of this noble effort to assure the equality of black Americans.

We like to think that we invented such great American institutions as the jury system, democracy, and the two-party system. This is not the case. The jury system that we use has been part of Anglo-Saxon culture since the Early Middles Ages. The bicameral legislature that we established with the Constitution is modeled after Parliament. And the two-party system also came from England, where Whigs and Tories have been around since the seventeenth century. What made our country unique is that Americans got a chance to try out Enlightenment ideas that others in Europe had only discussed. They also had the opportunity to create a society without much of the baggage that came with a hereditary aristocracy.

The rise of democracy began in England and was brought to America by the colonists or in the books that came to the colonies. The Enlightenment intellectuals, most often of the higher classes, talked of equality and rights. However, the definition of a citizen in those days was not the same as it is now. It was limited to males over the age of twenty-one, who owned property and paid taxes. When they talked of rights, there was little thought about women, the landless working class, or slaves. There is no stone tablet that defines equality. There is no set truth like one would find in math and science. Ideas of right and wrong are not human nature, but are part of a culture.

The British see democracy as their innovation, which historians call the Whig interpretation of history. According to them, it has roots in the democratic election of Anglo-Saxon chiefs, which occurred before they left Germany for England. The Middle Ages produced the Magna Carta, which legally limited the power of the monarch. The Glorious Revolution of 1688 increased the power of the legislature, with the passage of a law that called Parliament into session at regular intervals, regardless of the will of the monarch.

The main point I want to make at this time is that the notions of democracy, government by contract, jury system, equality of citizens, and such things came from England to all her American colonies. In the case of European culture, such things are in an ever-changing flux. We consider our morality of today to be superior. This is why we changed and adopted new ways of thinking and new ways of doing things. However, it does not seem right to condemn those of the past because their view of morality is not up to our standards. It does not mean that we should abandon our ancestors because they lived by a different code of morality.

Our Southern ancestors were not morally inferior to other Englishmen, or to Northerners. The concept of equality and rights that we have today is not the same as what they had at the time that the Constitution was drafted. It was not the same in 1861. The fact that Americans were still debating the limits of equality does not prove that Southerners, not even slave owners such as Thomas Jefferson, were morally bankrupt. As the times have changed, morality has changed. We should not judge those of the past by the standards or rules that we live by today.

This is a very important concept in our stand to preserve our Southern heritage. Those who condemn the Confederate flag and other symbols of our past make the assumption that these things represent part of the American past that was evil. To us, they are part of our heritage. The Sons of Confederate Veterans has passed numerous resolutions condemning those who use the flag of our ancestors to promote hate. My ancestors' concepts of right and wrong were based on a different code than we live by today. When we begin life we inherit the world we are born into. This has always been true.

SOME BACKGROUND ON SLAVERY

When the age of exploration began, Europeans did not have slavery. We know that England had about 10 percent slaves at the time of William the Conqueror. Shortly after that, the Pope decreed that slavery was wrong, so that by the fifteenth century there were very few slaves in Europe. When the Portuguese and Spanish increased trade with Africans, they did accept some slaves. Eventually is was discovered that the Carribean Islands were good for the growth of sugar. Since Native Americans were devastated by European diseases, there was a need for labour. Africans had traded in slaves for many generations before the age of exploration. Thus, the slave plantation system was well-established by the time the English began their colonies in America. The Jamestown settlement was established in 1607, and labour was supplied by indentured servants. Slavery was yet to come to England's North American colonies.

The age of conquest saw Europeans at war over trade and territorial issues. These wars spilled over into their colonies. Native Americans sided with the French during the French and Indian War, with the British during the Revolution, and most with the Confederacy. In all these instances, they fought against those they believed had stolen their land.

We also have a tendency to overlook the non-British colonies in America. Some were older than Jamestown and Plymouth. St. Augustine, Florida and Santa Fe, New Mexico are prime examples. These colonies rarely rate more than a passing mention in current textbooks. Those Spanish colonies absorbed into the South produced many Confederate soldiers with Spanish surnames. In this respect the South was more diverse than the North.

The founding of Jamestown in 1607 was a business venture. Captain John Smith had problems getting the gentry to work, finally saying those who do not work, do not eat. By the middle of the century Jamestown was a thriving tobacco colony. The two main issues were finding labour for the plantations and dealing with Native Americans. The first to arrive in Virginia were of three main social classes: gentry, middle class, and poor labourers. This latter group provided labour, paying off their passage by working for the gentry.

I, like many historians, lump Virginia and Maryland together and call them the tobacco colonies, or Chesapeake colonies. Maryland began as a refuge for Catholics under the leadership of Lord Baltimore. However, like the elder and larger colony, the economy was founded on tobacco and the plantation slave system became the method by which they produced the product. Let us not forget the basic assumption of Adam Smith; people operate on the principle of self-interest. The employer will try to get the labor as cheap as possible, and the employee will try to get as much as possible for his labor. On the surface, this seems like an objective situation. The reality is that the employee is quite often dependent on a job for survival whereas the employer is simply trying to accumulate surplus wealth. Thus, the wealthy employer has an advantage. This is how societies end up with slavery or some other form of exploited working classes. The worker who appears to have a choice is not necessarily better off than a slave.

Three-fourths of all new arrivals to Chesapeake between 1630 and 1680 came as indentured servants. There were numerous attempts by the landowner to take advantage of the indentured. However, since England was a land of laws, the laborer did have rights which enabled him to prevail at times. Many died from overwork or harsh conditions, but others served out their terms and became property owners themselves. The planters received fifty acres for every man they brought with them into the colony thus giving the well-to-do more motivation to bring in the poor. By 1675, the population of Virginia exceeded forty thousand, many of them former servants who wanted land. The landless poor became a source of problems.

The Dutch brought the first slaves to Jamestown in 1619. They needed supplies, and slaves were all that they had to trade with. English law did not recognize slavery, and so these first Africans were servants. Most Europeans of the time believed black Africans to be savages and inferior to white people. Even though at first they were not slaves in the traditional sense, they lingered in a gray area of English law and custom. Some acquired land and servants of their own while others lived a life that would approximate our traditional view of slavery.

Bacon's Rebellion probably had an impact on the shift from indentured servitude to slavery. By the later part of the century, the wealthy land owners became more concerned about maintaining peace with the Indians than in the further acquisition of land. Meanwhile, the population of freed indentured servants increased. Under the leadership of Nathaniel Bacon, who had his own motives, the poor of the colony rebelled. They burned numerous plantation houses and made it clear that they wanted land. The governor wanted them to leave the Indians alone but the rebels insisted in taking Indian land. With the death of Bacon, because of dysentery, the rebellion fizzled. The leaders of the colony realized that such problems would exist as long as they depended on poor whites for labor. The use of slaves would solve that problem. By 1660, slavery was part of colonial law. There is always an element of speculation in trying to understand why people did what they did. The fact is that in 1670, there were no more than two thousand slaves in Virginia; by 1700, the number increased to ten thousand, and in the next century, the South had 390,000 slaves. After Bacon's Rebellion, the planters preferred slaves to indentured servants.

The Carolinas

South Carolina was a restoration colony. After the end of the English Civil War, Charles II became king and rewarded some of his supporters with charters for colonies in the New World. By 1680, a colony settled in the present site of Charleston. Some settlers came from New England but more came from Barbados. They brought the slave plantation system with them. Rather than tobacco, they grew rice and indigo. They still required a lot of cheap labor. They settled on slavery. Some French Huguenots added to the population. They quickly assimilated to the ways of the English planters. Some drifted down from Virginia and Maryland, and a number of the Scotch-Irish would find their way to South Carolina as they flowed down the Appalachian valleys.

North Carolina was initially included in the same charter but it became clear that this older settlement had already started in a different direction. The first English colony of Roanoke had been established in the north, though it had disappeared before the settlement of Jamestown. Other settlements dated back to 1650 in a colony first known as Albemarle. By 1691, they officially took the name of North Carolina with the founding of permanent colonies by those who moved down from Virginia. They too had a slave labor based plantation system in the tidewater areas. Many of what historians call the yeomen farmers moved to the Piedmont and even the mountainous regions. North Carolina had some planter class, but not as many as South Carolina had. Both colonies had back-country middle and lower class settlers. The poor were drawn to the frontier regions where they had hopes of acquiring their own land, or at least squatting on the land that belonged to speculators or Indians.

GEORGIA

Georgia was founded for the purpose of providing a buffer between the Carolinas and Spanish Florida, and as a depository for the increasing London poor created by the Industrial Revolution. Despite earlier attempts, it was not until 1732 that the crown approved a charter granting the Board of Trustees a twenty-one-year lease. The next year 115 settlers led by James Oglethorpe laid out the town of Savannah. The first settlers consisted of artisans, trades people, and some of the poor. They were supplemented by Scottish and German settlers. The trustees tried to prevent Georgia from duplicating the tobacco colonies or the Carolinas by restricting exotic crops and slavery. With the expiration of the original charter, the new royal charter relaxed these restrictions.

NON-ENGLISH COLONIES

Florida had become part of the British Empire after the French and Indian War, but would be returned to Spain with the acceptance of the independence of the other colonies. Though St. Augustine was the oldest European city in the present United States, it remained a small settlement. Attempts to expand the colony failed and they never proved a threat to the English in Georgia, much less the Carolinas.

The Spanish took control of Louisiana after the French and Indian War and thus added their influence to what is one of America's favorite cities today. When the Spanish took command, New Orleans had only 9,500 people and the majority of them were slaves. The warm climate spurred the growth of profitable exotic crops, and like the rest of such colonies in the New World, the French and Spanish turned to slaves to fill the demand for cheap labor. Slavery in Louisiana did have a slightly different flavor than in those colonies founded by the English. Those who love to hate the Anglo-Saxons seem to feel that the Spanish and

French system was more humane. It is clear that there were more opportunities for free blacks, and the large Creole population indicates that they had a more relaxed attitude toward the mixing of the races

The far western limits of the South were part of Spain and stayed that way until the independence of Mexico in 1822. New Spain did not rely on slave labor as much as other American colonies, though there was a small black population. The new country of Mexico never did have slavery. When the territory became part of the United States, the only slaves to be found in Texas had been brought by Americans. Of course, their heavier economic dependence on cattle instead of crops such as sugar, rice, or tobacco did not make slavery as appealing.

SOME EIGHTEENTH-CENTURY DEVELOPMENTS

By 1700, most of the colonies had been well-established, and most of the Southern colonies had grown to depend on slave labor. By 1763, the planters controlled the tidewater and the middle class or small farmers dominated in the Piedmont regions. The Scotch-Irish, Germans, and an assortment of others moved into the Appalachian valleys and even began to overflow into the interior. On one hand, the class barriers were clear; but on the other hand, mobility was quite possible. Many of the Scotch-Irish became middle-class farmers also known as yeoman farmers. A few of these yeoman farmers even became wealthy planters, such as the families of John C. Calhoun and Andrew Jackson.

Few have failed to see a contradiction in the fact that Thomas Jefferson wrote "all men are created equal" while slaves worked his fields. Edmond S. Morgan saw the growth of slavery as an explanation for the growth of democracy in the Southern colonies. In eighteenth century England the ownership of property was one of the requirements to participate in the running of the society. The theory was that only those who owned an economic interest in the society could or should make decisions on the governing of that society. Since so many came to America to get land, they earned with it the right to participate in the selection of their leaders.

By 1763, the colonies, both North and South, had firmly established councils which they used to govern themselves. The British government left them to their own devices. The mercantilist economic theory that they operated under viewed the colonies as a source of raw materials. London seemed more interested in keeping the raw materials flowing than in dominating the colonies. It would not be until after 1763 that the British would again attempt to subjugate the colonists.

The Great Awakening of the eighteenth century was a religious revival that greatly impacted the common man. The preachers came from their ranks and not from the universities or clerical establishment. They even began the process of making the slaves Christians. This no doubt had a long-term effect on the attitude toward slavery. As the white men accepted the blacks into Christianity, it is only natural that more and more people began to see them as children of God. It would be a logical step to think it wrong to enslave one's brothers and sisters in Christ.

There were some other side effects of the Great Awakening that helped to lay the foundation for the movement toward independence. One is that as the preachers traveled up and down the colonies, as well as to England, they established more communication among those in the various colonies. This would be important as the subject of discussion changed from religion to politics. Another side effect of the Great Awakening is that the people began to show less deference to their superiors. It began with the religious leaders, and in time, it spread to political leaders or aristocracy. More and more of the common people refused to accept other men as their superior just because of their birth or greater wealth. Some believed it when Thomas Jefferson declared all men as being created equal.

As the population grew and the colonists traveled North and South throughout the colonies, they began to feel a bond with each other that was not felt with their fellow Englishmen. The fact is that in the late colonial and into the early Federalist period, the regional differences did not go from North to South as much as from coastal to back country. The middle-class farmer in Virginia might have more in common with his counterpart in Pennsylvania, whereas the wealthy planter in South Carolina would have more in common with the wealthy merchant in Boston. No doubt the wealthy of all colonies would be more educated and thus more familiar with the Enlightenment ideas that flowed from England, France, and Germany. I have little doubt that the interest of the middle and lower classes revolved more around land or business than ideas.

There are two main issues in the colonial period with which I take exception, and disagree with liberal revisionist historians and others overly critical of Southerners. The first issue is that many believe Southern distinctiveness to be a relatively recent development. The second issue is that the symbols of the South, especially the Confederate Battle Flag, represent a culture that was morally inferior to the North. *Librevs* often claim that all of the English colonies had much in common with each other and that any regional distinctiveness was not significant. I realize that we share much in common with those in the North, in fact we still have much in common with those in the old country. However, the colonists in the South, for the most part, came from different regions of the British Isles. Once they arrived here, they had a different purpose. Whereas the Puritans wanted to build a "city on the hill," those in the Southern colonies wanted land. Those in the North had small family farms, those in the South developed a plantation economy with many yeoman farms.

Those in the North were mostly middle class who divided themselves between saints and nonsaints. Those in the South quickly developed class distinctions with the main groups being planters, middle-class farmers, servants, and slaves. They started off different from those in the North, and the gap widened with each passing generation. When I speak of Northerners above, I am thinking of New England; those in the middle colonies were different even though they were considered the North in 1861. The people in New York, New Jersey, and Pennsylvania did not have the Puritan background of those in New England. Generally speaking, the people in these states would tend to be more sympathetic to the Confederacy, and even those dedicated to the Union would be less intolerant than their fellow countrymen from New England.

Obviously, the main reason liberals believe Southerners had lower standards of morality is because of the fact that they owned slaves. I do not believe that the difference was due to morality. Slavery was something that has existed since the beginning of history in many different parts of the world. When the English established colonies in America, all of them, North and South, had slavery to some degree. The reality is that in the Northern colonies it did not prove profitable, so they sold their slaves to the South, rarely granting them freedom. The morality that different cultures live under is defined for them by their codes of law or their religion. In the days that our ancestors owned slaves, both law and their religion told them it was right

SUMMARY OF AMERICAN HISTORY MYTHS IN COLONIAL AMERICA

The acceptance of some common myths in American history can get in the way of us defending our culture. I repeat that one of our biggest problems today is the fact that many of our own people are fully reconstructed, and therefore patriotic Americans first. Thus, they are often defensive of the propaganda interpretations of United States history. The view of so many of our detractors is that the Northern conquest of the South was part of the process of making the United States the greatest country in the world. There are many today, North and South, who believe in American exceptionalism. This is to say that they believe there is a purpose in our existence. For this reason many of our Southern people are willing to abandon our Southern distinctiveness. I believe American exceptionalism to be a myth.

The United States was not started with any great design. Like the rest of history, ours is the result of generations of struggle between those seeking their own self-interest. Some came for religious reasons, like the Puritans who wanted to build their "city on a hill," but most came for land. They did not come to build a democracy. Western European democratic theory is something that came out of the Enlightenment, and the English colonists brought it with them from Europe. There was no grand design and certainly not one that involved the abolition of slavery.

A very important myth is the idea that America developed a classless society. England had classes before the founding of the colonies, and they brought their classes to America with them even though they did not adopt the aristocratic titles. Those of the Northern colonies were no less class conscious than those of the South, even though they tended to have a greater percentage of middle class.

They even had slaves in the colonial period. The main difference is that they did not develop a plantation economy that created greater demands for cheap labor. This was not a decision based on moral superiority, but mainly because they could not grow those crops which were more labor intensive.

The colonists came to America because they were part of the British Empire. They worked for the building of that empire and, from their first days, continued to conquer land from the first inhabitants. The mercantilist economic theories dominated the colonial period, which were based on the idea that the colonies existed to provide raw materials for the home land, while the home land sent back finished products. We will see that the colonies continued to expand until they declared independence from the motherland, and that their propensity for territorial expansion did not diminish with the founding of the United States of America.

II: BIRTH OF A NATION, 1754–1789

T HERE ARE A NUMBER OF THEMES, issues, or assumptions during this time period important to understanding Southern history. First is the development of an American identity; none really existed before 1754. Second, we must remember the basic assumption of Adam Smith and the concept of capitalism; people do what they do out of self-interest. Third, we find that the question of states' rights came with the creation of the United States. In fact, when the colonists declared independence from England, they were taking the same stand as those who believe in states' rights—localism versus centralism. Fourth, we find that class has played a very important part in our history. Americans seem to avoid or ignore the question of class, and as a result, we miss some major issues in the development of our nation and of our Southern identity. Fifth is the role of black Southerners which is very much intertwined with the class issue.

The *Librevs* claim that Southern identity did not really exist until after the Civil War. Even if this is true, the origins of Southern culture predate American culture. I am referring to the Celtic fringe theory of Grady McWhiney. The seventh issue that is important to clarify is that the rise of democracy was not an American thing. It started in Europe, developed with the Enlightenment, and did not truly exist until the twentieth century, if even then. The reason it is important to understand this is that we Americans have often justified what we do on the grounds that it is all in the name of democracy and the American way. In the thinking of many, this has included the Yankee conquest of the South. The Yankees have justified their conquest of our native land on the grounds that it is they who were the torch bearers of democracy and the American way. The *Librevs* seem to have taken up the torch and added diversity to the battle cry. They assume that the North had to conduct their war and conquer the South so that we can have the racial equality we have today.

THE STATE OF GREAT BRITAIN IN 1754

Between 1754 and 1789, the people who had been part of the British Empire created a new nation and with it a new identity—Americans. Most of those living in the colonies, at least most of those who had a say in the colonies, had come from the British Isles. However, by the mid-eighteenth century, it had been several generations since they or their ancestors had left. During that time, things had changed in both Europe and America. The United States today, despite the population that has different ancestral origins, is still predominantly a European culture. We use the term "western" to include countries like America, which are basically of European heritage. We must remember that when we speak of modernization, we are talking specifically about progress in western civilization.

By the mid-eighteenth century, England had become the dominant power in the world-market economy. Like France, they trailed behind the Spanish and Portuguese in the beginning of the first true world market. After a series of world wars, they came out on top. This climaxed with the French and Indian war, which was called the Seven Years' War in Europe. In this last contest, not only did the British come out on top over the French, but the cost of empire also led to the conflict between London and the colonies.

THE RISE OF NATIONALISM

States' rights and localism are one and the same, the opposite of centralism. Centralism is a belief in a strong central government, which gives rise to nationalism. It is important for us to understand the development of nationalism if we want to intelligently discuss states' rights. Prior to the creation of nations, we had a world where most people identified with their local community. People living in the British Isles thought of themselves as being from Yorkshire or Cheshire or Devonshire rather than being English. Do not forget that Great Britain included the Irish, Scottish, and Welsh as well as the English. The common people looked to the local gentry to solve their problems and had little concern for global issues. The increase in the world-market economy produced a class of people who needed protection for their business activities, both within Great Britain and in other parts of the world. This resulted in a demand for the growth of the central government and of the militaristic capability to protect the merchants. The success of the British Empire hinged on their ability to create a powerful navy, which protected British merchants and built the British Empire.

The price of this strong central government is individual and community freedom. Common sense dictates that the larger the group, the greater the diversity. The greater the diversity, the less likely we will agree with each other. We are forced to compromise for the sake of unity. We are forced to surrender our local identity for the sake of a national identity. It is important to understand that when the North won the war, it was a big step toward centralism. Since it is the North that won, it is the Southern culture that has been sacrificed for the sake of unity. Today there are those who want to suppress what is left of our Southern identity so that we might have a stronger American identity. Unfortunately, many of our Southern people are contributing to the destruction of our culture as they swell with American pride and patriotism. It is difficult to serve two masters. It is even more difficult when one of those masters takes a dislike to the other.

THE RISE OF DEMOCRACY

Many Americans foster the myth that democracy came with the birth and development of the United States. This has become the justification we have used for territorial expansion. Today this type of thinking is probably even more popular in the South than the nation as a whole. This is the main reason that the biggest problem we have in preserving our Southern heritage is that many of our Southern people have become "American" and are willing to sacrifice our past for the sake of American unity. What the liberals have done is take this myth of American democracy and make the Civil War an important part of the progression. They believe that it was the United States and Abraham Lincoln who freed the slaves by defeating the rebels. They linked this war to the end of slavery and the ideal of American diversity. The neo-conservative Southern Republicans of today feel a twinge when they hear this but offer much less resistance than the Southerners of the past. Unlike our ancestors in 1861, they are American first and Southerners second. Those of us who are unreconstructed continue to be Southerners first.

The truth of the matter is that democracy grew out of the Enlightenment which began in Europe. England went through a real civil war and the Glorious Revolution of 1688. The power of the church was diminished, while the power of Parliament was increased. Though still not a true democracy, the foundation was being laid for progress toward that end. The scientific revolution and Enlightenment led to industrialization, capitalism and democracy.

The important thing to remember relating to Southern history is that these advances came about prior to 1776. The Americans became part of the movement, and the new thinking helped to bring about the move for independence, but they began in England and were brought to America. This means that they were no more Northern than Southern, and in fact, Southerners had just as much to do with the creation of the United States and the later rise of democracy as Northerners. George Washington, Thomas Jefferson, George Mason, and James Madison were all Southerners. This would mean that the idea that the United States had to defeat the Confederate States for the sake of the ideals we believe in today could not be true.

POPULATION GROWTH

Perhaps the most important variable related to the changes in America in the eighteenth century is the fact that the population continued to grow. This created the economic need to provide a home and sustenance before one could establish and expand their family. Most of the colonists had gone to America for the prospect of getting land. This not only would provide a home but, since many were still farmers, it would also be the way they would provide for their families. The colonists had land, they had hope, and they were optimistic about the future. One of the reasons Samuel Johnson did not like Americans is that he calculated that the way the population was growing in the colonies, they would soon exceed the population back in Great Britain.

Immigration into the colonies also continued at a good pace. The majority of immigrants did not have enough money to buy the higher-priced lands along the coast, either North or South, so many went west in search of more affordable lands. This included the Scots-Irish, an American term to describe those of Scottish ancestry who had lived in Northern Ireland for one or more generations. The Germans continued to pour in and likewise headed west and then south.

The Liberals of today lean toward creating a multicultural society. With this objective in mind they like to use the term "nation of immigrants." Those with this objective seem to despise the South, or at least the Confederate South, even more than their predecessors. They see the Confederacy as racist and a major barrier to their multicultural dream. Their claim is more myth than reality. On the surface this term sounds logical since our ancestors did immigrate to America from the British Isles. However, they were British subjects in Britain and remained such in the colonies. They migrated from one part of the British Empire to another and thus were not really immigrants.

Most of them landed in Philadelphia, the main port of entry in the eighteenth century, and then moved into western Pennsylvania. As that land filled up, they migrated down the Appalachian valleys to the South, all the way to Georgia. This helps to give credence to the Celtic Fringe thesis of McWhiney, who claimed that the South was primarily a Celtic culture. The South gained a large number of Scottish, as well as German and other migrants, but this meant that the frontier culture of America was heavily influenced by the Celtic culture.

The slave population also had a significant natural population growth. This was a major difference in the slave system in British North America as compared to other colonies. Most of the Sugar Islands of the Caribbean, whether French, Spanish, or Dutch, bought slaves with the idea that they would work for five to ten years and then die. This, combined with the importation of few women, limited the natural population growth in those colonies. Thus, they depended on the continued importation of additional slaves. When the importation of slaves was abolished in the United States, states that used slave labour depended on natural population growth.

DON'T FORGET THE NON-ANGLOS

There are significant portions of the South that existed before the establishment of the United States, which became incorporated into the South with American expansion. Not only are these areas an example of Southern diversity but also a reason why some Southerners would have been resistant to domination by the central government. With more diversity came the need to sacrifice more for unity. The stronger the central government, the more that is sacrificed for unity. A less centralized government would allow for the preservation of diverse cultures including the non-Anglo cultures. In other words, states' rights actually fosters diversity.

The least populated area of the non-Anglo South was Florida. In 1760, they had about three thousand settlers, mostly Hispanic but with some Africans. Florida was turned over to Britain at the end of the French and Indian War, and most Spanish left at that time. Texas and New Mexico had a few thousand Spaniards in 1760, and would continue as part of New Spain until they were absorbed into the South. Louisiana, with its mix of Spanish, French and Africans would be absorbed by the United States along with the Louisiana Purchase.

THE MYTH OF WHY THEY CAME

As an historian, one of the most irksome things I hear is when people claim that America was established by those seeking religious freedom, equality, democracy, or other such patriotic rhetoric. Some people came to America for other reasons, but the vast majority came to make their fortune. This is an important point since the subjugation of the Southern people was not over an issue of morality, but rather for economic and political power. The "middling" sort and the poor had more opportunity to become property owners in America than back in Europe. Though some failed to achieve this goal, others were successful. One of the main reasons that we have this myth of democracy as something American is that more people were able to vote in the colonies because more people became property owners.

The wealthy acquired prime real estate near the coastal ports, while the middle class and poor were forced to the frontier for land. This put pressure on the Indian lands and caused conflicts. It also created regional class divisions, and some power struggles between the wealthy and those new property owners, now voters, among the common people. We will see later that it is this drive to acquire land which led to the conflict over allowing slavery in the new territories, which led to the war.

THE RISE OF THE COMMON MAN

Much of the conflict that took place in England and the colonies was between the gentry and the common people. With the expansion of Enlightenment thinking, the commoners seemed to be more and more confident in demanding more say. In the colonies, much of this appears to be a conflict between the frontier and the coastal areas since it was mostly the commoners on the frontier. Some of these conflicts arose before the start of the Revolution. With the war, some felt that their interest lay with the planters fighting against the king, but others believed that the colonial aristocrats were their enemy. Many of those who did not see it as a class struggle in 1776 would realize it after 1783. The most famous examples of this in the pre-Revolution South is what we call today the Regulator movements. Historians have not always agreed to what degree these conflicts were class related; what is clear is that the common folk on the frontier demanded concessions from the aristocracy.

The Regulator movement in the Carolinas, which climaxed in the battle of Alamance in North Carolina in 1771, was an attempt by the frontiersmen and western farmers to gain concessions from the coastal aristocrats who controlled the government. They wanted lower taxes, fair elections, more representation, and relief from outlaws ravaging the frontier. The main point is that three distinct classes existed in the South, and at times this resulted in violence. The rich ruled and generally showed little interest in the welfare of the common people. The middle class were property owners. Some would struggle to become rich themselves while others simply wanted to have the independence to support their families. The poor were the outcast and some of them ravaged the countryside. Despite the class differences when the Revolution came, the former Regulators supported the local gentry against the English rulers.

THE FRENCH AND INDIAN WAR

The French and Indian War, the fourth in a series of world wars, became a turning point in colonial history. Before 1754, no one seriously considered the possibility of independence from England. The changes that came about because of the war led to the declaration of independence by the colonies.

This war began not in Europe; but in the colonies. The colonists were part of the British empire and they depended on London for protection. It is also an example of the importance of the colonialist greed for land. The Ohio Company of Virginia made plans to sell land near the present site of Pittsburgh in 1749. The French constructed forts to stop the incursion of the Anglo-American traders and Virginia land speculators. In 1754, the governor of Virginia sent a militia officer, George Washington, to construct forts to defend their interest. The 160 colonists under Washington's command lost to the French and their Indian allies. This sparked the fighting which, in 1756, escalated into the Seven Years' War.

There is evidence that, in the beginning, the colonists had no interest in being independent though they jealously defended their local interest. In 1754, seven of the colonies sent delegates to Albany, New York. They were able to negotiate an alliance with the Iroquois when most of the other Indians saw a greater advantage in backing the French. It was then that Benjamin Franklin came up with his plan for a unified defense. His proposal was not at all anti-British.   Even though the delegates supported the plan, not one of the colonial assemblies passed it. In 1754, most of the colonists did not want to abandon their individual colonial rights, a principle the Southerners continued to defend in the name of states' rights.

It is also clear that the colonies depended on London for protection from the French as well as the Indians. By 1756, the French penetrated into New England and dominated in the West. The tide changed after the British statesman William Pitt took command of the war effort. He poured British money and men into America, though he did expect support from the colonial legislatures. Success was achieved in 1763, with the French being forced out of North America.

There are three significant aspects of the war that would lead to conflict between the colonists and London, and to the creation of the United States. First, the four world wars of the late seventeenth and early eighteenth centuries left the British the most powerful empire in the world. However, they began to feel the financial burden of empire. They would turn to the colonies to help pay the tab. Second, with the French gone, the colonists did not feel the need for protection of the British Army and Navy. They still hungered for the Indian lands to the west, but the British army ended up becoming the ones who prevented them from taking what they wanted. The third aspect is more subtle and more difficult to document. The colonists had a greater exposure to their cousins from Europe, and this helped them to realize how much they had grown apart.   The colonial militias saw the British regulars as immoral, profane men who needed to be controlled with brutal discipline. The colonists had developed an identity distinctive from their cousins back in the old country.

TAXATION WITHOUT REPRESENTATION

Historians still debate the nature and causes of the American Revolution. Many Europeans even laugh at the idea of calling it a revolution; it was in fact a war for colonial independence. The wealthy gentry who dominated the colonies in 1763 continued to dominate in the new United States. Where is the revolution? However, there are historians who still defend the idea that it was a social revolution in the long run. If we have any hope of understanding what happened, we need to recognize that the American version of what happened has been based on radical rhetoric by those who promoted the idea of independence. It is true that the tax question is what upset many of the colonists. However, what the tax issue did is create a constitutional crisis which left many of the colonists feeling that the only solution would be independence. Some pushed for it from the start, but as things escalated, more and more supported the cause of independence.

The fact is that many people were involved, and they had varying reasons for their involvement. We must remember that not everyone favored the movement, and those who eventually went to the side of the Whigs did so at differing stages. John Adams said one-third favored it, one-third opposed it and one-third sat on the fence of indifference.

A CONSTITUTIONAL CRISIS

After the war with the French, the British government decided that the colonists should pay part of the cost of the empire. After all, this last of the four world wars began in America as the colonists attempted to expand into French and Indian territories. They tried various ways to raise the revenues. We have all heard about the dreaded Sugar Act, Stamp Act, and Townshend Revenue Act. Most of us were raised on the radical interpretation that the king was a tyrant and that the colonists should not have taxation without representation. As to the tyrannical government of London, they reacted to colonial protests by repealing the taxes.

The crux of the constitutional crisis revolved around the issue of representation and role of the colonial assemblies. The colonists claimed that their various assemblies were their parliament and that only their parliament could tax them. They said they did not have any representation in the Parliament in London. The British said they had "virtual representation." They did not have direct representation like the United States Congress of today, but rather each member of Parliament represented every British subject, including the colonists. They understood that the colonists had to pay taxes to support their colonial governments, and no doubt, this is the main reason London never taxed them at the same rate they did those back in England. The British government clearly attempted to keep the colonists happy. However, when they repealed the Stamp Act, they also passed the Declaratory Act which affirmed the power of Parliament over the colonies. Ultimately, the attempts to avoid a constitutional crisis failed.

THE PROCLAMATION LINE OF 1763

Most historians underestimate the significance of the Proclamation Line of 1763 as a reason that many of the middle class and poor joined the cause for independence. In my view, the majority of those who came to the colonies came for the opportunity to get land. By the time of the French and Indian War, most of the land in the thirteen colonies had been distributed or was still occupied by Indians. As the white population grew, the demand for new lands grew with it.

This is why most of the Indians sided with the French during the Seven Years' War. The French had a fur trading empire that did not require the white men to take possession of the land that the Indians had lived on for many generations. The English colonists were farmers and family men, and they valued the ownership of the land they lived on. The British created the Proclamation of 1763 to avert continued conflict with the Indians.. It forbade any of the English colonists to go west of the line that followed the crest of the Appalachians. So now, not only did the common people not need protection from the French who were no longer there, but they began to see the redcoats as the ones prohibiting them from getting the plentiful western lands.

The western lands issue affected those in the North as well as the South. A band of western Pennsylvania Scots-Irish marched on Philadelphia seeking military protection for the frontier. The legislature passed a bill to raise troops, but this showed that the class conflict between the frontier and the coast was not just a Southern thing. The fact is that the white settlers, North and South, wanted land and had no problem killing Indians to get it. It is also clear that the British government realized that this fostered conflict with the Indians, which in turn cost money. The government tried to stop the colonists from taking Indian land, and thus, the colonists began to see the British Army as a barrier, not as protectors.

THE POOR AND THE SEEDS OF DEMOCRACY

Americans like to think that the greatest thing about our country is that it has been a place where the common man could prosper alongside the aristocrat. Of course, many of our people deny that America had an aristocracy. This could not be further from the truth. Whether we are looking at the Boston merchants or the Virginia planters, the people with money ruled the land. The Enlightenment planted seeds of change, and the success of the Revolution fertilized these seeds. The rhetoric used to justify the move toward independence was taken to be reality by the people.

The wealth of many colonists grew as the colonies grew and prospered. Rather than a demise of aristocracy, there was merely a change in its composition. In this period between the end of the French and Indian War and the end of the Revolution, there is considerable evidence of a change among the common people, especially the poor. Deference declined, and the concept of democracy continued to be more inclusive. The growing middle class tended to see themselves as the successful people of the future; the poor saw themselves as those being denied the promise of the colonies. The belief in equality expanded. This included the growing working class of the northern and middle colonies, the landless and poor whites of the South and frontier, as well as the slaves. Some historians have seen this as the true revolution.

Several incidents, such as Charleston in 1766 and Philadelphia in 1779, hinted at a growing rejection of deference to the wealthy by the common man. Henry Laurens of South Carolina stated, "We are at this moment on a precipice, and what I have long dreaded and often intimated to my friends, seems to be breaking forth—a convulsion among the people." The number of wealthy men in the assemblies of Virginia, Maryland and South Carolina declined significantly after the War for Independence. With the end of the Anglican Church in America, the aristocracy lost a valuable crutch. Democracy and the rise of the common man were on the way.

TERRORISM AND THE BEGINNING OF THE WAR

The situation began to spin out of control as the colonists turned more toward terrorist tactics. In the Boston Massacre, an unruly mob was fired on, and five men were killed. The radicals such as John Hancock and Paul Revere exploited the situation as much as possible, even though the British government launched an investigation and put the soldiers on trial. Two were convicted of manslaughter and the rest acquitted with the help of their attorney, John Adams. It seems that a true tyrant would not have had an investigation and trial.

The Boston Tea Party, in December, 1773, saw a band of colonists destroy a shipment of tea. The British government passed a series of Coercive Acts, mainly aimed at Boston, to try to get them to pay for the damage. The colonists responded by forming the First Continental Congress in 1774 to find a course of action to what they labeled the "Intolerable Acts." In April of 1775, a British Army landed in Boston Harbor and marched toward the villages of Lexington and Concord in search of arms that they suspected would be used against the forces of law and order. The shot heard around the world was fired at Lexington on April 19, starting one of the most amazing military conflicts in history.

The Second Continental Congress met in Philadelphia on May 10, 1775, but it would be more than a year before they would take the step of declaring independence on July 4, 1776. The British objective was to restore control over the colonies while not yielding to acts of violence and rebellion. The colonists increasingly felt they were being invaded, and as things progressed, no doubt more and more supported the cause of independence. Another way to look at it is that more and more supported the cause of localism over centralism.

THE WAR

When George Washington was picked as the general to command the Continental Army, in May of 1775, the Virginian commanded an army that was basically made up of New Englanders. At first, the British efforts were centered on the North, after all, that is where the trouble started. They invaded and occupied New York and Philadelphia. There were victories on both sides, but the

British could not put down the rebellion. In February of 1778, the Americans forged an alliance with France, and most historians agree that this was a major turning point toward success in their bid for independence.

The British turned their attention to the South in 1778, having become convinced that there were many more loyalists there. So many Southern colonists had suffered at the hands of the Indians and outlaws that some petitioned the king for protection with a promise of loyalty. The British captured Savannah and Augusta, Georgia, in 1778 and by 1780 controlled the coast up to Charleston, South Carolina. The invasion helped to turn more of the Southerners to the Whig cause. The British army was stretched so thin they could not protect the loyalists. The Tories aggravated the situation as they turned to plunder and revenge. Banastre Tarleton's Tory Legion executed prisoners of war and destroyed houses and fields, leaving many homeless. By the time that the British moved on the interior in 1780, the Americans were able to achieve victories at King's Mountain and Cowpens.

Even though the British General Cornwallis won the Battle of Guilford Courthouse on March 15, 1781, his supplies were so low that he had to reach the coast for resupply. He then continued north, and reaching Yorktown, waited for the British Navy. The French Navy's defeat of the British Navy and Washington's arrival before Yorktown with a combined American and French Army decided the issue. The British surrendered in October of 1781, essentially ending hostilities.

AFRICAN-AMERICANS IN THE WAR

It is amusing that the *Librevs* most often reject the idea that African-Americans would have supported the Confederacy, yet they go out of their way to show how many had fought for the American cause during the Revolution. No doubt this is due to political correctness. It is also an example of why I claim that the *Librevs* are not as objective as they like to think they are. On one hand, they don't want to show any support for the Confederacy while on the other hand, they want to talk about the contributions made by African-Americans. The fact is that the British promised freedom to those slaves who supported the king. The Union in 1861 did not even let blacks join their all-white army, much less promise them freedom. Why did the slaves support the slave owners in 1776 but not in 1861? My answer is that in both cases they believed they were part of a homeland that was being invaded by foreigners, and supported the defense of their homes.

In 1775, blacks made up 20 percent of the 2.5 million people living in the colonies. Most were Southern slaves, but free blacks lived in the North and the South. Lord Dunmore, royal governor of Virginia, declared "all indented servants, Negroes, or others" who would support the king would be free. The American planters considered this foul play and assumed that the objective was to generate a slave rebellion. Many African-Americans took advantage of the offer, and no doubt, their knowledge of the countryside gave the British some assistance. The rumors spread among the slave population and many began to "believe that their freedom depended on the success of the king's troops."

In contrast, African-American support for the Revolution received little welcome. Boston excluded slaves and free African-Americans from participating. As it became more difficult to achieve their recruiting quotas, many Northerners accepted African Americans. In Virginia, some masters sent their slaves as substitutes. An estimated five thousand African-Americans served in the Continental Army and state militias, or at sea on American ships. At the end of their service, many of the slaves who fought received their freedom.

When talking about the Indians or African-Americans, we must remember the principle of self-interest. The Indians were not motivated by the same issues as either the British or the colonists. They tried to determine which would benefit them the most. Likewise, African-Americans, free or slave, had to decide which would be best for them. The bottom line is that it is not logical that so many *Librevs* can promote the idea that African-Americans fought for the American side in 1776 but refuse to accept that some freely chose to fight for the side of the Confederacy in 1861. The planters and slave owners of 1861 were Americans in 1776.

THE ARTICLES OF CONFEDERATION

States' rights would continue to divide Americans because the new government of the United States was very weak. The name tells us a lot about the situation—our nation does not really have a name like most others. It is simply called the United States of America. (originally the united States of America, emphasizing the States) This is the root of the issue that was not resolved until 1865, and has lingered to a lesser degree after that. Did this new government have power over the individual states of America that had united to fight for a common cause—independence from London and the king?

In the beginning, it was not a matter of North versus South but the general question of centralism versus localism that existed among the modern western peoples. The common man had few concerns outside his local market. This is why the Federalist Alexander Hamilton did not want to see political power in the hands of the common man.

In many ways, Alexander Hamilton was the founding father of the modern United States. He was the major spokesman for those who wanted the see the new nation become a mercantile and industrial power, an active competitor in the world markets. He understood that success in this endeavor required a strong central government. Since he believed the common man could never comprehend this, the aristocrats should be the movers and shakers. Not only did he become the spokesman for a strong central government, but he also became the leading opponent of democracy. As the North became more industrialized, Northerners would have a greater interest in the world markets and thus more of an interest in a strong central government.

Thomas Jefferson opposed Hamilton's views. In many ways, the main controversy among the founders of the United States could be summed up by the conflict between these two men. Jefferson did represent an element of modernization, but not the big business side that obsessed Hamilton. Jefferson was concerned about the Enlightenment ideals of human rights, democracy, and personal freedoms. He pictured an idyllic nation of farmers and artisans armed with certain rights. He believed that the best government was that which governed least. He became the defender of states' rights as well as personal rights.

THE CONSTITUTION

There were two main variables that convinced many in the new nation that the central government needed to be stronger. The first and most important was economics. This not only meant the capability of the government to pay its bills but also to create the best opportunity for Americans to compete in the world markets. The second is related to the first—the ability for Americans to protect themselves. For the wealthy, this included protection abroad. The first American military engagement outside of the United States was the attack against the North African pirates who had made a living out of demanding ransoms from European ships. No farmer in Tennessee could have much of an interest in this. And no merchant in New York could have much interest in protection from Indians. Both might support a military out of patriotism and self-interest.

Once it was determined that they would create a new document of guidance rather than simply revise the Articles of Confederation, the biggest issue was how to see that all states had fair representation in the central government. For those with large populations such as New York or Virginia, this meant that representation should be based on population. Smaller states had feelings of equality regardless of how many people they had. This was resolved with the Great Compromise. In the upper house, which would be called the Senate, all would be equal. In the lower house representation would be based on population.

It is interesting that many people today do not understand why we have the Electoral College in which a candidate for president can have more popular vote and still lose the election. That is part of the Great Compromise. The nation is made up of states, and each state is voting for president. Some of the electoral votes are based on population, the same as the number of congressmen in the House of Representatives. Other electoral votes are the same for all states, the same as the number of senators. This is called the Great Compromise.

After resolving this as well as a number of lesser problems, the Constitution was sent to the states for ratification. After much heated debate between those supporting and those opposing a strong central government, it was ratified and went into effect in 1789 with George Washington elected as first president. Let us not forget that consent was not unanimous among the people, nor among the states. North Carolina and Rhode Island did not ratify immediately. They were also not invaded and forced to join the new union.

The split was not so much along North-South lines as it was along the frontier versus the coastal areas. The fact that the South ratified the Constitution means that they accepted the sacrifice some states' rights which came with its adoption. Keep in mind that those along the coastal counties from Boston to Charleston were dominated by the older, wealthier families. Those on the frontier were the poor and middle classes who, for the most part, had not yet made their fortunes. Obviously, the wealthy coastal dwellers were more interested in the world markets and thus would benefit the most from a strong central government. It is interesting that when one looks at the presidential election results today broken down by counties one can see a similar pattern: urban areas versus rural areas. To understand the South as well as the North, it is necessary to recognize the class differences in America, and to understand that these differences also correspond to a large degree to rural areas versus urban areas.

Please note that this document did not create a democratic nation. Alexander Hamilton, one of the northern Federalist most responsible for the Constitution, said "It has been observed that a pure democracy, if it were practicable, would be the most perfect government. Experience has proved that no position is more false than this." He added, "The ancient democracies in which the people themselves deliberated never possessed one good feature of government. Their very character was tyranny: their figure deformity." He made this speech on June 21, 1788, to endorse the Constitution. He obviously did not see this document as one that made the United States a democracy. I see this as an important point because the *Librevs* like to see the War of Southern Independence as something created by the planters, and they assert that the common Southerner was not so much in favor of it. The point is that in 1789, it was still the aristocracy, North and South, which ran the country. These are trends in the entire United States, not just in the South. Curiously, the *Librevs* seem to accept the idea that democracy rose in the South.

UNRESOLVED ISSUES

After the Constitution was ratified, there were issues that remained unresolved, some because they seemed insignificant and others simply a classic case of agreeing to disagree. First would be the amount and type of taxation. The poor rebelled when their lands were confiscated for taxes or when they had to pay too much for whiskey tax. Chronic problems arose related to tariffs. The

North had more manufacturers who wanted American industry to be protected by tariffs. The South had more consumers who wanted limited tariffs. The Constitution proclaimed taxes should be uniform.

A matter of little concern in 1787 which would increase over time is the question of internal improvements. This would include turnpikes, canals, and later, railroads. Of most concern would be those passing through two or more states. What would the role of the central government be in the development of these important links of trade? Southerners tended to view internal improvements as something that benefitted the Northern states.

How would the new territories be administered? This question grew over time and eventually added to the division between the states. The Northwest Territory, between the Great Lakes and the Ohio River, was opened for settlement after states extinguished their claims to the land. The Ordinances of 1785 and 1787 set up the system by which it would be surveyed, distributed and eventually become states. It was also one of the first territories to prohibit slavery. Controversy would grow not just over slavery, but mainly the status of slavery in the territories.

AFRICAN-AMERICANS

When the patriots and founders of America spoke of equality and rights, they were speaking of propertied white males. These are the only ones who could vote, the theory being that these are the people who owned an interest in the society. They were like stockholders. This is the main reason I have pointed out that our country was not founded on any principle of democracy. The nation was founded by propertied men, and it was designed to be run by such men. They ignored women, Indians, poor whites, and the slaves. This also shows how our nation had classes. The founders, Northern or Southern, did not think in terms of the all-inclusive, nondiscriminatory democracy that we at least strive to have today

Enlightenment thinking, along with basic Christian philosophy led more and more people to question slavery and its relationship to this new democratic thinking. Most Europeans of the time assumed that white people were superior to people of color. It was assumed that they were more intelligent and were believers in the true God. This included those in the North, in Europe, as well as Southerners. There were a few exceptions, such as the Quakers, but most believed in white superiority. Even with the Quakers some were slave owners at the time of the Revolution. Anti-slavery movements were popular in the South, and there were attempts to limit, or even eliminate slavery. The big question was what to do with the freed slaves. It was thought, by people North and South, that the white race could not coexist with a large, free black population.

The Quakers were the first to take steps toward doing something about it. They began by condemning the owning of slaves among their own members, but even then, it took some time to convince all of them. In 1780, Pennsylvania passed laws to eliminate slavery in that colony. Massachusetts followed in 1783, Connecticut and Rhode Island in 1784, and later Vermont and New Hampshire. New York did not introduce a gradual abolition until 1799 and New Jersey in 1804.

There were many Southerners of the day who questioned the morality of slavery. Patrick Henry wrote, "Would anyone believe that I am Master of Slaves of my own purchase! I am drawn along by ye general inconvenience of living without them, I will not, I cannot justify it." He admitted that he depended on the profit even though he cannot justify it. He also pointed out that he inherited the system. Thomas Jefferson blamed the king in an earlier draft of the Declaration of Independence. There are numerous examples of Southerners who freed their slaves so that by 1860 about 10 percent of the black population was free, half of those in the South.

Southerners did not create slavery, but were victims of their age. Most, though not all, profited from slavery because fate had given them a plantation economy that demanded a cheap labor force. It was whites of an earlier age who chose to meet that demand with slavery. There were attempts to limit the importation of slaves before the break with England, but Northern slave merchants and royal authorities opposed the loss of revenue. The quotes are numerous from Southerners who felt that their inheritance was more of a curse than a blessing. I firmly believe that in time they would have condemned the institution, as others before them and after them did.

CONCLUSIONS

The period between 1754 and 1789 was a time of great change, but my focus is on those changes which had the greatest impact on Southern history. The most important is the rise of American identity. Americans lived at a time when Enlightenment thinking generated beliefs in equality and democracy. The move toward independence started because of taxes but was fueled by the principle of self-interest. The colonists increasingly felt that their interest could be better served if they were on their own. There were also feelings of being different from their kinsmen back in England. The wealthy merchant may have been concerned about the taxes, but the poor and middle class probably resented the fact that the king would not allow them to take the Indian's land more than anything else.

The *Librevs* like to point out that Southern identity is something new. I believe it increased in the struggle for independence, but its roots go back to the differences between Anglo-Saxon and Celtic Britons. They started out different, and after arriving in the colonies, the gap only widened. States' rights at first was a local issue, more in tune with frontier people and issues they had with the planters of the coastal areas. Over time, states' rights became more of a Southern political principle, with Thomas Jefferson being the champion of limited government. Alexander Hamilton was the chief proponent of a strong central government, in tune with the wishes of the banking, business, and mercantile class.

African-Americans were Southerners, too, though they lived in a society controlled by white men. They still were influenced and had influence on Southern culture. We will see in future chapters that most Northerners did not want to abolish slavery, and many of those who did, wanted to send African-Americans back to Africa, or some other foreign shore. They certainly did not want freed slaves living in their states. We will find that they did not vote for Lincoln and the Republicans to abolish slavery, but rather to stop the spread of slavery into the territories.

III: EARLY CONSTITUTIONAL UNITED STATES, 1789–1848

NATIONALISM WAS ONLY BEGINNING during the early days of the United States, and the rise of regional identity is my main point of focus in this chapter. The fact is that as of 1789, a national identity of any kind was vague at best. Apparently, many did not have a strong British identity, which is why they could sever their ties with our nation of origin. Most of the colonists had the greatest bonds with their respective states. The North and South found that they had enough in common that they joined together to declare independence from England and to form a new nation. The main reason for joining together was for the sake of a military alliance; it was the only chance that they had for success.

National identity comes about when a people see a reason to be united. It is very much tied to the issues of localism versus centralism. Feelings of identity are the result of individual perception. Unification occurs when those unifying have feelings of commonality. Disunion occurs when individuals see some of their fellow citizens as foreigners. During the period between 1789 and 1845 we do see an increase in a regional split. The gap between North and South widened so that by 1845, it became obvious to some that the South would have a difficult time maintaining equality in the newly created nation. This chapter deals with some of those changes.

If we look again at Woodard's view of eleven nations, then the events that unfolded in the early and mid-nineteenth century can be more easily explained. There are some historians who noticed that with western expansion there arose new economic centers that challenged those established in the east. Those living in various spheres of economic influence had their own self-interest to look after. This is one way in which slavery played a critical role. As people went west, the role of slavery was becoming a national issue since they differed on whether it should be allowed in the western lands. The Free Soil Party and Republican Party would be founded on the idea of halting the western expansion of slavery, not the abolition of the institution.

The United States grew economically, geographically, and in population. Economic opportunity abounded for people in all regions of the rapidly growing country. After a brief period of Federalist rule, Thomas Jefferson and his Republicans, or Anti-Federalists, predominantly Southerners, seized control, and it appeared that their dream of America would be the way of the future. The Federalist Party, of which Hamilton was a leader, faded away; however, those who wanted the United States to be a nation of business that would actively compete in the world markets did not go away. During the period covered by this chapter, most of them found a new voice with the Whig Party. In the next chapter, we will see that the Northern businessmen, or Northern Whigs, will band together in the Republican Party. What happened to the Southerners who had ambition to find economic success in the world markets? They had problems finding a political party that could fill their needs all the way up to the beginning of the war.

On the eve of the Mexican War, the sun would be setting on Southern domination of the central government. Meanwhile, it was clear that even before the conflict between the regions began, the North was growing in population and as a result would be able to seize control of the federal government. Those of the South, especially the planter class, would begin to realize that such trends had all but solidified. During the war, both Union and Confederates would claim that it was "a rich man's war and a poor man's fight." They were both correct. The growing gap between North and South began with the upper classes. Do not be misled into thinking that all rich white Southerners supported the Whigs. Only those who comprehended their role in the world market embraced the Whig philosophy. Some planters remained with the Democrats. As long as Southern businessmen saw future economic success with the Union, they were Whigs. As the perception of Northern aggression increased, Southerners rejected the Whig Party, which contributed to its collapse. The Northern businessmen turned to the Republicans. The failure of the Southerners in finding a party contributed to Lincoln winning the election of 1860.

The support for the Constitution came from those who expected to benefit the most from the world markets. They were called Federalists. Some of the Jeffersonian purists may have understood this too, but they feared the loss of personal liberty as part of the price tag for economic success. This is one of the things which separated Yankees from Southerners. The historical fact is that Alexander Hamilton and his Federalists supported the Constitution; Thomas Jefferson and the Anti-Federalists opposed the Constitution. A myth has grown around the belief that the Federalists were Northern and the Anti-Federalist were Southern. A more accurate distribution would be that the centralist businessmen supported the Constitution, and the localist and those most interested in protecting their rights opposed it. Many of the common people, North or South, also opposed it. The common people tended to be localist. This is what Hamilton did not like about them.

Though both sides talked about the preservation of liberty, it is clear by the programs proposed by Hamilton that the real issues were economic. The first step in his plan would be the federal assumption of state debts. Economic strength lies in good national credit, which can only be achieved if all the states enjoy good credit. A national bank would be necessary to maintain economic strength. This would produce a major political issue as the Americans debated the Bank of the United States. Hamilton saw the future in manufacturing. Only by joining the Industrial Revolution could American business compete in the world market. Tariffs would provide a source for national revenue and protect domestic manufacturing. More merchants, shippers, financiers, and manufacturers came from the North, and thus, there would be more support for the Constitution from that region.

The fact that the South ratified the Constitution tells us that support for a strong central government was not restricted to the North. George Washington did much to lend support to the notion of a stronger central government. The fact is that the planters had ruled the Southern colonies and that for many years to come they would dominate in the Southern states. The early nineteenth century would see a growth in the power of the common man, what historians would call Jacksonian democracy. However, the planters would retain power and influence that far outstripped their meager numbers. Washington was one of this class. Most of these men were educated and had at the least a basic understanding of the growing field of economics.

Adam Smith published his *Wealth of Nations* in the same year that the United States began. The capitalism that Smith wrote about is the only thing that has been a part of this country since its founding. The planters were just as much a part of American business and the world market as the Northern manufacturer, though in a different way. The planters wanted free trade, to trade their crops for manufactured goods. The North wanted high tariffs, which protected their profits, while providing revenue for the central government to spend on internal improvements which also benefited them. For the North, it was a win-win situation. For the South, it was a lose-lose situation. The South remained predominantly agricultural throughout the Nineteenth Century, producing tobacco, rice, indigo, sugar, and cotton for the world markets.

Thomas Jefferson and his Republicans have become regarded as the founders of Southern states' rights and the opponents of centralism. His dream for America, at least the South, would be a nation of farmers. He also talked of the possibility of more than one republic on these shores. Jefferson had seen the Industrial Revolution of Paris and London and had no desire for manufacturing to come to his country. He loved to putter around Monticello and develop his plans on how to improve productivity. He also loved to philosophize on things like the rights of man, government by contract, and other Enlightenment ideas that stood against the forces of tyranny. Jefferson and his Republicans lived in fear that the Federalists were the enemy of his ideal America.

Just as there were those in the South who favored a strong central government, the North also had a class of people who defended localism, though they did not often refer to it as states' rights the way Southerners would. Anytime they believed their Northern values were threatened, they too spoke of nullification, and even of secession. The first such talk came from New Englanders who resented Southern domination.

Another theme I will cover throughout this book is the conflict between rich and poor. I am writing about Southern history, but this division exists in the North too. The New Englander maintained a more homogeneous population because of the common Puritan background. Whenever I talk of New England, I am usually speaking of the Puritan elite, not the working-class immigrants or others who happen to live in New England. Even on the Mayflower not all were Puritans, they had almost as many of what they called "strangers." The Puritans dominated, but it was not always easy for them to do so. In the North, it is the small farmer, Puritan or not, who was the beginning of a working class, and more often opposed a strong central government.

THE GEORGE WASHINGTON YEARS

George Washington was a Southern planter and a believer in the principles of the Constitution, and thus became a great unifier for the new nation. If any other man had become the first president, perhaps the nation would not have survived the difficult first decade. Southerners have always been proud to claim Washington as one of their own, but the fact is they never have looked to him as a defender of states' rights the way they have regarded Jefferson.

Washington was a military hero and was "first in the hearts of his countrymen." He was aware of the party differences around him; and in fact, when he left office, he warned Americans of the dangers of political parties. He apparently felt that some difference existed between North and South as he kept a balance between the two regions in his cabinet. Most historians would agree that he had Federalist sympathies, but also some misgivings about too strong a government. He made the effort to appear nonpartisan.

THE FEDERALISTS BLOW IT IN THE FIRST ROUND

The election of 1796 reflected a pattern that can still be seen in elections today. The Federalists represented the forces of centralism, and their support came primarily from New England and the North. The Republicans represented the forces of localism, and most of their support came from the South and the West. Nonetheless, the Federalist made some advances in the South in the election of 1798 and 1799, even in Virginia. In 1799, the old dominion state sent eight Federalists and eleven Republicans to Congress. Adams appealed to the Southern Federalists when he avoided being drawn into a war with France. However, he blew it when he attempted to stifle dissent.

For those who are not historians, I feel obligated to point out that the Republicans of Jefferson are not that same as the Republican Party of today. The Jeffersonian Republicans were the ancestors of the Democratic Party, whereas the Federalist were the forerunners of the Republican Party. The thread connecting the Federalist with the later Republicans is centralism and the thread running through the Jeffersonian Republicans and at least the early Democratic Party is localism. Both parties change through the years, so this does get complicated. Today no major party stands for the Jeffersonian principle of states' rights and limited government.

In 1798, Congress pushed through the Naturalization Act, Alien Act, and Sedition Act. The Federalists wanted to limit immigration because of a fear that they helped the Republicans more in election time. The Sedition Act made it a crime to attack government officials. This was no mere bluff. Government lawyers prosecuted Republicans, especially newspapermen, and Federalist judges sent them to jail. In the process, Jefferson and James Madison established another precedent for Southern politicians; they advocated the notion of nullification. Madison wrote resolutions for the Virginia state legislature proclaiming the Alien and Sedition Acts unconstitutional and stressing states' rights. Jefferson took a similar position for the state of Kentucky. These Resolutions made the states' rights issue a Western thing as well as a Southern thing. They both took the position that the states could nullify laws passed by the federal government that were deemed to be unconstitutional by the states. This helped to solidify Jefferson's association with the issue of states' rights.

THE SOUTH TAKES COMMAND

Southern Federalists did not disappear with the election of 1800, but the Republicans won fifty-three of the region's sixty-three electoral votes. Nationally, Jefferson, the Republican presidential candidate, won by only eight votes since New England remained solidly Federalist. The Republicans gained some support from the central states with New York giving Jefferson all twelve of their votes, and Pennsylvania contributed eight of its fifteen electoral votes. There would be many times in American history that Southerners would find some support from the central states. The greatest conflict between North and South would be focused on the differences between New England and the Deep South. This again is an example of those ideas presented in Woodard's book, *American Nations*. There are more than just two nations in the United States.

THE SOUTH, THE WEST, AND NATIONALISM

All three of the main regions in the original thirteen states would contribute to western expansion; however, Southern influence would prove to be greater. The plantation economy increased the Southern demand for land which would send more people from that region over the mountains. This helped to cement a bond between the South and the West. Historians tend to overlook a powerful variable of which genealogists are aware—the familial bond. Those from New England had the greatest influence on the Northern tier of new states and territories, while those from the Southern states pushed westward in the Southern tier, preferring those lands with a long growing season. Those from the central states could go either direction.

The Northwest Ordinance of 1787 kept slavery out of the Northwest Territory; however, this did not bother Southerners much since most of this land had limited growing seasons. Slave owners found new land in Kentucky and Tennessee and later in Mississippi and Alabama. Thomas Jefferson gave them more territory with the acquisition of the Louisiana Purchase in 1803. It would be the Mexican War and another major increase in the size of the country which would generate the final point of contention in the contest for regional expansion.

The Republican success in the elections of the early nineteenth century, along with the Louisiana Purchase, helped to instill in Southerners a sense of nationalism. They began to become more and more aggressive in their territorial ambitions and, in fact, had dreams that never materialized such as the acquisition of Cuba, Mexico, and other places in Latin America. In the early nineteenth century, the drive for territorial expansion of the United States came from the South. The North was critical of expansion and the militarism that was a part of it.

SOUTHERN FACTIONS

Three distinct groups developed among the Southern ruling class. The first group, the most conservative, called themselves the *tertium quids*. They felt that Jefferson did not live up to the principles of the Kentucky and Virginia resolves. They were led by John Randolph of Roanoke and Nathaniel Macon of North Carolina. They called on Republicans to never desert the principles that had given birth to their party: local power, small government, and a just fear of the executive. They became symbolic of those Southern planters that lacked the more pragmatic American philosophy. No doubt they were the beginning of those romantic planters that viewed themselves as the vestiges of Southern aristocracy. A step above everyone else, they saw themselves as the defenders of honor and nobility.

Henry Clay was a representative of the second group. He was typical of those Southerners who wanted to see their region participate in the Hamiltonian dream of American leadership in the world markets. Clay began his life in Virginia but moved to the West at an early age. He married into a prominent family and became a planter and slave owner in Kentucky. He was one of those men who tried to become president on many occasions but never succeeded. Though he did not remain with the Whig Party, he was typical of those who facilitated American business regardless of the region they came from.

The third group included the likes of John C. Calhoun of South Carolina. He had a Scotch-Irish background; however, his family became wealthy planters. He is evidence that refutes the view of the planter as the defender of an aristocratic past. He had risen in social class and ran his plantation more like modern agribusiness. He was also one of those rare people who could see into the future by using logic rather than any clairvoyant ability. He seemed to be motivated by regional economic competition rather than romanticized defense of feudalism. He never lived to see Southern independence; however, he realized that the North was growing, and even though the South dominated the federal government most of his lifetime, he knew that her days of glory would be limited.

THE EUROPEAN THEATRE

Americans could not find complete isolation. The European affairs continued to impact their own in two main ways. First, European powers maintained colonial interest in America, which would put them in possible conflict with the United States. Second, the wars that resulted from the French Revolution and subsequent European expansion would interfere with the American desire to conduct free trade. The French Revolution added a philosophical tint to the situation.

The Federalists tended to support the French loyalists on the idea that it is they who had helped the colonies to achieve independence. The Republicans defended the Enlightenment principles of the revolutionaries. Both parties tried to prevent the United States from entanglement in European alliances, of which Jefferson warned us. In 1798, the Adams administration conducted a quasi-war with the French while Jefferson resorted to peaceful persuasion with his Embargo Act.

Despite American isolationism, the European wars threatened the new nation. Napoleon was no doubt motivated to sell Louisiana to Americans to keep it out of the hands of the English, or other European rivals. Even though the French were gone, other European powers remained in America. Spain would be a potential threat from either Florida or the West. The British continued to occupy Canada and the Pacific Northwest.

THE WAR OF 1812 AND NORTHERN RESISTANCE

In 1860, Northerners would be willing to kill Southerners rather than allow them to go their own way in peace. They seem to have forgotten that the first serious discussions of secession came from the New England states. These days, there are many of us who think of war protestors as unpatriotic. The fact is that for every war this country has fought there was a significant segment of the population which objected to it. There would be times when those of the North disagreed with the war path, and other times the South would not agree. Despite claiming that they represented states' rights in the early nineteenth century, it is the South which led the way in American nationalism. There are numerous examples of the different regions demanding states' rights when talking about something that was not in their best interest. The South wanted to see the country expand and therefore supported the wars of the time. It is primarily opposition to American expansion that led the Northern states to threaten secession.

The first bid came following the Louisiana Purchase of 1803. New England Federalists feared that the addition of new western states would diminish the power of the Federalists since westerners seemed to prefer Jeffersonian philosophy. The plan known as the Essex Junto began in Massachusetts. A group of the most extreme Federalists concluded that the only hope for New England would be to form a Northern Confederacy. They believed that it could succeed only if joined by New York and New Jersey. They turned to Alexander Hamilton for leadership who condemned "dismemberment of our empire." He went on to say that it would be "a clear sacrifice of great positive advantages without any counterbalancing good, administering no relief from our real disease, which is democracy." After that, the group turned to Aaron Burr, who ran for governor of New York. Hamilton, like many others, believed Burr supported the move for independence. It was Hamilton's accusations of treason which led to the famous duel between the two men. Burr fled to the West, where he got involved in another plot to carve a new nation out of United States territory; meanwhile the New England movement faded into the pages of history. This would be forgotten by the New Englanders who labeled Southerners "rebels" and "traitors" in the 1860s.

A second movement began in Massachusetts and again sought New England independence; this time it would come about because of disagreements over the War of 1812. The governor of Massachusetts secretly contracted a separate peace with the British. In late 1814, a group of Federalist organized the Hartford Convention and issued a report supporting the right of states to declare federal laws "unconstitutional." This was the same states' rights position laid down by Jefferson and Madison in the Virginia and Kentucky resolves.

The list of demands made by this convention gives us a clear picture of the main disagreements developing between the North and South as of 1814. The only reference to slavery as a problem is the three-fifths rule, which counted the slave population in the distribution of congressmen. Other items on the list included a two-thirds majority in Congress to declare war and admit new states, a one-term limit on the president, and a ban on presidents from the same state succeeding one another in the office. They also prohibited naturalized citizens from federal positions since most were Republicans. In fact, their concerns did not come from slavery but rather the fact that the South was dominating the federal government. This is a prime example of why I believe that the main cause for the bloodshed and destruction of the Civil War and Reconstruction is that the North seized control of the United States government, which had previously been in the hands of Southerners. The South preferred independence over submitting to Yankee domination. I also believe that the main motivation in their different perspectives was economic interest. Much behind the regional divide came from economic competition. More on this to come.

SOUTHERN POWER AND WESTERN EXPANSION ARE THE REAL ISSUE

Southerners needed land for their plantation economy and growing population, which led to territorial expansion and a trend toward Southern domination of the West. Many viewed the South as the more rural part of America. This is true; however, it is not until 1920 that more Americans lived in urban areas rather than rural areas. Until 1920 the majority of the US population were not city slickers. Industrialization and urbanization grew more rapidly in the North; however, in the early nineteenth century, the American dream for most still revolved around the family farm. It is the Northern desire for farmland that caused them to compete against Southerners in the west and inspired them to limit the expansion of the planters and their slaves.

Ironically, in the years after the War of 1812, Southerners seemed to abandon their desire for small government. No doubt this came about because the South was gaining control of the central government. It seems that some Southerners did not object to nationalism and centralism if they were in control and could make federal policy match their understanding of the Constitution. Keep in mind, too, that just as some Northerners yearned for land, some Southerners recognized the benefits and the economic advantages of a strong central government. Southerners in the House voted in favor of the national bank at a two to one margin. The tertium quids' objections based on Republican doctrinal purity held little sway. Southerners did oppose tariffs and internal improvements, but not all Southerners adhered to the Jeffersonian ideal of remaining an agricultural nation.

The Southern resistance to the new nationalism was centered in Virginia, though not all Virginians shared their sentiments. They no longer went by the name of quids. Thomas Ritchie, editor of the *Richmond Enquirer*, spoke for the new group known as the Richmond Junto. He warned his readers that the nationalist cause undermined the hallowed truths of the 1790s.

Jeffersonian traditionalists lost out in the South to the vigor of nationalism under Southern leadership of such men as Henry Clay and John C. Calhoun. These younger men had not been around for the debates in the 1790s, and the prosperity that came with western expansion strengthened Southern control of the central government. It became increasingly clear that the philosophical questions addressed by the traditionalists played second fiddle to regional economic competition. The reality is that most questions of war and peace, whether talking of the War of 1812 or of the Civil War, revolved around economic competition; ideology was mainly used as a propaganda tool. The South dominated in the early nineteenth century, and its growing strength led to a decline of Jeffersonian values. The regional conflicts between 1789 and 1848 had much to do with economic competition and little to do with the morality of slavery.

WESTERN EXPANSION AND SLAVERY

The first serious debate over the expansion of slavery into the territories came with the admission of Missouri as a state. The two regions that became known as North and South were better known at this time as slave states and free states. They had achieved peace by keeping an equal balance in the Senate between the number of senators representing slave states and free states. This is itself an example of the power struggle between the North and the South. The admission of a new state as a slave state would jeopardize this balance. That balance was maintained by the admission of Maine as a free state. Before this compromise, a congressman from New York named James Tallmadge proposed an amendment to the Missouri statehood bill. His proposal had two parts. First, no more slaves would be allowed to enter Missouri. Second, all slave children born after statehood would become free at age twenty-five. The issue was resolved with the Missouri Compromise of 1820, but not without beginning a national debate that would escalate after the Mexican War.

The Tallmadge Amendment sparked concern among Southern slave owners. First, they began a tradition of objecting to outside interference with slavery. Second, they did not want to see any barriers to the expansion of slavery. They knew that their domination in the federal government came with their growing strength in the West. Third, supporters of the amendment denounced slavery as an aberration in the United States or any nation dedicated to freedom and liberty. Their conclusion would be that the slave owners were immoral. As of 1820 abolitionists were a minority, but their numbers were increasing.

A curse that came with the Missouri Compromise was the restriction of slavery to South of Latitude 36°30'. This would be a major part of the debates that would rage after the Mexican War. We will see later that this issue of the expansion of slavery into the territories is what sparked the war, not the institution of slavery where it existed.

The most important issue that separates those who condemn Southern and Confederate symbols from those who claim that these icons are merely part of our heritage is the invalid assumption that the Confederate symbols represent a nation that was based on the defense of slavery. This is the main reason they use to justify the destruction of our heritage. Northern liberals, blacks blinded by NAACP rhetoric, and now Southern scallywags claim that the war was fought to free the slaves. Most Americans are taught in school that the Civil War was a war to end slavery. Southerners have always claimed that the war was fought over states' rights and the principle of self-determination. Part of the reason for this disagreement is failure to understand that the issue of slavery may have been what sparked the crisis over states' rights, but that does not negate the latter issue. What we see in this chapter is the dispute over the spread of slavery into the territories, not the abolition of slavery.

Lincoln and Congress would support the Corwin Amendment, which would have protected slavery, where it existed, from federal interference. Most *Librevs* either don't know their history, or hide this fact, as it destroys their false narrative. The belief that the federal government was denying the South its Constitutional rights regarding taking slaves into common territories is what led to Southern secession. This, in turn, caused the North to invade the South in their determination to preserve Union control of the South and the tariffs which fed the central government. It was all about economics. Neither Republicans nor Abraham Lincoln spoke of abolishing slavery until the war had dragged on for many months, and it became increasingly clear that the war would not end until the entire nation abolished slavery. Even the *Librevs* will agree that the issue that fueled the debate over states' rights was not the abolition of slavery but rather the spread of slavery into the territories. Most Americans of 1860, including those in the North, were not abolitionists.

The minority in the North who sought abolition; however, most objected to the spread of slavery into the territories for two other reasons. First was economic competition. They feared that they could not compete with the planter and his slave labor, and therefore if the planter went into the new lands, the small independent farmer would be shut out. Second, the North did not want blacks living in their states and territories. Most people, North and South, in the Antebellum period believed blacks to be inferior to whites. In fact, many in the North thought that Southerners were degenerate because they lived in close proximity to blacks. Northerners passed laws to prohibit blacks from settling in parts of the North. A good example is the territory of New Mexico. They never had slavery before American occupation, yet they passed laws preventing blacks from settling in the territory. Other Northern states and territories also tried to prevent blacks from making a home in their lands. It is difficult to prove why people did what they did, but it seems clear to me that such laws were motivated by what we today call racim. The problem with using a modern term like this is that for the most part, the world- Europe, Africa, Asia, the North and the South, held these views Therefore, it is useless to blame the South for this, or to dwell on something that was near universal at the time, but does not fit into our culture today. That was then, this is now.

THE JACKSONIAN ERA CONFLICTS

The years 1824 to 1840 reveal a conflict within Southern society. The period brought Jacksonian Democracy, the Democratic Party, and the rise of the Whigs. Remember, Jackson was not only a Southerner, but also a planter and a slave owner. I will discuss the various classes, ethnic diversity, the Indians, and slavery in separate sections; for now I will talk only about the political changes.

Jackson had more votes than any other candidate in the election of 1824, but too many candidates and the resulting political bargaining put John Quincy Adams in the White House. All the other candidates were Southerners, which only serves to support my previous claim that the period was fraught with conflict within the region. William Crawford was from Georgia, but represented the Virginia dynasty. Henry Clay represented the West. John C. Calhoun, though he would later be the champion of nullification and states' rights, wanted a stronger national government, and supported internal improvements and tariffs to protect American industry.

The other candidates and their supporters believed Jackson a potential military despot. Jackson won the election of 1828 with support from parts of New York, Pennsylvania, and the former Northwest Territory. His support in the South was nothing less than impressive. He won in Alabama by more than eight to one, in Tennessee by twenty to one, and in Georgia he got 100 percent. Southerners believed that Jackson would deliver them from the evils of a strong central government, though they would later find that this may have been an invalid assumption. New England was not totally for Adams, but did distinguish itself from the rest of the nation by offering him the greatest support. Remember this election when I later speak of the division between the rich and poor Southerners.

The biggest contest during the Jackson administration was the battle between Jackson and Calhoun of South Carolina. The latter served as vice president during Jackson's first administration; however, some personal issues and the nullification crisis led to the selection of Martin Van Buren for the second term. Jackson sided with Peggy Eaton when the ladies of Washington rejected her while it was Mrs. Calhoun who led the attacks. Jackson also found out that Calhoun had tried to get Jackson punished for his military aggressiveness in Florida following the Battle of New Orleans. These personal conflicts just fueled the main issue which centered on tariffs.

Jackson inherited the situation but was determined to enforce the tariff voted in before the presidential election of 1828. Calhoun became the leader of the South Carolinians who turned to the Virginia and Kentucky resolves for support in their nullification of the tariffs, which they considered extreme. Calhoun argued that the states had created the Union, and as creators, they were sovereign. He also said that the states gave the federal government only those particular powers specified in the Constitution and nothing more. Jackson took the same position that another Southerner, Abraham Lincoln, did in 1861; he threatened to use the United States military to enforce federal law. A crisis was averted when South Carolina and the Federal government compromised. But the question of states' rights would not go away, and South Carolina would again stand up to federal threats.

WHIGS, SOUTHERNERS, AND ECONOMICS

The support of economic growth is the connection between the Whig Party and the later Republican Party. The main support for the party came from those men who believed in American business and that a strong central government was necessary. What separated the two, so that Southern Whigs could not support the party of Lincoln, is that fact that the Whigs catered to the planters and thus the slave owners as well as Northern businessmen. The common man in the South continued to look to the Democratic Party of their hero, Jackson. About three quarters of those in the South never owned a slave and therefore would not have the same concerns as the planters. So, why did many of them relate to the interest of the planter? Perhaps they hoped to become slave owners themselves someday. Perhaps, they might have feared the economic competition that would come with millions of freed black men.

When the Southern Whigs arrived at the national convention in Harrisburg, Pennsylvania, in December 1839, they supported the candidacy of Henry Clay. Clay had dumped his American system, which supported economic nationalism, and he advocated states' rights and condemned abolitionists. When Clay lost out to William Henry Harrison, the Southerners had no major problem with that choice. Harrison had become associated with Indiana; however, he was a native Virginian. His father was active in that state's politics and was a signer of the Declaration of Independence. As a congressman, Harrison supported the South during the Missouri crisis, and he also denounced abolition. His running mate was another states' rights Virginian, John Tyler. Harrison carried seven of the slave states and won more than half of the popular vote in the region.

Harrison died after his first month in office, and the first vice president turned president, John Tyler, took his place. Tyler seemed in many ways to carry on the conservative states' rights philosophy of Jefferson and the Quids. Soon Whigs, including Southerners, did not consider him one of their own, especially after he opposed a national bank and their policy of economic nationalism as unconstitutional. Whigs had considered Harrison a yes man for their programs. In Tyler, they found a man of principle who was a strict constructionist regarding the Constitution. They turned to Clay for leadership since this was the basic idea of his American System.

The revisionists have been right in identifying the growing significance of slavery in the nineteenth century politics. Both the Democrats and the Whigs knew that they needed the support of Southerners if they hoped to win national elections. Calhoun was among the first to realize that if the population in the North continued to grow at a greater rate, it would just be a matter of time until a party might win with Northern support only, and threaten slavery and support oppressive tariffs. For now, I wish only to make the point that the Whigs were not perceived to be a threat to slavery, whereas the Republicans would be.

It is not easy to distinguish Southern Democrats from Southern Whigs. Both parties had a large number of planters and slave owners among their ranks. The Democrats tried to present their party as the one which advocated "equal suffrage." At this time this meant equal suffrage for white males. The Whigs responded by claiming that the Democrats kept the voters "laboring under tyranny and oppression." The best explanation for the regional divide is that the Whigs were more commercially oriented and lived in more commercially oriented towns and counties.

ETHNIC DIVERSITY AND REGIONALISM

I have mentioned before that part of the stereotype that justifies those who attack the South today as a bastion of racism is the fact that the region is less ethnically and racially diverse than the North. I have also pointed out that this is somewhat true today; however, at the time of the Civil War, this was not the case. I am now going to give some specific examples for this time period. The South was especially more diverse than the bastion of Northern righteousness, New England. In the first census of 1790, the country was 47.9 percent English. In New England, the percentage was 82 percent, and in the South, they were only 35.7 percent, less than the population with African ancestry. The *Librevs* like to refer to the central colonies as more diverse, but the Anglo-Saxon population in the mid-Atlantic region was slightly more than in the South with 36.9 percent. The central states had only 5.3 percent African population.

This is based on the 1790 census; by 1860, there was even greater diversity in the South compared to New England. Both regions removed Indians, one way or another; however, many of those in the South married Indians. I have seen nothing to contradict that common claim of Indian blood for many with Southern ancestry. The records on the removal of Indians to present-day Oklahoma indicate a considerable number of mixed- bloods. Significant areas of the South had an existing Hispanic population, which became absorbed into the future Confederate states including Florida, Alabama, Louisiana, and Texas. Let us not forget the French population of Louisiana as well as the number of Huguenots who immigrated into the South. Only one-third of the American Jewish population lived in the South, but the majority of Northern Jews were not in New England. As to Southern bigotry, it is interesting to note that half of the Jews who held congressional seats came from the South. I recognize that the numbers are too small to have any statistical significance, but from the small sampling we have, the indication is that Jewish politicians found a greater acceptance among Southerners. It apparently was not a fluke that the first Jew to hold a cabinet post in America was with the Confederate States of America.

We are often misled by the popular boasting of America as the land of immigrants and diversity. The fact is that prior to 1830, there was very little immigration into the United States. Immigration increased between 1830 and 1860, but we are talking about a virtually all-European population. The English only accounted for 18 percent of the new Americans, but the rest also came from Northern Europe. This included 27 percent German, 43 percent Irish, and the remaining 12 percent from the rest of Northern Europe. With increased immigration, the North became more diverse, including New England.

The Celtic population was British, and so in some ways it could be argued that those of Irish, Scottish, or Welsh backgrounds are not part of American diversity. The diversity of America at that time was mainly the same as Britain. Nonetheless, the Celtic population of New England in 1790 was only 11.9 percent compared to 21.8 percent of the South. The Central states had the highest with 24.6 percent, less than 3 percent more than the South. However, the common immigration pattern for the Scottish in the late eighteenth and early nineteenth century was to land at the port of Philadelphia, move west in search of affordable land, and as that filled up, move South through the Appalachian valleys. From there they migrated west along with the established population. The Celtic fringe theory claims that the Celts were the dominant population in the South. These statistics suggest that they were not necessarily more numerous than the Anglo-Saxon; however, they may have been. The key word in the theory is "fringe." This means that many of those of English background came from the north or west of England and not the predominantly Anglo-Saxon southeast. Most of the New England Puritans came from the southeastern parts of England.

THE NORTHERN ECONOMY AND CHEAP LABOR

I will overlap into the time period covered in the next chapter, but that is because the labor demands were changing throughout the nineteenth century. The condemnation of all things Southern, and especially Confederate, is based on the assumption that this region had slavery and that the Confederate nation existed for the preservation of slavery. The North, on the other hand, did not have slavery and even harbored the majority of the radical abolitionists who wanted to rid America of the evil institution. The conclusion of those at the vanguard of eradicating our Southern heritage is that the Northern way of life was morally superior and that they were right to kill our ancestors, burn their cities, destroy their crops, and leave millions dead, crippled, or homeless. This is absurd in the face of the fact that Lincoln and his government simply sought to continue to transfer money from the South to the federal government, and were content to let slavery remain. Many people believed slavery would not last much longer if kept within the states where it then existed.

It is difficult to prove, but I firmly believe that the Northern choice for non-slave labor was more of an economic decision than an example of the moral superiority of the Northern people. In the colonial days, New England was a land of family farms, whereas the South began to develop a slave plantation economy. This was not due to any moral depravity of those settling in the South, but rather that the climate of the Southern colonies was more comparable to the warm climate of the Caribbean islands. This is where the plantation slave economy thrived in other English colonies. The children of the prolific puritans met most of the labor demands of that population. New England had some slaves, including Indians, but did not have the same scale of agriculture as the plantation South.

By 1840, New England businessmen began to construct manufacturing facilities, and naturally, the demand for labor increased. At first, their needs were satisfied by their own female population. Going back in the Middle Ages, young women were used to meet cheap labor demands. Because of the nuclear family that existed among most Northern Europeans, the females had a time where they often sought employment outside the family. One of the most common jobs was as domestic servants in the homes of the wealthy, but they did other work as well. They started working when they were old enough to make a significant contribution and quit when they married and went off into their own family unit. Like most nuclear family cultures, they married at an older age, which means that they worked for several years before starting their own family. It was tradition for those of New England to look to this source of labor. These daughters of the puritans were not exploited the way cheap labor often is. The first manufacturing plants in New England, such as the facility in Lowell, Massachusetts, were idyllic communities which were more humanely run than those found in most European industrialized cities.

Between 1840 and 1860, manufacturing increased dramatically and with it the demand for cheap labor. By that time, the Northern businessmen had found a source far superior to the slave labor of the wealthy Southern planters—the rapidly increasing immigrant population. Generally speaking, it is the manufacturers who wanted to allow the increased immigration while the majority of the older American population wanted to stop them from coming in. Those who did not like the foreigners formed a political party, the Know Nothing Party, whose main political platform was to put an end to the great influx of immigration. Whereas the manufacturer saw a source for labor, the rest of the population saw a threat to their way of life. On the lower end of the socioeconomic ladder, they thought of the Irish or Germans as competition for jobs and housing. For the more middle class, they saw a growing voting population that could steal elections. In the larger cities, the immigrants outnumbered the native population and thus dominated city politics. They even became a significant number of votes in the state and national elections. This is also the time period when many refugees from failed socialist revolutions in Europe arrived, eventually causing serious trouble for the country.

The *Librevs* help us here because they were the first to point out that the wealthy controlled America in the colonial period and continued to do so after the formation of the United States. This is why the immigrants continued to come in despite the objections of the more numerous lower and middle-class population. In 1840, manufactured goods in America stood at $483 million; by 1850, it was over $1 billion, and in 1860, it doubled again to $2 billion. In 1860, seventy-four thousand of the factories in the Northeast accounted for two-thirds of the output. Of the 1,311,000 American factory workers, 938,000 were employed in the mills and factories of New England and the mid-Atlantic states.

The growth in the immigrant labor force created a system in which the Southern planters could argue that their slaves were better off than the Northern workers. This was not just a rationalization of their labor system. Remember, Charles Dickens and Karl Marx made a living writing about the deplorable conditions of the nineteenth-century working class. Some claim that the American working class was better off than their counterpart in Europe, but nonetheless, most lived in flimsy shanties and in grim conditions that were hazardous to their health and that of their families. The slave owner offered healthcare for their slaves; the manufacturer just replaced a sick worker with a healthy one. The slave owner provided food and housing for their slaves even in the off season, whereas the factory owner left the workers to fend for themselves when the factory shut down production. The diets of the average slave was better and the size of their living quarters was larger than what the average immigrant worker experienced. No one can put a price on freedom; however, when it comes to the physical comforts, there was much to be said for the argument that the slaves were better off than the Northern working class.

The bottom line here is that the situation does not seem to imply that Northerners, especially the wealthy manufacturers and businessmen, were morally superior to the Southerners, but rather that they developed a different system for meeting their demands for cheap labor. Slaves may have been on the lowest social level in the South, but the same was true of free blacks in the North. It is not a matter of moral superiority which led to the different ways of meeting demands for cheap labor. The Southerner inherited a system that dated back to the early days in the New World, whereas the Northern businessman did not have the same needs for labor until after European philosophy questioned the morality of slavery.

I will emphasize that my point here is not to justify slavery or to suggest that slaves were happy. The point I am trying to make is simply that the Southern slave system was not the product of a morally bankrupt slavocracy. There is no evidence to accept the difference between the two cultures as being the result of anything other than an economic decision, not superior morality. If one wants to take a socialist perspective in which the wealthy are the enemy of the working people there is no reason to condemn the Confederate States of America anymore than the United States of America.

There was manufacturing in the South too, but more money could be made growing cotton. Remember that cotton is produced to supply raw materials for the textile industry. Not only was cotton a major product in the Southern economy, but it was also a major product in the American economy. The Northerners depended on the production of Southern cotton for their textile mills. One major error Confederates made in their decision-making was that the Europeans, especially the British, would intercede on their behalf because their textile industry would not be able to survive without Southern cotton. The fact is that the British had already begun to find other supplies of cotton in places like Egypt and India.

There are two reasons the *Librevs* do not like to talk about the fact that the Northern textile industry depended on slave-grown Southern cotton. First of all, this means that the Northerners who condemned slavery depended on slave labor as much as Southerners did. This means that they were participants in slavery and certainly not in a position to feel morally superior. Second, this dependence on Southern cotton could explain why the North was determined to keep the Southern states in the Union. They like to think that the Northern states invaded the South to free the slaves. The reality is that Northern businessmen and politicians were well-aware of the consequences of losing Southern resources. I have already explained how the rise of nationalism is the result of the growth of the world-market economy and the need for protection of businessmen. In the modern world-market economy, and in fact in most other times and places, most wars have been fought for the benefit of businessmen. And of course, as has already been mentioned, the North depended on the South to pay for the federal government that benefited the North. Northern newspapers and politicians' speeches leave no doubt that the tariffs would be collected. In fact, Lincoln said there would be not violence as long as the tariffs were paid.

The relationship of the Southern economy to slavery is more complex than it might at first appear. Prior to the nineteenth-century increase in cotton production, many Southerners questioned the benefits of slavery. This is when they first created the colony of Liberia and entertained the idea of returning the slaves to the land where they came from. The plan never worked, mainly because of the high price tag, and in fact, the number of slaves continued to increase at a much higher rate than the exodus. Yet the South led the way in the number of abolition societies early in the republic.

As the planters increased cotton production, the dependence on slave labor increased. In 1840, there were 2,487,213 slaves, and the number increased to 3,957,760 in 1860. Because of the growth in cotton production and the resulting growth in slavery the antebellum period was not a good time to talk about abolition. There were too many influential men making too much money. These men were from the North as well as the South. What we do not know, and will never know, is how slavery would have ended if the Northern hordes had not invaded and killed hundreds of thousands of the Southern people. There is general agreement that slavery would have died out in the South by the end of the Nineteenth Century. I can never accept the idea that it was necessary to kill hundreds of thousands of Americans to end slavery. This did not happen in any other country. Many countries had slavery at one time, and do not have it today, and in no other case did they kill hundreds of thousands of their own people to achieve abolition.

I have always thought of Maryland as an example of how modernization took its toll on the institution of slavery. Slavery still existed there in 1860; however, they had the highest population of freedmen. One reason for this is that there were a significant number of Quakers who lived in Maryland at the time that church urged manumission. There was also a greater dependence on manufacturing in Maryland, especially in Baltimore. Another trend in Maryland was toward the production of specialty crops. This industry did not lend itself to slavery as easily as tobacco, rice, cotton, or sugar. Cotton did not do as well in Maryland and Virginia. Many of the slave owners in those states were selling their slaves to those in the cotton belt. Virginia also had a large number of freedmen. They were not that far behind Maryland on the path to industrialization. Louisiana also had a large free population. Historical differences are probably the main explanation for this. Slavery had been different under the French and Spanish.

When we look at these various locations, we can see the possibility that slavery would have died a natural death. Another possibility is that as the Northern businessmen capitalized on the cheap labor of immigrants, the Southerners might have realized the economic advantage of this system. As we will see when we get to discussing the postwar South, the sharecropping system offered advantages over slavery. First, it increased the labor supply by taking in a number of poor whites in addition to the African population. Second, numerous expenses went away, such as providing housing, food, clothing, and medical care. The greatest advantage came when it was necessary to cut production because of a declining economy. Slave owners had to take care of their slaves or dispose of them when production was cut, compared to the sharecroppers of the twentieth century who simply lost their jobs and homes and were cast out upon the highways of America to fend for themselves.

Librevs especially like to think that these various classes banded together to defend slavery in 1861. I, for one, find it difficult to believe that the average Southerner would have been willing to fight simply so that the rich guy could keep his slaves. If you read the reasons they gave for banding together, it was to defend their homes and Constitutional rights. I will talk more about this later. The non-slave owner might fear economic competition if the black man entered the free labor market. Many feared what the society would be like if bands of free blacks roamed the countryside unrestrained by the slave owner. This is also true for the working and middle classes of the North. They imagined large numbers of blacks would head to the North looking for jobs and housing. They did not like the idea of black people living among them as can be seen by the laws passed in several Northern states which prohibited free blacks from settling within their borders.

THE SLAVES

This is not a book about slavery; however, I feel that I must give a brief overview of the institution during this period. Every *Librev* historian is aware of the fact that the slave population in the United States grew mainly because of natural population growth. Why is this important? It is rare for any human population to grow when they live in deplorable conditions. The fact is that even though only 5.4 percent of the slaves brought to the New World ended up in the area now called the United States, by 1860 the slave population in the country accounted for 60 percent of the slaves in the Americas. Remember, in 1808 the United States banned the slave trade. Most historians accept the research that claims only about fifty thousand were smuggled in illegally. Therefore, most of the population growth was due to natural growth. I have always found it amusing how the *Librevs* avoid discussion of these facts; they must know what the implications are. When you look at the average life -span of slaves in the rest of the Americas, it is even more astounding.

Who were the slave owners? Only 25 percent of the Southern population owned slaves. Of those, only half owned more than five slaves, and only a quarter owned more than ten slaves. The planter class is defined as those who owned twenty or more slaves. Of the one quarter of Southern whites who owned slaves, only 12 percent fit in the class called planters. Only 1 percent of the 25 percent owned more than one hundred slaves. Remember, that 75 percent of Southern whites did not own a single slave.

The "our family treated their slaves well" defense which I just said we must avoid, is recognized by the *Librev* historians; they call it paternalism. They freely accept that many of the planters had this attitude. However, we must also realize that there were planters who had the opposite attitude. There are men today who abuse their wives and kids; there is no reason to doubt that some slave owners abused their slaves. Paternalism was part of Anglo-Saxon culture. Even in the Middle Ages, the wealthy considered their servants as members of the household. The philosophy of *noblesse oblige* made it good manners to treat your servants well. This tradition carried over to the planter class in the colonies. We know from interviews with former slaves that most were treated well. There were laws against slave abuse, though as with all laws it is the enforcement that is the true measure of its effectiveness.

As Southerners became more businesslike, they learned the principles of good management just as the Northern factory owners did. A common expression which has been around a long time is "you get more flies with sugar than with vinegar." Fear can be a management tool, but it is much more limited than treating people with some respect and allowing them some dignity. There is no doubt that most used some combination of the "carrot and stick approach." Even today managers use this, even if the stick is nothing more than dismissal or lack of promotional opportunity.

Looking at the situation from the slaves' perspective, this means that even though most slave owners owned less than ten slaves, most slaves came from large plantations. Most were field hands; the lucky ones worked in the big house. On many large plantations, the head-house servants had positions of considerable responsibility and respect. The larger plantations would have some skilled workers, such as carpenters or blacksmiths.

The significance of owning twenty or more slaves is that this is considered to be the point at which the slave owner would need management help. The first level would be the overseer. This was most often a white man, but on some plantations, a trusted slave might have the job. The overseer was often not respected by either the slaves or the owners. They were usually from the lower classes. The overseer handled discipline, including whipping. In *Gone With the Wind,* the overseer was the one who became a scalawag and tried to steal Tara from Scarlet by merely paying back taxes. This was an accurate reflection of the image that many whites had of these men. The overseer might need formen, which they called drivers. The drivers were usually slaves. The wise master or overseer who could find the right man would pick one who had the respect of his fellow slaves. The driver usually received preferential treatment, perhaps the best cabin or a few more rations.

The purpose for slavery was to provide cheap labor, so the work is the main part of slave life. Most were field hands. They worked in either the task or gang system. The former was prevalent in the rice-growing areas where they worked at a specific task. The slave had to finish the task assigned to them, which might take a few hours or most of the day. Some slaves were allowed freedom to hire themselves out to other farmers in their freetime to earn money, or to raise livestock or vegetables for sale. The hardest work and longest days came at different times of the year, depending on the crop being cultivated. The gang system was more popular among the cotton growers. This was simply slave gangs supervised by drivers and overseers.

The foundation of the slave diet consisted of pork and corn. Some could get more variety, and many would be allowed to have a patch of ground where they could grow their vegetables of choice. Like the average white farmer, they might get an occasional chicken, and in fact, the slave diet was not generally much different from that of whites. Like the white population, some slaves supplemented their diet with fish or wild game. Hunting was a sport liked by all Southerners, and many times master and slave hunted together. We can see this today as Southerners have pretty much the same taste in food, regardless of race. Malnutrition was rare, and most masters realized that the well-fed slave would be the best worker.

Clothing was pretty basic, with typically two allotments a year. They received a set of lightweight clothes for the long summer months and something a little heavier in the wintertime. In either season, it would be coarse and plain. Children often went naked while some wore a cotton shirt that covered them similar to a dress. They often received hand-me-downs from the whites. Many of the slaves tried to design their own clothes, introducing more color and variety.

Housing varied from substantial brick structures to barely adequate shacks. Most lived in a small wooden cabin with a fireplace. They were usually grouped together in a small village. By 1860, many slave owners understood the importance of housing. As pointed out before, the average slave had more sleeping room than the average immigrant in New York, and might be comparable to a backwoods frontier cabin.

Much of the research today focuses on the cultural life of the slaves, which of course includes the family life. In the 1960s many sociologists claimed that the high divorce rate among black Americans was a byproduct of slavery. They assumed that the family unit suffered under slavery. Recent research indicates that the antebellum family unit was stronger back then than it is today, with fewer out of wedlock births. There were tragic times when families were torn apart, but most masters sought to avoid this as much as possible, despite what many critics claim. Most slave owners tried to keep family units together. They knew this made the slaves happy, and they knew that that a happy slave was a better worker. The division of families was the worst part of slavery and no doubt the greatest source of pain and suffering among the slave population. Another factor not often mentioned is that many plantations were owned by absentee owners, many times Yankees. These might have a harsh overseer trying to make a profit and not a family living in close proximity to their servants.

The year I lived in Africa has given me considerable insight in understanding the influences of African culture on Americans today. The cultures of Eastern and Western Africa are as different from each other as the cultures of Eastern and Western Europe. The great majority of the slaves came from Western or Central Africa. Researchers have traced the influences this had on American music, dance, architecture, diet, and overall lifestyle. We have always understood the obvious cultural impact of the European masters on their slaves, but few realize how much the African population influenced the white Southerners. I repeat, I am a firm believer in the Celtic fringe theory, which claims that Southerners and Northerners were different from the very start. I also believe that the differences increased over time. Much of the reason for this is that Southern culture and lifestyle borrowed considerably from the black Southerners.

I have always looked at the music as the best example. The world listens to Southern music, including blues, jazz, gospel, country, bluegrass, and rock. This music is a blending of African melodies and rhythms combined with the folk music of England, Scotland, Wales, and Ireland. Though the British have imitated it since World War II, it is still distinctly an American music which cannot be found in either Europe or Africa. It is the combination of the two. I believe this to be true about much of Southern culture. This is why Southerners differ from Northerners and from Englishmen, Australians, or other British colonial cultures. Southern culture is a melding of Anglo-Saxon, Celtic, and African culture with a trace of French, Spanish, American Indian, and other influences.

FREE BLACKS

In 1860, the black population of America was about 4.5 million. Of these, about a half million were free. Of the free blacks, about half of those lived in the North and half in the South. North or South, the free blacks were considered second-class citizens, a status that would continue in both regions until after World War II. The free population grew with time. We have few accurate statistics from the colonial or Federalist period. Maryland had 1,817 free blacks, and as late as 1780, Virginia had even fewer. By 1790, Maryland had 8,043, and Virginia had 12,766. Much of the increase came with the revolutionary rhetoric of liberty, but some also came because of the large Quaker population in these two states. Quakers freed their slaves with the encouragement of the church. Contrary to popular belief, Southern states such as Virginia had abolitionist movements, and even attempts to legislate an end to slavery. Unfortunately, these failed, especially after radical abolitionist in New England grew more violent in their rhetoric. The French and Spanish influences accounted for much of the free population in the Southwest. Regardless of where they lived, they were rarely considered equal to free whites. They were often barred from trades; had restricted access to theaters or railroads; and their legal status in things such as serving on juries or voting was usually very limited.

Some slave owners were black. This is a select group of Americans, but it does mean that there is a possibility that some of those who want to ban our heritage may be condemning their own ancestors. There were 3,600 black slave owners in 1850. Seventy percent of South Carolina's black masters lived in Charleston. They were also among the small group of slave owners who used slave labor in manufacturing. One of the latest *Librev* trends is to point out that by 1860 some Southern states did take steps to rid themselves of free blacks. Arkansas passed a law that they must all leave the state by January 1, 1860. They had a choice—choose a master or be sold into slavery. Florida passed a similar law, and Mississippi was on the verge of it. This does not justify or condemn the attacks on our Southern culture. The North also made it clear that they did not consider blacks to be of full citizenship status, and some prohibited free blacks to live in their states too. Few of the Northern freedmen owned property or businesses; most worked at menial, low-paying jobs. In most parts of the North, blacks could not vote, could not attend public schools, or use any of the public services available to the white population. Many of the abolitionists wanted to end slavery coupled with the idea of returning them to Africa. This is called the colonization plan, which I discussed earlier. Mr. Lincoln was a firm believer and advocate for this plan.

ABOLITIONISTS

I have often challenged my students to provide a biblical scripture that condemned slavery. So far, I have not received a good answer. The fact is that there has not been any literature from the Roman Empire that morally condemned slavery. In those days, it was accepted as a way of life. In the eleventh century, the Pope spoke out against slavery, and because of the position of the church, European societies ended the institution. As I have already pointed out, it was reintroduced in the early days of the Age of Exploration. With the Enlightenment, more and more people began to consider the institution morally wrong. Some spoke out at the time of the Constitution, but they clearly did not garner enough support to condemn it. It may come as a surprise to many, but some of the support for accommodating slavery the Constitution came from New England slave trading states. In 1804, New Jersey became the last Northern state to outlaw slavery.

The failure of the colonization movement served as a slight setback to abolitionism. The establishment of William Lloyd Garrison's abolitionist newspaper, the *Liberator*, in 1831, began a period of growth for the movement. By 1835, there were more than 400 chapters and, by 1838, 1,350 chapters with more than 250,000 members. Though growing, there were numerous riots that began in Northern cities by those who did not support abolition. Many had fears of hordes of freedmen moving North. The growing immigrant population feared the competition for jobs and housing. The reality is that most Northerners were racist, even some of the abolitionists. Abolitionists were a minority, and the Republican Party knew that an abolitionist would not have a chance of getting elected to the White House, even in the North. The *Librev* historians have often stated that the abolitionists were less than 5 percent of the population.

As the attacks escalated against slavery, Southerners became more creative in their defense. I do not present this section as any attempt to justify slavery, but simply to understand how people thought during this time period. Their defensive arguments fall into five categories: historical, racial inferiority, equality of whites, comparison to the conditions of the white working class, and religious.

We must also keep in mind that there were Southern abolitionists. The first abolitionist newspapers were printed in Tennessee. Southern abolitionists outnumbered those in the North for much of the early republic. Since colonial times, there have been many examples of Southerners who freed their slaves because they believed it to be wrong to keep them. This was the main source for the free blacks living in the South. Some worked in the Underground Railroad. Levi Coffin, so-called "President of the Underground Railroad," came from North Carolina. Even after he moved to Indiana, he still defended Southerners to his Northern friends. Like most Quakers, he hated slavery, but he did not hate the slave owner.

Slavery defenders who used historical arguments pointed out that slavery had been an integral and legitimate part of western history. It was around in the Greek and Roman civilizations. Belief in racial inferiority justified the reintroduction of slavery by Europeans after the papal ban of the eleventh century. In the early days of exploration and colonization, such attitudes were based on the fact that the Africans were not Christian. In the nineteenth century, Southerners as well as others of European ancestry, used science to try to prove the inferiority of Africans as well as the others. Southerners pointed out that all civilizations had class differences, and this, of course, meant that someone had to occupy the bottom rung of the social ladder. Southern whites had a political democracy unmatched anywhere else in the civilized world. Southerners argued, "the poor white laborer at the North is at the bottom of the social ladder, whilst his brother here has ascended several steps and can look down upon those who are beneath him, at an infinite remove."

John C. Calhoun defended slavery on the grounds that the slaves of the South lived in better conditions than the working class of the North, which I have discussed to some degree above. Karl Marx and Charles Dickens became famous for pointing out the deplorable conditions of the working class of the Industrial Revolution. Neither wage worker nor slave lived in fancy houses nor wore fine clothes, but I have little doubt that the slave was much more of a stranger to hunger. An injured or sick wage earner would most likely be unemployed, whereas the slave owner had money invested in his slaves and would see that the slave got medical attention. A factory owner will lay off a worker in idle times, whereas the master must maintain his slaves even at times when there is little work for them to do. I have noticed many examples in the slave narratives recorded during the depression years in which the interviewee admitted that he longed for the economic security he had in his earlier life. However, most denied any desire to return to slavery despite physical comforts. We must realize that few men would prefer a life of comfortable servitude over a more stressful life of freedom.

Disputes about the morality of slavery caused splits among the Methodist and Baptist and threatened such a split for the Presbyterians. There may be no direct condemnation of slavery in the Bible, but some clergymen used the golden rule or other such scriptures to support their point of view. The Southern preachers not only gave the slave owners religious justification, but they were a source of consolation for the slaves. The preachers would emphasize the importance of the afterlife over any burdens that we might have to bear in this world. The stories of Moses and how his people eventually found freedom helped to serve as a source of hope. It could also give a boost to their self-esteem knowing that even God's chosen people had at one time been slaves.

No one today would accept these arguments to justify slavery; however, I point these out to show that the defense of slavery in the early nineteenth century was not due to moral inferiority of the Southerners. Most Northerners and Europeans, even some abolitionists, accepted some aspects of these intellectual defenses. I do not see any justification in the scrapping or condemning of our heritage just because many of our ancestors believed in things that we do not believe in today.

THE INDIANS

White people in both regions had been less than kind to the first inhabitants of the land. The Cherokee had learned to write, built schools, and publish newspapers in an attempt to adapt to the white man's civilization. This did them little good when they were forced from their ancestral lands as the white man sought wealth from gold or new lands to farm.

The history of the federal government's failure to live up to treaties made any alignment with the North unlikely. Several of the tribes also held slaves, which tended to tie them to the South in the struggle. The plains Indians experienced very harsh treatment during and after the war as the United States sought westward expansion and the building of a transcontinental railroad.

Many of the Indians allied with the Confederacy, partly because those in the South sought an Indian alliance, and the North did not. The actions of the Indians were not unanimous, and even those who did support the South did so because they saw it in their best interest to do so.

Andrew Jackson maintained a favorable image among Southern whites when it came to his policy toward the Indians. Though Cherokees had fought with him, when the white man thought it was necessary, they were removed to the West. Like the Southern attitude toward blacks, Jackson took a paternalistic view toward the Indians. He believed that whites were better guardians of the Indians' welfare than the Indians themselves. He believed that they could survive if they kept their traditional ways, but they would have to do so in the West.

CONCLUSIONS

The period 1789 to 1845 began with a Federalist victory and the ratification of the Constitution, but concluded with Southern domination of the United States government. It is true that some Southerners had become a force for nationalism, but they used it to their benefit while in power. This is contrary to the defense of states' rights—what Jefferson had stood for in 1789, and what the South would stand for again in 1861. It would appear that everything was going their way with the victory in the War of 1812 and the acquisition of new land for the rapidly expanding cotton industry. Some, such as John C Calhoun, had visions that the Southerners were riding the crest of a wave that was about to break in a big crash. The North was growing faster, and it would only be a matter of time until they dominated the House of Representatives. They would have enough votes to take control of the White House, a predominately Virginian residence on Pennsylvania Avenue, without Southern support. To make matters worse, those in the North began to speak out against slavery. Many Southern planters began to see them as a threat to the labor system that they had depended on for generations. Ironically, their territorial expansion, fueled by greed, would eventually lead to a war which they would lose.

IV: NORTHERN HATRED OF THE SOUTH AND SOUTHERNERS, 1848–1860

URING THE YEARS AFTER the Mexican War, Northern hatred for the South escalated and gave birth to the Republican Party. There appears to be consensus on this, although many would use different wording. The main interest of the *Librevs* in their studies of this period is to prove that the war was caused by slavery. Their "proof" lies in the argument that regional conflict grew during the post–Mexican War period, climaxed with the secession of South Carolina, and the majority of the issues which generated the conflict revolved around slavery. They look more specifically at the development of the political parties beginning with the 1844 election in which both major parties had supporters from both the North and the South, but by 1860 this was no longer true. The Whig Party vanished because of regional division, the Republican Party arose with Northern support alone, and the Democratic Party was divided into Northern and Southern factions. The gravitation to political parties was based on issues related to slavery, tariffs , and the size of the central government. Their arguments have some merit.

If the question is "did slavery lead to secession of the Southern states?" then the *Librevs* might be correct. When we look to the cause of the war, it is more difficult to find a simple answer. According to Lincoln there would be no war if the central government could collect its tariffs (needed to run the government). The problem was those states which paid the bulk of the tariffs were no longer in the union. It is interesting to point out here that the question of slavery in the territories was no longer relevant, as the seceded states had no connection to the territories. Therefore, the continued threats against the seceded states can only be explained by a lust for money by the banking-mercantile-government interests in the North. As I pointed out in the Introduction, there were other variables, too, and there are plenty of those who claim that one or more of these other variables were the main cause. Many do take the stand that slavery was the main one. Regardless of which position one takes it cannot be considered "proven," and the debate will likely continue.

I also pointed out in the Introduction, both the President and Congress of the United States said that the war was being fought to preserve the Union, not to end slavery. Most of the *Librevs* do not accept the word of the politicians. They seem to be possessed by the arrogant and self-righteous assumption that the "Lost Cause Myth" of a war over states' rights has been shattered. Though they still argue among themselves over other topics, in their eyes the states' rights position has been reduced to "myth."

Way back in the 1890s, Major Jed Hotchkiss of Virginia expressed the same thesis in his history of Virginia, as it appeared in the *Confederate Military History*. These volumes of Southern history, as told by the former Confederates, are a prime example of what the *Librevs* have labeled the "Lost Cause Myth." Hotchkiss began, "While the war of 1861-65 between the Union, or Northern and non-slaveholding States, and the Confederate, or Southern and slaveholding was not fought by the South as a whole, and certainly not by Virginia, for the perpetuation of slavery, nor by the North, at least in its inception, for its abolition." Most good *Librevs* should be frothing by now as they shout "Lost Cause Myth." However, Hotchkiss went on to say, "yet every candid student of the history of the colonies and the States must admit that the slavery question, often under the name of 'State rights' of one kind or another, was a dominant factor making issues that led to the temporary disruption of the Union."[12]

In 1828 tariffs came close to causing South Carolina to secede. If they had, and Jackson had used military force as he threatened, then that war also would have been over states' rights, not tariffs. Likewise, I believe the war which began in 1861 was fought for states' rights. It was not fought by the North to free the slaves, and the South did not fight to preserve slavery. I also pointed out in the introduction that my view is economic. I believe that economic competition was part of why the issue of states' rights became so important.

No doubt, the *Librevs* would claim that they are only interested in presenting an accurate history of the United States. I believe it to be much more than that. I believe that historians which I have labeled *Librevs* are not as objective on this topic as they claim to be. I see much of what they do as a perpetuation of the Northern rhetoric, which began with the Republican South haters during the period of impending crises covered by this chapter. The supporters of Mr. Lincoln blamed the whole war on the planters of the South, which has become known as the planter conspiracy. I do believe there is much to be said about the influence of the planters.

I also believe that it is the planter class which led the South down the path of secession. However, it is Lincoln and his Republicans who turned it into war. It is they who killed, maimed, and destroyed their fellow Americans. The South

---

12. Maj. Jed Hotchkiss, *Virginia, Confederate Military History* Volume III. (Atlanta: Confederate Publishing Company, 1899), 17.

haters prior to 1861 had one thing in common with the South haters of today—a feeling of moral superiority based on their despising slavery. They totally reject the Quaker attitude that it is slavery that is to be hated and not the slave owner.

The *Librevs* continually vote for Lincoln as the greatest American president. I find it ironic that liberal university educators in America today project an image of not only being unpatriotic but have also been called "America haters." The *Librevs* do not reflect any of this attitude when it comes to talking about the Civil War. They praise Abraham Lincoln as the leader of the United States in what many of them would consider one of the few justified wars in American history, the crusade to abolish slavery. Therefore they endorse the slaughter and crimes committed by the United States military as a necessity in ending the institution of slavery. To them, cherishing any symbol of the Confederate cause is to worship slavery and to endorse the views on race that the institution was predicated upon. This is really the main point that those of us whom they like to call neo-Confederates have disagreement with. Their views help to fuel those who seek to erase all memory of the Confederacy from public view.

I have covered the current thinking along these lines in my Introduction. I cover the history of this critical antebellum period here only as a refresher. I covered my personal beliefs on the cause of the war in the Introduction. Whether one agrees with the *Librev* theory, accepts my beliefs, another explanation or combination of explanations, the fact is that there are none which can claim their view to be proven. It remains one of the most disputed topics in American history. Therefore, it is not adequate grounds to destroy monuments to those Confederates who gave their all to defend their homes and families.

THREE AMERICAN MYTHS

At times, I have been accused of being one of those liberal America haters by my students. The fact is that we cannot understand the true story of the South if we continue to accept the patriotic rhetoric which has become so much a part of our history. There are three myths most relevant to the historical era covered by this chapter. I have already discussed all three to some degree but feel I should repeat them again here as I discuss how they are related to this period. First is the idea that this country was founded on any principle other than the making of money. Second, is a myth which has become most popular today: the idea that we are a land of immigrants and that as such we stand for "diversity." The third is the denial of the fact that the United States is an empire. The first myth is that many Americans believe that our nation was founded on some noble principle that makes us all Americans, such as a love of freedom and democracy. We often hear "that is what this country is all about," yet there does not appear to be any consensus on what that is. I believe this is important to understand because that is why there are those who insist on making this later war about slavery rather than a conflict over economic issues. I believe that most people came to this country to make money. There have been those who came for other reasons, but by far most came for economic opportunity.

Economic differences were among the most important that separated Northerners from Southerners. The most obvious of these in early America was the Southern dependence on slavery for a source of cheap labor. We must realize how important the plantation economy was to the Southern way of life, and that the system of slavery served no purpose other than economic. The other side to this coin is that the North could not easily accept the loss of the Southern states. Northern cities depended on the Southern resources. Cotton was an American product, not just a Southern one. Without the Southern states, the federal government was broke. This would end most internal improvements.

We must also realize that the political competition reflected in the development of the political parties was based on economic competition. The cities and states of America compete against each other, and any notion of an American economy is dependent on their individual profits. Who in Atlanta would be happy with a prosperous American economy which neglected Atlanta? Who in Boston would live in poverty so that the rest of the country could prosper? Regardless of region, the average American looks after their personal interest first. Any concept of American prosperity is based on what most benefits the individual, who is part of an economic community. A continuation of unity of the regions is based on the assumption that all are better off if we remain united. When this is no longer true, then they will consider the possibility of terminating that Union.

The second myth is that we like to think of America as a land where people of all nations are welcomed. This is the belief of most of those who want to erase our heritage. This is an important point because it relates to the *Librev* belief that the Confederacy is evil because it was in opposition to the nation of immigrant multiculturalism which most liberals believe in today. This is what they believe the country to be all about. It has been a popular subject relating to debates on the role of immigrants today, but they connect it to race issues in the past. They like to think that it has always been a nation of immigrants, and therefore the North stood for good and the South stood for evil.

The fact is that in the 1830 census 99% of the population were native born. Most were descended from the British colonists who established the colonies and then turned them into an independent nation that spread to the Pacific. A large segment of the population in 1830, about 7%, were Germans. They had immigrated to the British colonies, and for the most part they assimilated into the British population. Another large segment of the population was African. There were an assortment of others, mostly Europeans and relatively few in numbers. Between 1830 and 1860 immigration increased, but 85% of those were German or Irish. The latter were also from the British Empire, as most of the colonist were. It was not at all the "nation of immigrants" or the multicultural dream that some like to think America has always been. The United States of 1860 was basically a British nation which had gained independence from the empire. Except for the German, African, and Native American populations, most of the diversity in America was that which existed in the British Isles.

When it comes to the immigrants in the early days it was the Northerners who had the greatest problem accepting them. They were the ones who promoted the Alien Act of 1798. Keep in mind that at that time the immigrants were mostly Irish and German, not anything like the multicultural dream many have today. There were merchants who wanted the cheap labor, but probably most of the population was not accepting of immigrants. The Know-Nothing Party was founded in the 1840s on a desire to exclude the growing population of immigrants. It was the supposedly morally superior Northerners who led this fight. Southerners may have not liked the immigrants any more that they did, but they did not fear them as much as Northerners did.

I accept the assumption that this kind of hatred is the result of feeling threatened, whether it is real or imagined is not important. People who hate other groups of people feel that the objects of their hatred pose a threat to their way of life. Immigrants did not pose as much of a threat in the South. This is the same principle as to why Southerners have expressed more concern about blacks. The African population did not pose much of a threat to most Northern communities. The fact that this nation has blacks and those descended from immigrants is not due to any brotherhood of freedom lovers. The diversity in population we have is the result of the rich, both North and the South, who had a demand for cheap labor. The rich Northerners wanted cheap immigrant labor. The rich planters wanted slave labor. The general population did not care for either of these groups living among them. In the minds of most of the native population, the foreigners with their strange ways appeared to be a threat.

I believe it important to clarify these first two myths because I believe that economics is behind the regional conflicts. As we explore the impending crisis of 1848 to 1861, we are talking about a time in American history in which many prospered. Various communities in America found their niche in the increasingly prosperous young nation. They unified when they saw an economic advantage in doing so. By the mid-nineteenth century, it was becoming increasingly obvious that the central government, once dominated by the South, was falling into the hands of the North. By 1860, some in the South believed it to be to their advantage to extinguish the alliance that had been known as the United States. The rich of the South, mainly in the tidewater plantation areas, led a crusade for secession to protect their economic interest. The rich of the North, mainly from New England, chose to kill the Southern people to protect their economic interest. The average person in both North and South rightfully called it a rich man's war and a poor man's fight. This is why in both parts of the country there were many who did not like the way things were going. Many of the Southern poor, and even yeomanry, did not want to secede from the country they grew to love. Many of the Northern people did not want to go to war to force the southern states to remain in the union. This is why the election of 1860 was so complicated. The election of a candidate whose support was totally from one section of the country was ominous.

The disagreement over slavery, the points of contention, were related to American expansion, or imperialism. The Republican Party did not come into being to abolish slavery, but rather to stop the spread of slavery into the territories and to represent the interests of big business. The expansion of empire is what gave us the territories. In the days before the Civil War, it was the South which pushed for territorial expansion. Most objection to the Louisiana Purchase came from the North. I have already discussed the attempted movement for independence that came in 1814 because of the New England disagreement over the War of 1812. Though the North did not threaten secession, they objected to the Mexican War while the South not only supported it, but insisted on it. During the antebellum period, the South abandoned some of the Jeffersonian principles. They fostered nationalism, even though that might lead to a stronger central government. This is a great irony; they pushed to acquire the territory which would lead to their discontent and subsequent secession. Of course, Thomas Jefferson thought the expansion of the country would lead to secession and more than one republic on the continent. Indeed, he saw several republics springing up, and prospering in mutual trade and friendship.

The journalist John L. O'Sullivan gave us the name for antebellum American nationalism when he wrote a column about Manifest Destiny. This Jacksonian Democrat voiced the attitude of American imperialism which justified the aggressive actions the country took. His philosophy appealed to Southerners, and the Democratic Party adopted it as a way to woo Southern voters. O'Sullivan created an American myth that is alive and well today. He claimed that Americans are not like the Europeans, "our national birth was the beginning of a new history, the formation and progress of an untried political system, which separates us from the past and connects us with the future only." We do not conquer for kings "but in defense of humanity, of the oppressed of all nations, of the rights of conscience, the rights of personal enfranchisement." The planters might acquire new lands that would expand the production of cotton, but that is not our objective. The contradiction in what O'Sullivan said is that "we are the nation of progress, of individual freedom, of universal enfranchisement." Like Jefferson, he said, "all men are created equal." This is the philosophy which would make it more and more difficult to justify slavery.

The greatest fallacy in this belief is thinking that the profits from expanding cotton fields did not motivate the antebellum American expansionist any more than oil fields motivate U.S. foreign policy today. In other words, it seems most likely that American imperialism has been and still is fueled by the desire for profits. Occupation of Canada had been a dream of pre–Civil War Americans. A group of Americans in 1854 drafted a private document in Ostend, Belgium, that has become known as the Ostend Manifesto. They made a case for purchasing Cuba from Spain, and if they refused to sell, then they advocated seizing the island by force. Americans had the same problems then that we have today; not everyone in the world comprehended the nobility of our mission. Some called it a "buccaneering document" or a "highwayman's plea." Southern expansionists worked elsewhere. In 1857, William Walker gained control in Nicaragua, and his new government was immediately recognized by President Pierce. Congressional resistance dried up financial support for Walker's enterprise, and by 1857, the American president of Nicaragua was ousted.

Most resistance to territorial expansion came from the North, but not all of them had a problem with it. Some Northerners also wanted expansion as they took their apples and moved to Oregon. People of all regions rushed to the gold fields of California, Nevada, and other western states beginning in 1849. Henry Clay was one man who correctly feared that territorial expansion could lead to scraping the scab known as the Missouri Compromise.

The profit motive led many in the South to support territorial expansion, just as it did in the North. The conflict had always been Southerners wanted the option to take slaves into territories, while the North wanted the territories to remain the province of white men. Unfortunately, many believed the Constitution did not allow the prohibition of slavery in territories. This did not stop the North from pursuing this course.

Hoping to stimulate economic expansion and provide a buffer between Indians and Mexico, the Mexicans offered considerable rewards in land to any who would move to the area known today as Texas. Stephen Austin led a band of Catholic, primarily Southern pioneers who hoped to find new land to settle.

Austin sought self-government within the country of Mexico, but following his imprisonment in Mexico City, and the overthrow of the republican government by Gen. Santa Anna, the Texicans declared independence. After defeat and annihilation at the Alamo and Goliad, they captured Santa Anna and won their war at San Jacinto in 1836. They immediately sought annexation by the United States; however, the passive Congress feared that it would lead to war with Mexico. Again, most of the resistance was from the North. Some feared that it would upset the balance between the slave and free states. Then along came John Tyler.

Tyler had been elected vice president with the Whig victory of 1840; however, the sudden death of William Henry Harrison made him the first man to become president because of the death of his predecessor. Some even questioned the line of succession, but Tyler remained in the White House. In many ways, the Virginian Tyler stood for traditional Jeffersonian principles more than the modern business interests promoted by the Whig Party. He had alienated other Whigs, and he accepted the fact that he would not win the nomination of that party in 1844. His adherence to the letter of the Constitution lead some historians to list him near the top of the list of our greatest presidents. He fantasized about beating out Martin Van Buren for the Democratic nomination, but Northern

Democrats feared domination by the Southern slaveholders, and many objected to territorial expansion. Tyler hoped to win support of the Southern Democrats by pushing for the annexation of Texas.

John C. Calhoun banded together with Tyler in advocating the annexation of Texas, which they assumed would become a slave state. Some advanced the belief that Great Britain had its eyes on the land and that if the British acquired it, there would be no room for the slave owners. The annexation question became a slave issue as well as an expansion question. Van Buren did not support the idea, which led to his political death among the Southern Democrats. Tyler had hoped to win the nomination of that party, but instead, it went to James K. Polk. Tyler supported Polk with the assurance from Polk that he would support Texas annexation.

As we will see by the end of the chapter, the main argument of the *Librevs* is that slavery polarized the political parties. With the election of 1844, we can see that there were other issues which separated the two regions. With the nomination of Polk, the Democratic Party adopted a platform to annex Texas. Meanwhile, the Whigs nominated Henry Clay, and Southern Whigs feared that the party would lose to the Democrats over the issue of Texas. Clay did not oppose the idea but apparently did not come across too convincing as he won only four states in the South. The *Librevs* would have us believe that the Texas question was a slave issue; however, there is no way to know the significance of slavery compared to the general imperialism that had become known as Manifest Destiny. Congress passed the annexation of Texas before the election so that the campaign slogan "54° 40' or fight" could rally Polk to victory. The lack of Southern support for Clay would have had nothing to do with the acquisition of Oregon. The pressure to acquire Oregon came from Manifest Destiny only and was not in any way related to slavery.

THE MEXICAN WAR

The Mexican War divided North and South, and at first glance there is little to suggest that slavery had much to do with the philosophical disagreement. The Southern quickness in answering the call for volunteers demonstrated the regional support for the war. Tennessee was asked to provide three thousand troops, but nearly thirty thousand came forward. Kentucky filled its quota within two weeks after Congress declared war. Baltimore took only thirty-six hours to raise its allotted number. In the first year of the war, forty-five thousand Southerners had joined compared to only twenty-four thousand from the North. One reason Southerners supported the war for Manifest Destiny was the fact that Texas was settled by Southerners.

The Texas question and lack of support for the Mexican War had weakened the Whig Party. The Whigs became critical of Polk and his policies, which alienated many Southern Whigs whose patriotic feelings demanded that they support their country while at war. As stated above, there was more dividing North and South than simply slavery.

THE WILMOT PROVISO

The Wilmot Proviso is one of the most important, if not the most important, piece of failed legislation in American history. It also began making slavery a critical issue relating to the new territories which came with victory in the war with Mexico. David Wilmot proposed an amendment to an appropriations bill that would forever prohibit slavery in any territory acquired as a result of the Mexican War. This would not only begin a string of crises in American politics that would dramatically change party alignment in the country, but would also climax with the election of Abraham Lincoln and the subsequent secession of the Southern states. Southerners would remain united up to the War for Southern Independence in their resistance to the Wilmot Proviso. They saw that not only would this proposal limit the freedom for the Southerners to move into new territories which had been won largely with Southern blood, but that it would also suggest that the Southern system was morally tainted. This will be discussed later when I talk about the growth in Northern contempt for Southerners.

This proposed amendment would disrupt the existing political parties as they would divide based on region. The Southern Democrats not only opposed the proviso, but they also made it clear that they would not support any candidate "who does not unconditionally, clearly, and unequivocally declare his opposition to the principles of the provisions of the Wilmot Proviso." The Democrats would straddle the fence as much as possible, until their selection of Stephen Douglas divided them in 1860. The Whigs, however, were on the path toward extinction as they too split by region. The Northern Whigs supported the proviso as adamantly as the Southern Whigs objected to it. After the death of the party, the Southern Whigs would seek a new party elsewhere while the majority of the Northern Whigs would be the foundation for the Republican Party.

THE COMPROMISE OF 1850

The admission of the state of California would be the next major blow to the Whig Party as well as the next cut in severing the South from the Union. President Taylor surprised and annoyed his Southern supporters by proposing the idea of dividing the entire Mexican acquisition into California and the New Mexico Territory, with the idea that both would be admitted to the Union and that both would be free states. Even though Taylor was a slave owner himself, he did not believe in the spread of the institution into the new territories. Then came Henry Clay with one of his compromises.

The Clay proposal called for a number of measures that would appeal to both factions and thus the term compromise. First, California would be admitted as a free state, the obvious choice of those living in the territory at the time. Second, the remaining territory would be divided into Utah and New Mexico, and that the residents of those territories would decide for themselves whether to be slave or free. Third, the slave trade would be abolished in the District of Columbia. Fourth, it called for the passage of a new fugitive slave law to enforce the constitutional provision to return those slaves living in another state. Fifth, it also settled a border dispute between Texas and New Mexico.

Each side found a particular aspect of this compromise that would become a point of contention. The Southerners liked the idea of "popular sovereignty," which they saw as a way to end the restriction of 36° 30' that they inherited from Clay's 1820 Compromise. This opened any new territory as a possible place for Southern expansion. All future political aspirants would insist on the adoption of popular sovereignty if they had any hope for Southern support. Many of those in the North, especially the abolitionists, would have a problem with the fugitive slave law. Not only did the nation maintain the institution of slavery, but also anyone, black or white, who helped runaway slaves would become criminals themselves.

The proposed compromise widened a growing regional split in both of the major parties. The Northern Whigs backed Taylor who opposed the idea. The Southern Whigs supported Clay. The Northern Democrats considered it reasonable and backed it while the Southern Democrats followed the lead of Calhoun and said that Clay had sold out the South. The Calhounites cried "never" to the notion of admitting California as a free state. In the Deep South, the parties broke down all together. A minority of Democrats joined a Whig majority and promoted Union parties while minority Whigs joined most Southern Democrats and looked to states' rights parties.

Taylor found an easy way out when he died, and thus, the crisis had passed. Each part of the compromise had been divided into a separate bill. Congress passed each part; and the new president, Millard Fillmore, signed them into law. Calhoun was a minority in recognizing that the future for Southern influence in the national government appeared bleak. Most Southerners were still proud to be Americans and were pleased with the outcome.

KANSAS

The next battleground was not the newly acquired Mexican lands but rather involved those yet unsettled parts of the Louisiana Purchase, more specifically Kansas and Nebraska. Stephen Douglas was chairman of the Senate Committee on Territories and pushed for the organization. When he began, he assumed that the Compromise of 1820 meant that slavery would not exist there since both were above 36° 30'. Southerners rallied around their new platform—popular sovereignty. Douglas accepted their argument. If it was okay in New Mexico and

Utah, it should be good in Kansas and Nebraska. Douglas saw an opportunity to unify the Democratic Party as the proposal served to further divide the Whigs. The Northern Whigs to the man opposed the repeal of the Missouri Compromise and made support of Douglas's Kansas–Nebraska the only issue. Instead of unity, Douglas had created a split in his party. He got it through the Senate easily enough; however, the House took ten weeks to settle the debate, which ended up taking a toll on party unity for the Democrats and the Whigs. The passage ended up a Pyrrhic victory for Southerners. It ended the 36° 30' restriction; however, it had aggravated Northern hatred for Southerners which would eventually lead to the formation of the political party that had no interest in the feelings of those Americans in the South.

Shortly after its passage, settlers began to stream into the new territory. Most were motivated by personal interest as they simply hoped to acquire a family farm; instead they became soldiers in the first battles of the war. Some expected Kansas to become a slave state as it was assumed that those who would vote on popular sovereignty would be settlers who had migrated west from the slave state of Missouri. The abolitionists of New England hoped to prove that assumption wrong when they created the New England Emigrant Aid Company. Through this organization, they helped to finance Northern settlers who would vote for Kansas to become a free territory and eventually a free state. This led to a countermove in which Southerners would go into Kansas, even if it was only at election time.

The land of dreams turned into a nightmare in what became known as Bleeding Kansas. Both sides turned to violence in the struggle, which resulted in death and destruction of property. John Brown first attained national attention as he and his sons not only murdered supporters of slavery, but also hacked their bodies to pieces with his sword. Though a mere handful acted this way toward Southerners at the time, Brown eventually grew to be a highly admired martyr to many radical Northerners. He also was a terrorist to many, North and South, who were shocked by his actions.

In 1856, the violence spread to Washington. Senator Charles Sumner of Massachusetts made a speech against what he called the "rape" of Kansas. At one point, he made a derogatory reference to a senator from South Carolina, Andrew P. Butler, which angered his cousin, Representative Preston Brooks. Brooks proceeded to the Senate where he confronted Sumner with his cane. The beating not only destroyed the cane but also left Sumner incapacitated for a few years. The battle cry of the newly formed Republican Party became "Bleeding Kansas, Bleeding Sumner."

A nearly fatal blow came to the Democratic Party in the form of the Lecompton Constitution of 1857. The slave supporters held an election in which they hoped to make Kansas a slave territory. The free soilers assured its passage when they boycotted the election which they considered illegal. Douglas and the Democrats had adopted a platform of popular sovereignty; however, they saw the Lecompton Constitution as a bogus document. Douglas led a crusade for the Democratic Party to reject the admission of Kansas with Lecompton, which turned a friend of the South into a man they could not vote for.

SOUTHERN ECONOMY

I began the discussion of the economy in the previous chapter, but at that time I was mainly interested in the source of labor. I talked about the fact that the North found immigrant labor while the South not only continued to use slaves, but that it was even more profitable to do so in the antebellum period. I also pointed out that this was not a matter of defending a feudal way of life, but that they were part of the nineteenth century capitalist system.

The reality is that the South was as much involved with the modernization process as the rest of America. Like those in the North, their ancestors came to make their fortunes and those who succeeded were those who found a niche in the modern world-market economy. At the time that the South seceded, the Confederate States of America was the fourth wealthiest nation on earth. There are statistics which can make it appear that the South was falling behind in industrialization. While they were still on the path of industrial and urban development, the reality is they were not entering the new stage as rapidly as the North. I will continue with what I began in Chapter 3.

Between 1840 and 1860, the South declined from 20 percent to 16 percent of total manufacturing in the United States, thus making it appear that the South was resisting modernization. Other statistics suggest that this is not the case. Southern manufacturing increased, but at a slower rate than in the North, and that is why the percentage of total manufacturing declined. Manufacturing below the Mason-Dixon went from $53 million invested capital in 1840 to $93.6 million in 1850 to $163.7 million in 1860. In the 1850s, manufacturing output increased 79 percent to $186.9 million. This was less than other regions but still clearly growing. The per capita manufacturing output in the South was $17.09 compared to $37.33 in the Northwest, $96.28 in the Middle States, and $149.47 in New England. These are per capita statistics, and of course, the population in the North was growing at a more rapid rate. The bottom line is that the South was modernizing, just not at as rapidly as the North.

The fact remains that there were those in the South who promoted modernization and sought to profit from the world markets. Railroad mileage in the South increased five times in the 1850s. The South lacked the banks that the North had, but they did grow. In 1846, James D. B. De Bow brought out the first issue of his journal *De Bow's Review*, which promoted commercial development in the region. The more popular industries included iron works, tobacco processing, and textiles. The South remained agricultural, but more and more of the crops produced were for the world markets, not eating. The South actually had food shortages during the war because they could not eat tobacco, cotton, hemp, or indigo. The successful planters were those who ran their plantations like a business, such as Jefferson Davis. Most of the men who promoted modernization were Whigs, like their counterparts in the North.

The South remained more agricultural, but that is not to say that it was in the same way as their ancestors did during the feudal era. Cotton alone, but also other plantation crops such as tobacco, sugar, rice, and indigo, made for greater profits in agriculture for the Southern farmers. I mentioned in the previous chapter how the South was making a lot of money from the growing of cotton. Why would someone seek to find an alternative when they are making so much money doing what they already know? It is not resisting industrialization, but more the result of the great profits they were acquiring with their crops in the world market. Some studies show that Southern farmers, especially those outside the large plantation economy, were happy with their lifestyle and level of wealth. They did not see acquiring more money as desirable if it interfered with their lifestyle and culture. Let the Yankees work themselves to death, the 'Plain Folk' would continue in their traditions.

PARTY REALIGNMENT

The *Librevs* support the notion that the war was fought over slavery. Yet other issues such as tariffs, internal improvements, and the role of the central government versus state government affected voters. With each issue the political parties evolved toward becoming regional parties. In the case of the Whigs, the split led to its demise. The Democrats split into two parts, thus allowing the new strictly northern Republican Party to win with less than 40 percent of the vote in the 1860.

THE WHIG PARTY

It is tempting to describe the Whig Party as one made up of men with money, but it would be more precise to look at the Whigs as those who aspired to make money by seizing the opportunities of American participation in the world markets. Whigs would not be the descendants of Jeffersonian Republicans, and thus would not represent a dominant view in the South since the formation of the United States. They would instead be those who tended to support a more centralized government since such a government would be more protective of the American businessman in the world market. Remember, the South did have enough Federalists that they ratified the Constitution. The best way to understand them is to reject any image of them as defenders of aristocracy, but rather as being predecessors of the modern American agribusiness. They did not run their plantations like a feudal lord, but rather as a businessman who produced cotton instead of widgets.

Henry Clay's American System is a good example of what I am talking about. He was a Southern planter, but he was a businessman. This is why at first, Southern Whigs stood behind him in the election of 1844. They supported the economic policies of Clay, but they could not support him after he came out as opposed to the annexation of Texas. The Southern plantation economy was dependent on expansion. He carried only four states in the South as the Democrats adopted a platform of annexing Texas.

The next blow for Whigs came with the Wilmot Proviso. Southern Whigs opposed the Proviso while Northern Whigs just as adamantly supported it. The party took no official position on the issue, and until it did, the Southerners would not abandon the party. With the Whig nomination of Zachary Taylor, the party remained alive. Taylor had been a hero of the Southerners who supported the Mexican War, and he was a planter and slave owner.

The 1852 nomination of another Mexican War hero, Winfield Scott, delivered the final death blow to the party in the South. Scott was a Southerner; however, unlike Taylor he did not seem to represent planters and the Southern interest. In the South, he carried only Tennessee and Kentucky. No Whig presidential nominee had ever done so poorly in the slaves states. Not only that but the Whigs did poorly in the state elections of 1852 and 1853; the only houses they controlled were North Carolina and Tennessee. In the Congressional elections of the same year, only fourteen of the sixty-five representatives were Whigs. Almost all in the South blamed the antislavery Whigs of the North for their demise. By 1854, the party was virtually dead in the South. Some Southern Whigs turned to the Democrats while others hoped to mold the new Know-Nothing Party into a Southern party.

THE DEMOCRAT PARTY

The Democrat Party, like the Whigs, began to divide along regional lines, which does support the *Librev* view that slavery contributed to the growing divide. One could argue that the trouble began with the elections of 1840 and 1844 in which the Southerners led the way in defeating Van Buren in the first election and the selection of James K. Polk as the Democrat candidate in the latter. The dumping of Van Buren for Polk had much to do with the Texas question, which in turn had a lot to do with the expansion of slavery and states' rights.

The party definitely began to divide after the Wilmot Proviso. Those in the North tended to support it while those in the South rejected it. The main reason that the Democrats did not share the same fate as the Whigs is that they found the policy of popular sovereignty. As the Whigs declined, more and more Southerners turned to the Democrat Party. In the elections of 1852, they picked Northern candidates Franklin Pierce of New Hampshire and James Buchanan of Pennsylvania. The radical abolitionists would have to look elsewhere, but the more moderate Northern voters could support these candidates who gave the Southerners the popular sovereignty they demanded. In 1852, Pierce won his party the most Southern votes since the days of Andrew Jackson.

Even Stephen Douglas yielded to Southern desires when he included popular sovereignty in his 1854 Kansas–Nebraska Act. While the Southern Whigs would continue to shop around elsewhere, most Southerners seemed content with the way the Democrats were going until Douglas took a stand against the Lecompton Constitution. After that, most Southerners refused to back the man that the Northern Democrats insisted on in their 1860 convention.

THE FREE SOIL PARTY

With the fall of the Whigs and the path taken by the Democrat Party, the Northern abolitionists and anti-Southerners also shopped around. In 1840, the Liberty Party ran a candidate who did not advocate abolition but did preach against the spread of slavery into the territories. When Taylor ran in 1848, the "Conscience" Whigs, some remnants of the old Liberty Party, and a few Northern Democrats formed the Free Soil Party based on the principles of the Wilmot Proviso. Their slogan became, "free soil, free speech, free labor, free men."(they might also add 'free from blacks' as they opposed blacks immigrating North) In the 1848 election, they nominated Van Buren, who won one out of seven of the Northern votes. They did not come anywhere near winning, but they did win ten seats in Congress and demonstrated a growing demand for their way of thinking.

THE KNOW-NOTHING PARTY

Most Northern bigotry was aimed at the ever increasing immigrant population, mainly because they were Catholic. The South had some immigration and certainly had some anti-Catholic prejudice; however, the South did not receive as many of the newcomers. Though almost all of the new Americans came from Northern Europe, and did not come close to the population diversity we have in America today. Those in the Know-Nothing Party sparked many a riot and succeeded in passing legislation barring Catholics from public office and unsuccessfully sought to increase the residency requirement for citizenship from one year to twenty-one years.

Southerners, especially Southern Whigs, looked to the Know-Nothing as a new party that could represent their interests. Even some in Louisiana, which had a large Catholic population, backed the alternative. Most of the sugar-planting Whigs in that state were also Catholic, but they were willing to ignore the anti-Catholicism if the new party would adopt a platform of popular sovereignty in all the territories, and back the Fugitive Slave Act. These are the issues that racked the national conventions of 1855 and 1856. In 1855, it looked like the Southerners would get their way, but in 1856, the Northerners won out. This caused the failure of the Know-Nothings in the South.

THE REPUBLICAN PARTY

Northern Whigs and some Northern Democrats became the foundation for a new party, which would not only survive but also find success while making no effort to appeal to the Southern voter. The prophecies of Calhoun relating to the Northern population growing to the extent that they would not need the Southern vote had come to pass. In the 1860 census, the Northern population was more than twice that of the South, including the slave population. Initially, it required the split of the Democratic Party to win the White House for the Republicans, but as we will see, by the end of Reconstruction, the new party had become solid without any Southern support and eventually would even be able to abandon the black Southerners, who had been "encouraged" to vote Republican.

The mere existence of the Republican Party affirms the *Librev* interpretation of antebellum politics and the role that slavery played. The Whig party did divide and die as the Southern Whigs deserted them since they could not adopt a pro-slavery platform. The Democratic Party would split since the Northern choice of Stephen Douglas refused to support the pro-slavery Lecompton Constitution. The Know-Nothings would not conform to the slavery platform. In the election of 1860, the South would secede from the Union as it became clear to them that they could not retain any power and influence in the national government. Not only did the Republicans have no concern for the Southern voter, but they also became more and more aggressive in their criticism of Southerners. Led by the abolitionists, they used strong language in their condemnation of slavery in which they clearly expressed feelings of moral superiority. This is the same attitude many Northerners continue to embrace in their attacks on our Southern heritage today.

SOME OTHER SLAVERY ISSUES

Some other national issues helped to fuel the political divide between North and South. The Dred Scott case drew national attention. When the Supreme Court backed the Southern slave view, it further agitated Northern hatred and prejudice. More and more writers expressed their contempt for Southerners, the most famous being Harriet Beecher Stowe and her book *Uncle Tom's Cabin*. Though the book was not based on any first-hand knowledge of Southern slavery, it was popular even outside the United States. Some Northern writers attacked the Constitution, and some even the Bible, for not condemning slavery.

The Lincoln Douglas Debates of 1858 helped to bring national attention to the future president and the man who would lead the way in the destruction of the South. Perhaps the most devastating was the raid on Harpers Ferry.

John Brown had demonstrated his hatred for Southern slave owners in Kansas, but in the fall of 1858, he attempted to lead a slave rebellion. Though the terrorist was tried, convicted, and hung for treason, many in the North looked at him as a martyr. It was bad enough that Northerners would politic to limit the spread of slavery into the territories. It could even be understandable that some would campaign to end slavery in America. . But with the venom put out by some writers, the support of many for Brown, and his determination to not only terrorize, but kill Southerners, it was becoming clear that there was no future for the South in the United States of America. It is interesting to note that the first man killed in the raid by this madman was a free black man.

NORTHERN HATRED OF SOUTHERNERS

Many, if not most, Northerners would protest my accusations that they hate Southerners today almost as much as their ancestors did more than a century and a half ago. The more liberal-sounding would simply call it disagreement, or better yet, they would say that we Southerners are still fighting the Civil War. The fact is that, like our ancestors in the 1860s, we are simply defending ourselves. The battles that we fight today are a defense against Northern aggression. The verbiage of the South haters who attack our heritage is very similar to the language used by the Northern abolitionists and the radical wing of the Republican Party of 1860. Northern identity was founded on hatred of Southerners, and it is alive and well today.

I find that the following words from Major General Isaac Ridgeway Trimble best sum up the Northern attitude. Keep in mind that Trimble was born a Quaker; raised in the border South; and that neither he nor his family owned slaves. He graduated from West Point, but spent the thirty years before the war working for the railroads, the vanguard of modernization in America:

Our Connection with you never had, from the early settlement of the colonies till now, any bond but that of political interest. Your bigotry [sic] & hatred of everything Southern drove us from you-the Union was at variance with our feelings, tastes, pursuits, honorable aims & religion and time instead of removing these, has strengthened them, untill [sic] on the great principles of self preservation and self respect, the Union has been sundered forever. Let the calm verdict of a future age, be awarded on the merits of this contest. The South has no fears for her reputation either on account of the wisdom of her statesmen or the valour [sic] of her soldiers-If she perish, she can go down to the grave of nations, with the proud boast that she has abundantly nourished with her blood the seeds of Liberty, which will spring up & bear fruit to bless mankind in comeing [sic] time.[13]

Since it fits in here I will repeat some of what I said in the introduction. I feel confident that the majority of *Librevs* would disagree with what I am saying on this subject, but there are those who have covered this topic. Eric Foner claimed "Northerners came to view slavery as the very antithesis of the good society, as well as a threat and an affront to their own fundamental values and interest."[14] Howard Floan studied Northern literature in *The South in Northern Eyes* and concluded that the Northern view of the South was basically a view of slavery. A more interesting account can be found in *North over South* by British historian Susan-Mary Grant. She saw the Republican Party as the origin of a national identity which, because of their success, became a Northern identity. This is what Lincoln was doing when he created the national holiday we now celebrate as Thanksgiving. The first declaration of such a day for thanks did not occur in Massachusetts, but in Virginia. However, the creation of this national holiday has altered reality by generating the myth that the United States began in Massachusetts and New England. Thus, many think that the founding of the United States was Puritan, even though Jamestown predates Massachusetts Bay. This holiday became more powerful since it combined the patriotic founding of America with the religious sanctification of the Puritans. This was what Lincoln and the Yankee Army fought for.

In the words of the most famous Southern historian, C. Vann Woodward, "the South has long served the nation in ways still in great demand. It has been a moral lightning rod, a deflector of national guilt . . . a floor under self-esteem."[15] He also said, "the legend that the Mason and Dixon Line not only divided slavery from freedom in antebellum America, but that it also set apart racial inhumanity in the South from benevolence, liberality and tolerance in the North." He continued "Looking back through the haze of passing years that obscured historical realities the myth-makers credited the North with the realization in its own society of all the war aims for which it fought."[16] If you doubt my word, a humble California Okie, perhaps you will believe Woodward, generally acknowledged as one of the greatest historians on the American

---

13. Isaac Ridgeway Trimble, "The Civil War Diary of General Isaac Ridgeway Trimble," *Maryland Historical Magazine*, March 1922, 15.

14. Eric Foner, *Free Soil, Free Labor, Free Men: The Ideology of the Republican Party before the Civil War* (New York: Oxford University Press, 1970), 9.

15. C. Vann Woodward, "From the First Reconstruction to the Second," *Harper's Magazine*, April 1965, 133.

16. C. Vann Woodward, "The Antislavery Myth," *American Scholar* 31 (spring 1962): 316.

South. This is pretty much the same concept that I am trying to express with the scapegoat theory. There are those who want to put the sin of American racism on the symbols of Southern culture and then sacrifice the goat to the gods of history.

THE FIRE-EATERS

As hatred of all things Southern grew, so did the number of those in the South who preached secession; we call them fire-eaters. They were still a small band, but they were the seed from which the creation of the Confederacy sprouted. They had the most influence in the states which had the most slaves, which again lends some credibility to the *Librev* point of view. They doubted the South could retain its Constitutional rights in the face of a government run by a sectional party, and they awaited the outcome of the next election. With their leadership, South Carolina began the secession parade following the election of Lincoln in 1860. The issue of slavery was not the immediate fuse that ignited secession, that was the election of 1860.

THE ELECTION OF 1860

Lincoln and the Republican Party came to power without winning a single Southern State. In fact, in the month after the election of November, 1860, South Carolina seceded, and before Lincoln took office the Confederate States of America had come into existence. South Carolina was joined by six more lower-South states: Georgia, Alabama, Florida, Mississippi, Louisiana, and Texas. Since the states had ratified the Constitution in conventions, they had to hold conventions to vote to rescind the ratification in order to secede. There likely would have been no more secessions, as Tennessee and Virginia had voted against secession, if not for the events which unfolded.

The Republican Party, unlike the Democrat Party and the Whig Party, represented a sectional interest, the interest of a large segment of the population of the North. The Republican Party never adopted a platform to abolish slavery; they merely wanted to limit its spread into the new territories. Most of the abolitionists joined the new Republican Party, but the majority of Republicans were not abolitionists, and there is little doubt that the party would not have succeeded with an abolitionist platform. I pointed out in the Introduction that Lincoln stated in his First Inaugural Address that he had no intention of interfering with slavery in the states where it existed. I also pointed out that Congress passed a resolution saying that the war was not about slavery. The fact that Congress and President Lincoln supported the Corwin Amendment, which would have protected slavery from federal interference, leaves no doubt the war was not started because of slavery. Lincoln sent letters to Southern governors to entice them back into the union, to protect slavery AND collect the tariffs the federal government was so dependent on.

I believe that the *Librevs* are right when they claim that many in the South, especially the lower or middle classes, did not support the notion of secession from the Union. I also believe many in the North had no problem with the South seceding. Many Northern newspapers from the time carried headlines wishing their Southern brothers well, until the new government in Montgomery passed a low tariff. That sent shock waves through the North. One thing the North could not support was free trade, or anything resembling it. With prompting from Lincoln, their protectionist instincts led to a quick change of policy. Now they had to defeat the South to save their economic lives.

The mood in the country was against war. Congress was out of session, so Lincoln had a window of opportunity to plunge the two countries into war. Lincoln needed the South to fire the first shots, to give him an excuse call for troops to invade the South. The United States withdrew its forces from all other forts in the South except Forts Pickens and Sumter. Through deceit and treachery, Lincoln was able to put South Carolina in a position where they either had to fire on Ft. Sumter or let the United States Navy resupply it. The resulting bombardment touched off a series of events, culminating in invasion. Nonetheless, most people at the time did not accept the notion that it was the South who was the aggressor since their only objective was to end the occupation of a fort in their sovereign territory by a foreign army.

Lincoln's call for 75,000 volunteers to suppress the free will of the people of the South was the final straw for many. Support for the union in the border states dwindled as states such as Tennessee and Virginia, which had recently voted against secession, prepared to vote for secession. Most citizens, regardless of their support for or against the union, felt that the president did not have the power to call for an army to invade the South. His expectation that sister states would contribute troops to such an undertaking shows his lack of understanding of the basic view most people had of the Constitution at that time. If Lincoln really believed that those states had not left the union, then his action would be called treason under the Constitution. The only reason he would have to send troops into a state is if that state's legislature or governor requested assistance. No such request was ever made.

The reasons for Southerners to fight the war changed dramatically since the first votes for secession, not only with the demand for 75,000 troops but also the subsequent invasion of the Southern states. I think it is also safe to assume that many of those in the Deep South who originally opposed secession now supported their new nation. By the time of the first real battle in July 1861 many, if not most, Southerners saw the issue as one of defense against a foreign army invading their land. They needed to defend their homes and families—a situation in which war is undeniably justified. I am quite ready to concede to the *Librevs* that secession was led by the planter class; I will never accept any claims that the majority of the Southern people did not believe in their cause. What may have begun as a heated debate over the spread of slavery into the territories was now a war of defense for the Confederate soldier. It is the North who turned a declaration of independence into a war.

CONCLUSIONS

The period that we now call antebellum is crucial in the defense of our Southern heritage since it is the time that we look to in searching for the causes of the Civil War. The main reason that so many hate Southern icons, especially the Confederate Battle Flag, is that they see them as symbols of slavery. The liberal-revisionist historians, *Librevs,* know that Abraham Lincoln and the Republican Party never promoted abolition. They claim that they are merely objective historians searching for the truth in history. I do not believe them. The vast majority of these open minded and objective historians support the attempts to exterminate our culture, and many of the studies focused on the antebellum and Reconstruction periods in American history seem to be attempts to discredit the Southern perspective. They have labeled the traditional Southern historical interpretations as the "Lost Cause myth." It seems to me that they have reasons for what they do which include more than just good history. It seems clear to me that they have an agenda. They like to say that those who sympathize with the Southern point of view are the ones with an agenda, which they have labeled the "Lost Cause myth."

Most *Librevs* would choose Abraham Lincoln as their choice for the best president in American history. I do not agree with them. If you use upholding the Constitution as the measure of a president's success, Lincoln is a failure. His violations of the Constitution are well known. When I hear that Saddam Hussein was an evil dictator who killed 300,000 of his own people, I think to myself, that is what Lincoln did. Lincoln created the War of Northern Aggression. They both did so for the same reason, to retain control of those people who did not want to submit to their control. This 300,000 figure is based strictly on those Confederate soldiers killed and does not include the 300,000 plus Yankees who died in the process. It also does not include the thousands of civilians, black and white, who were killed or starved to death as a result of Lincoln's war.

It is amusing that the South haters of today want to condemn Southerners for owning slaves at a time when it was legal and accepted as moral by many. This is called presentism. They condemn Southerners from 150 years ago for having values that we do not have today, yet seem to condone Lincoln and his Yankees who held values we do not have today. When they chose to kill rather than to accept the Southern states desire for independence, they did not follow what is considered acceptable today. Their attitude was based on lust for money.. When the colonies seceded from England in 1776, England chose to kill them rather than to recognize their independence. This is not the attitude today. When Quebec wanted independence from Canada, they voted on it. When Scotland wanted independence from the United Kingdom, they voted on it. If we are going to hold the slave owning Southerners to the standards we have today, why not hold Lincoln and his Yankee invaders to the standards we have today? Is it because many support and benefit from the strong central government we have as a result of that invasion?

V: THE WAR, 1860—1865

THIS CHAPTER IS ABOUT the War for Southern Independence. It is strictly from the point of view of the relationship between the war and the attacks on our Southern heritage. There are thousands of books out there that go into the details on the military and political aspects of the war. My objective is neither to repeat or dispute military strategy or such aspects of the war. I will offer a brief account of the highlights for the sake of those not familiar with it. It is such a large part of Southern history that I do not want to make the assumption that all readers are well-versed on the subject. For those who are well read on the subject my brief description will make my interpretation clear just to make sure we are on the same page. Any disagreement with my interpretations of the battles or military aspects of the war are not relevant to my objectives in this book.

One of the most fascinating aspects of the Librev view on the war is that this seems to be one of the few cases in which the liberals support the idea of war. Though generally pacifists, most of them look at what they call the Civil War as a just war because it liberated the slaves. They are well aware but seldom mention the fact that the United States is the only nation on earth which found it necessary to kill hundreds of thousands of their own people to end slavery. The Librevs consistently vote Abraham Lincoln as the greatest American president, even though he created the most devastating war in the history of North America. In fact, more Americans were killed in the War for Southern Independence than all other wars combined up until Vietnam. This is to say more than in the war for American independence, plus the Indian Wars, plus the War of 1812, plus the Mexican War, plus the Spanish–American War, plus the First World War, plus the Second World War, plus The Korean War, and finally with the Vietnam War the death toll exceeds that of the US invasion of the South. In addition, many more were left crippled and maimed. The southern countryside was in near total desolation as the army of Lincoln destroyed towns, houses, farms, and even fences. I cannot cite reliable statistical proof; however, I have little doubt that if we included the civilian loss of life, the American death toll would be considerably greater for this war than all others combined. It has always amazed me that the pacifist liberal American historians most admire the man who generated such death and destruction.

SOME ASSUMPTIONS

As I composed my opening comments for this chapter, I realized that there are three main issues I need to discus before continuing. Entire philosophies often rest on a handful of assumptions. The history of the war is important when addressing the attacks on our heritage and I believe that these assumptions are important in discussing the war. There are many things which are difficult to prove, so we are forced to accept assumptions. It seems to me that most of those who arrack our heritage have accepted their assumptions as facts. If they could only recognize that their assumptions are not proven, then maybe they would be able to see why it is wrong to destroy our heritage.

First, the liberals have convinced much of the American public that liberalism is synonymous with intelligence or education and that is why their interpretation is the correct one. Second, the significance of the name "Civil War" and why Southerners continue to object to that moniker. Third is a reminder of the basic assumption that Adam Smith made in his book *Wealth of Nations*—that people are motivated by the principle of self-interest. In other words, as stated in the Introduction, I see the main cause of the war as economic competition and not slavery.

FIRST: LIBERALISM IS NOT GENIUS

This is an important issue because it is probably the main reason so many accept the excuses given by the liberal population in general for the destruction of our heritage. This includes the liberal historians and liberal media who play key roles in the distribution of this thinking. This is why so many accept their interpretation as gospel. In the Introduction I presented a current historiography on the causes for the war. I have shown that there is disagreement as to what the war was all about. Not all historians agree that the war was caused by slavery, much less that the Confederate States of American was all about slavery and racism. Therefore, there is a disagreement as to the meaning of Confederate symbols. The liberal interpretations have strength because so many believe that the liberals are smarter and better educated, and therefore their point of view is the correct one. There have actually been studies to try to prove this belief, and some claim success at doing so. I am not convinced that there is evidence to support the idea that liberals are smarter or better educated than conservatives. Therefore, this is not a reason to accept their interpretation relating to the war and the Confederacy.

I recall a survey of Mensa members done in the 1990s in which the split between those who labeled themselves liberal or conservative was very similar to the same division among the general population. Since Mensa members are chosen for their above average IQs (the top 2 percent), then it seems logical to assume that intelligence is not a significant variable in determining why people lean one way or the other in the political spectrum. In other words, it would seem that liberals are no more intelligent than conservatives, nor for that matter, the other way around.

Of the many studies and articles which have been done over the years to prove that liberals are smarter, as well as those trying to disprove this, I like the conclusion reached by Scott McGreal in a essay for Psychology Today. He said "The findings discussed illustrate a number of key points. Firstly, highly intelligent individuals may ctually support right-wing views, not just left-wing ones, contrary to claims that support for right-wing positions reflects a lack of intellectual sophistication." He went on, "It seems fair to say then that not only liberals, but conservatives (and those with other positions, such as libertarians) can have intellectually sophisticated reasons for their political views." He explained his reasoning, "The second point is that categorizing people simply as generally liberal or conservative may mask differences in people's views on social versus economic issues." He added,, "Therefore, in order to better understand how political attitudes are related to intelligence, a two-dimensional model that separates social and economic attitudes may be preferable to the traditional yet overly simplistic left/right distinction." He concluded, "Finally, the relationship between intelligence and political attitudes is most likely not fixed in some simple way, but probably changes across time and context."

I can see why so many liberals have this belief; the leftist view does dominate American academia. This is important since liberal bias means Northern bias when it comes to Southern history. This is especially true when it comes to the war and Reconstruction. Liberal bias in education, like liberal intelligence, is another subject of debate. This subject has been discussed since the 1950s, and there have been many studies done since then in an attempt to prove it. I will say that this is no more proven that those studies which have claimed that liberals are smarter.

The liberal interpretation of the war is not the only one, but it would appear to be if one listens only to the SPLC and other enemies of our heritage. I repeat, I have covered the historiography of the war in the Introduction and showed that there are many professional historians who have alternative beliefs to those used as battle cries of our enemies. Not all intelligent and educated scholars agree that it was all about slavery, which is the main point used in the attacks on all symbols of the Confederacy.

According to Wikipedia, Sociologist Paul Lazarsfeld and Wagner Thielens, were the first scholars to conduct a systematic survey of the politics of American university professors. The research was commissioned by an arm of the Ford Foundation in 1955 as a response to McCarthyism, and focused solely on social scientists. Lazarsfeld found that just 16% of the social scientists he surveyed self-identified as Republicans, while 47% self-identified as Democrats. 67% said they were "more liberal" than the average person in the community where they work. A 1999 survey conducted by Stanley Rothman, S. Robert Lichter, and Neil

Nevitte found that professors with liberal socio-political views outnumbered their conservative counterparts by a ratio of 5 to 1 in the United States, with the former constituting 72% of the faculty body and the later representing 15%. To be fair, this study was criticized by political scientists Barry Ames, David C. Barker, Chris W. Bonneau, and Christopher J. Carman, who argued that it was "plagued by theoretical and methodological problems that render their conclusions unsustainable by the available evidence." Rothman, Licther and Nevitte's study was later revealed to have contained a coding error, which exaggerated the percentage of professors holding liberal views by 12%. It is not conclusive; however, there are many who believe this bias in education exist.

Liberal bias in educations cannot be considered proven, but I will explain why I believe it to be true. It has become a self-perpetuating system. A good example of this came with the passing of Grady McWhiney. The Journal of Southern History wrote about the death of "an influential if controversial historian of the American South. . ." They mentioned his "provocative work" Cracker Culture and later described the historian as "an interesting mix of devotion, gentility, controversy, and dedication to his craft and to his students."[17] [I emphasized the word controversy] However, when the self identified communist historian Elizabeth Fox-Genovese died, they described her as being of "fiercely independent mind."[18] Perhaps it is just me, but "fiercely independent" sounds more respectful or at the least less euphemistic than "controversial." I remind the reader that Grady McWhiney is the historian who wrote Cracker Culture. He obviously did not accept the Librev conclusion that Southern identity was created during and after the war. This is why he was "controversial." He dared to disagree with the liberal academic elite. Again, it may be just me, and this is only anecdotal evidence, but I felt that they were saying that not only was he controversial but that he was also wrong. The communist historian, on the other hand, was just "fiercely independent." A book could be written on this debate alone.

It seems to me that the liberals have seized control of the top jobs in the great Northern universities, such as Yale and Harvard. They influence the hiring process so that it is difficult for a conservative historian to find a job at such a school. Perhaps some of the less prestigious Southern or western schools would hire the more conservative, but as for credibility among the intellectuals how could they compare to a Harvard or Yale professor? As these professors seek publication of their research, they cannot expect to be received in the same way as those who work at Harvard or Yale.

---

17. "Obituaries," *Journal of Southern History* (August 2006): 738–9.

18. "Obituaries," *Journal of Southern History* (May 2007): 516–7.

Peer review is another process by which the liberals dominate academia. To be given credit as a legitimate historian one must publish with the academic presses. To get accepted the author is subject to peer review. I can understand the desire to maintain quality within the profession, but it is also a way to maintain a consistent point of view, a liberal point of view.

This liberal academic attitude spread southward shortly after the end of the war. Two of the first Southern universities to win the prize of being respected by the Northern educators were the University of North Carolina at Chapel Hill and Louisiana State University. These schools have become liberal anchors in the conquest of Southern history. They are respected in the North but could never compare to the holy shrines of Harvard or Yale.

This Librev thinking has spread throughout the South like a cancer. Those Librev historians who could not get a job in the North, or at least the prestigious Yankeefied schools of the South, are forced to settle for positions in the less-prestigious Southern universities. They might accept jobs with the state schools such as the University of Oklahoma, or Arkansas, or Tennessee, but often do so with the hope of escaping north some day. When they move down South they carry their Librev culture with them in their carpetbags.

I do not believe that the liberal Northern intellectual elite are any more intelligent or educated than the more conservative historians who have achieved the same educational level. Merely being on the faculty at Harvard or Yale does not mean that their interpretations are more correct than a conservative-thinking historian, only that they have achieved acceptance by the intellectual elite. They may offer Southern history with a Northern slant, but not necessarily a better slant.

SECOND: WHAT'S IN A NAME?

The name used to describe the war is important because the name alone generates a level of bias. Many are aware that there is controversy over the generally accepted name "Civil War," but most find it nothing more than an amusing disagreement. Historians refer to the events of 1776 as the "War for American Independence" or "Revolutionary War," even though when it started there was no declaration of independence. Why do they refuse to call the war which started in 1861 the War of Southern Independence? The Southern states stated their intent of Independence from the beginning They wrote a constitution, elected a president, printed their own money and stamps, and built an army, and yet it has become generally accepted that this war for independence is called the Civil War.

Why is the name important? Since it is commonly accepted that it was a civil war and since they lost, those who fought and died for it are reduced to treasonous rebels. Washington and Jefferson are patriotic heroes while Davis and Lee are rebels. From 1860 until today, the loyal Confederate Southerners have viewed the conflict as one between two independent and sovereign nations and not as a civil war. Therefore they prefer the name War of Southern Independence over Civil War. Some like to call it the War of Northern Aggression since it was the North which invaded the South and made it a war. The only difference I see between 1776 and 1861 is the outcome of two wars which were fought for independence. This is key as to why there are those out to remove all symbols of this war while honoring those of the first war for independence.

THIRD: WAR OF ECONOMIC OPPORTUNITY

I also covered this in detail in the Introduction, but I feel that it is important enough to give a reminder and recap now that I am at the chapter on the war. I believe that the main causes for the war are economic. The liberal prefers to think of it as a war to free the slaves. I have previously stated that I do agree that slavery had something to do with the war; however, there were other variables of importance, such as states' rights. Even if it is conceded that slavery had something to do with the war, it does not negate the importance of states' rights. If one accepts that it was states' rights it does not negate my belief that it is economic. I see slavery as a catalyst which sparked the issue of states' rights, but I see the latter as the product of economic competition.

Most Americans, liberal or conservative, like to think that any war we fight must be over some noble cause. They prefer to believe that their nation's soldiers fought and died for freedom and democracy, not imperialism or money. This creates a dilemma when we try to evaluate the War of Southern Independence. This is probably the main reason so many want to see it as a war to free the slaves. The fact is that the war was one in which the business-driven Republican Party of the North conquered the South. Their main reason was to protect Northern business interest. It is true that it was, as many said at the time, a rich man's war and a poor man's fight. The planters of the South were convinced that it was no longer to their advantage to remain with the Union. The northern businessmen chose to invade and conquer rather than to allow them to go their own way. The war was a battle of the business interest of the Southern planters versus the Northern merchants.

I also believe Colin Woodard was right in his book *American Nations*, in which he claimed that the United States of 1860 was divided into more than two parts, North and South. He identified eleven separate nations. His view is that it was New England in the north and the Tidewater and Deep South nations in the south who were primarily responsible for the events which produced the war. On both sides these leaders sought alliances from the other "nations." From the election, to the decision to secede by some of the southern slave states, to invasion of the South by the United States Army, most of the other regions were not as aggressive. This becomes clear when we look at how it all started. Woodard's view helps to explain the series of events.

This was the idea behind the Constitutional Union Party which was founded on the belief that slavery was no justification of secession. They were able to gain support from those non-slave states which did not think secession was reason enough to go to war. This is why most of the slave states did not secede after Lincoln won the election. This is why both sides found in necessary to draft soldiers to fight the war. In New England and in the Deep South there were those who enlisted immediately. In other parts of the once United States the motivation to fight evolved as events unfolded. There were many in the other regions who never approved of the war. It was the radicals in the South which led them to secession, and it was the radicals of the North which led them to war.

It is interesting that in most other cases the liberals will not only admit to the idea that American wars have been fought for selfish gain, but they will often promote that theory. Librevs talk about how the United States military stole land from Indians; unjustifiably invaded Mexico; fought the Spanish in Cuba because of the capitalist newspapers; and entered World War I for the sake of the bankers and munitions manufacturers. They seem a little more hesitant to blame World War II on American imperialism, but there have been some who at least leaned in that direction in that war too. Of course many, if not most, of the Librevs see Vietnam and the recent wars in the Middle East as the product of US imperialism.

The Librev historians do recognize the economic importance of war, even the one they call the "Civil War." They will use the expression "a rich man's war but a poor man's fight." Most often they are referring to the planter conspiracy, but they do accept and mention the fact that wealthy Northerners sent immigrants to do their fighting for them. They at least mention the draft riots of New York City and of the immigrant attacks on blacks living in that city. That does not deter them from picking Lincoln as the best American president. They tend to focus on the evils of the slaveocracy and seem to be in general agreement that Mr. Lincoln's war was a rare example of a "good war" to end slavery. In their logic, it is only later that Republican Party exist to represent business and United States imperialism. I believe that the Republican Party has always represented the interest of businessmen, Northern businessmen, and that is the main reason for war. This is the view I accept, and this is what I will expand on the rest of this chapter.

THE LIBREV ISSUES

There are a number of issues relating to the War of Southern Independence which we should be aware of. They have become part of the Librev historiography which relate to the attacks on our heritage. These are also the topics which relate to the Librev term used to describe any interpretation of the war sympathetic to the South as the "Lost Cause myth." This term is their way of discrediting the stands we take in attempting to preserve our heritage. There are six important points of dispute and these are thus the ones I will focus on in this chapter. First, the war was caused by the planter conspiracy. Second, the war was fought to free the slaves. Third, the poor Southerners, who they have labeled the "pine-barrens folk," did not support the Confederacy or the war. Fourth, they like to emphasize the role that blacks played in winning the war for the North while generally rejecting that notion that blacks played any significant role in defending the Confederacy. They say that any claim that there are blacks who fought for the Confederacy is a myth. Fifth, they have even begun to peck away at the near-deity status of Robert E. Lee. Sixth, and most important for us today, is that they clearly support the idea that Confederate symbols, especially the battle flag, should be thrown on the same historical rubbish pile as Hitler's *Mein Kempf*.

FIRST: PLANTER CONSPIRACY

The view of a planter conspiracy is often seen as an example of how the South was resisting modernization. As stated previously, I believe that the war was mainly economic in nature. I cannot deny the idea that the planter class of the South are the ones who initiated the momentum which led to the declaration of Southern independence. I believe the idea that most American wars, including this one, were fought to protect the interest of American businessmen. What the Librevs overlook is that the planters led the conflict in the South because they were the leading businessmen in the region, just it was the businessmen in the North who led their faction. The issue of slavery was the result of economic competition. The distinction I wish to emphasize now compared to what I said earlier is that it was competition between regional markets, not a Southern resistance to modern capitalism. The South was part of the modern world market economy, they had different ways of competing and slave labor was part of that difference.

Where I see bias in the Librev interpretations is that they emphasize the role of the planters in the South and generally down play the role of the rich in the North. The North and the South were both capitalistic societies. I have already pointed out that Southerners have been as guilty as Northerners in looking at the South as a region which resisted modernization. I have discussed how the South was still predominantly agricultural, but not in the same way as a feudalistic society but rather as an agribusiness, a part of a capitalist economy. As N. S. B. Gras, the founding father of business history at Harvard, said in his book *Business and Capitalism*, "A study of the history of capitalism shows that major struggles do not occur between capitalism and some other order of society but between two rival forms of capitalism." Gras's view would indicate that tariffs and other economic issues may have been as important as slavery. And even the issue of slavery was more likely an economic issue rather than due to moral superiority. The South had dominated the federal government and was losing out to the North. They finally became convinced that they would be better off on their own, better off economically. The Northern businessmen could not lose the supply lines for their textile industry. They were determined to retain them even with force. "One group of capitalists may win over another and the victory may be progressive or retrogressive, but some form of capitalism will remain triumphant." Gras did not specifically refer to the War of Southern Independence, but apparently, if he was correct, he would probably agree that the South was not a premodern society. "To be sure, force could be attempted, but a seizure of a capitalistic society without a preparation in the use of investment of capital is like an invasion of an orderly state by Huns and Vandals."[19] From his theories, it would seem logical to view the war between the states as one between two differing capitalist factions.

SECOND: THE WAR TO FREE THE SLAVES

This point too has been covered in greater detail in the Introduction and expanded on in the previous chapter. The Librevs still argue that the war was fought over slavery while recognizing the facts that suggest it did not start out that way. This is why I do not see them as objective as they see themselves. They know the numerous quotes from Northern leaders including Abraham Lincoln and Ulysses S. Grant in which they said they did not fight to free the slaves. They know that the Emancipation Proclamation did not free a single slave at the time that Lincoln signed it; however, they argue that it is still a great document because as the North conquered the South, the slaves became freed. They ignore the fact that the masters in the North held on to their slaves. They are all aware that it was the Thirteenth Amendment which freed the slaves and that it was not ratified until after the war was over. The war resulted in the end of slavery, but that was not the reason that the North started it.

THIRD: THE PINE BARREN (POOR) FOLKS DID NOT SUPPORT THE CONFEDERACY

Librevs, like other liberals, like to think of themselves as caring people who are the defenders of the poor, and thus, they do not like to think of the poor as being capable of doing wrong. It takes a rich man to be a sinner. This is why it is important for them to show that the poor of the South did not support the Confederacy. This is tied to the planter conspiracy theory, but there are a number of books which have focused on the unwillingness of the poor to fight in the war. I agree with them that in the North and South, the average man is not the one who led the nation into war. I feel that it is safe to say that this is the case for most wars throughout not only Western history but world history. The leaders are usually rich, and the rich are usually the ones who have the most to gain or lose at time of war. I believe that the poor too are motivated by self-

---

19. N. S. B. Gras, *Business and Capitalism: An Introduction to Business History* (New York: Augustus M. Kelley Publishers, 1971), vii-viii.

interest, but they are the ones who are expected to give up their lives to fight the wars. They are the ones who lose the most when they have to leave their jobs and homes to fight the wars. But, there are times when they see the need to fight.

In this case, their self-interest came about when the blue hordes moved south. I will never believe that the poor will not and did not fight to protect their homes from invaders. Many did not see the election of Lincoln as a threat to their home and families, but when Lincoln's armies crossed their state lines the threat became obvious. It may be true that most did not desire secession, but once they were invaded it was a matter of self defense.

The Librevs like to look at the election of 1860 in determining the Confederate supporters. They assume that the Breckinridge supporters were those who led the way to independence and thus the war. The election results do indicate that the average middle-class Southern farmer and even many of the wealthy feared a movement toward a declaration of independence. The Constitutional Union Party was formed by those who could not support the black Republicans but feared a split in the Union. The supporters of Breckinridge did come from those areas with the most planters. I can see no reason to disagree with this Librev assumption. I do believe that many did not support secession, and then the war. However, I believe that this changed after April of 1861. I have already discussed this.

Prior to then the majority of the slave states were still in the union. The fact is that after the firing on Fort Sumter and the subsequent demand for seventy-five thousand troops and the invasion of the South by the Northern army, it became a different question. It is true that many deserted as they did in the North. It is true that many resented the draft as they did in the North. It is true that the common farmer was worried about the welfare of his family and the protection of his property as they were in the North.

The bottom line is the most men in the South did fight in the war, the majority of whom never owned a slave in their life. They fought long and they fought hard, and it took the North four years to defeat them, even though they outnumbered them two to one and possessed more weapons and supplies. I cannot accept the idea that this would have been true without the support of the common man. They were the ones who made up the vast majority of the population. Seventy-five percent of the Southerners did not own a single slave. If they had not fought long and hard it would not have taken four years to conquer the Confederacy.

FOURTH: THE ROLE OF BLACK SOUTHERNERS IN THE WAR

One of the main objectives of the liberal revisionist since the 1960s has been to include the stories of all Americans, not just the middle-class Anglo-Saxon population. This is a noble objective. All people are part of history, not just the wealthy and powerful and not just the whites. I finished my undergraduate studies in history in 1970 and never heard of the role that black soldiers played in the War of Southern Independence. Even though Elkin's book about the black soldiers, *The Sable Arm*, had been published in 1957, it was not required reading in the university I graduated from. It is a good thing to realize that the blacks were part of American history too.

In more recent times, there are those who have studied the black support for the Confederacy. The Librevs generally dismiss this as a statistically insignificant anecdotal collection of accounts of blacks who fought because they were forced to. I do not understand how they can be enthusiastic in recalling the black role in the war for American independence and yet say that they did not participate in defense of the same states when they were part of the Confederacy. The stories of Revolutionary War soldiers involve the grandfathers of the 1860s' slaves helping the grandfathers of the 1860s' planters. The British crown promised them freedom if they supported the king in 1776, the Union offered them nothing in 1861. I will never understand why it makes sense that blacks fought for the United States but not for the Confederate States. This is another example of why I am convinced that the Librev scholars are not as objective as they claim to be.

Related to this topic is ethnic diversity. The emphasis on blacks is really an emphasis on race. Those out to destroy our heritage believe that the South is bad because they represent attitudes contrary to multiculturalism. Today there is no disputing that the North is a more diverse population than in the South. This was not true in 1860. We will see in this chapter that not only was the South more diverse, but that there were people from many ethnic groups who helped to defend the Confederate States of America. To these people the Confederacy was not a nation of racism any more that the United States.

FIFTH: THE SAINTED MARSE ROBERT

Lately the Librevs have begun attacking the name and image of Robert E. Lee. General Lee is the only man in the history of the world to be offered command of opposing armies. He has been one of the most respected historical figures, not only in the South but also around the world. He has been a symbol of integrity as well as a military genius. He has been such a powerful image that his existence alone justifies respect for the Confederacy. I have no doubt that this is the main motivation for attacking his good name. This is why they have put him in the basket of icons they call the "Lost Cause myth."

The only thing I have to say is that General Lee did not suspend the constitution, order an invasion, encourage state-sponsored terrorism, nor oversee the destruction of millions of acres of private property including cities, farms, homes, and businesses. The man who appears on the five dollar bill and the one-cent coin, whose monument looms over the city of Washington, and the continued Librev's favorite president did do all of these things.

SIXTH: BURY CONFEDERATE SYMBOLS

In the end, the Librevs have endorsed the attacks on our Confederate symbols, especially the battle flag but also including monuments, place names or even simple things such as cotton plants. Most of the previously mentioned objectives of the Librevs seem to be aimed at the principal target of Confederate symbols. The Librevs look at organizations such as the Sons of Confederate Veterans or the United Daughters of the Confederacy as defenders of the Lost Cause who are "still fighting the Civil War." Some seem to accept our pleas that to us the flag is a symbol of "heritage not hate" and that it does not represent racism. Nonetheless, they say that "at issue is not just history but whose history." So while they endorse ideas such as Black History Month, they urge the sacrifice of our heritage. As one college history book explained, "In the interests of reconciliation, it's surely time for Southerners to follow Robert E. Lee's final order to his men and 'Furl the flag, boys.'"[20] What more do I need to say. I, for one, do not believe that I should be expected to sacrifice the memory and honor of my ancestors to the gods of political correctness and diversity. No one should be made to feel ashamed of their heritage, black or white.

THE WAR - DISADVANTAGES FROM THE START

We may not like to admit it, but we lost the war. People like to look for simple one-line answers to questions, including the answer as to why the South lost. We all know that the North outnumbered them two to one and that they had more factories, railroads, and munitions from the start. They also had a navy, which allowed them to build a blockade and thus limit the ability to acquire the needed weapons and other supplies. These all fit into the category of military causes for defeat.

Less frequently discussed are the political problems. The South had to create a new government along with all of its' infrastructure, whereas the North already had a government. It dramatically changed with the parting of the Southern states, but nonetheless, it had been operating for many decades. It was more difficult to make up for this problem because of the issue of states' rights.

Some like to say that the South just copied the government of the Union. Even if one accepted this charge as true, do not forget that government was partially constructed by Southerners. A Southerner, James Madison, is called the father of the Constitution. The few changes made highlight what the Southerners saw as problems with the old government which needed to be fixed. These included a nonrepetitive presidential term of six years, line-item veto, limits on federal

---

20. David Goldfield et al., The American Journey: A History of the United States (New Jersey: Prentice Hall,), 560.

taxation, and limits on the central government interference with slavery in the states or territories. Clearly we cannot deny that slavery played a role in the issues that led to disunion. That is not to say it was the only issue.

The Southerners' reasons for fighting were a big part of their problem. They claimed that they stood for states' rights, which means that they stood for a weaker central government. Like most controversial issues, there is some good and some bad to be said for each point of view. A weaker central government affords more individual freedom, but it can be a problem in times of crises, such as a war. There were times when the states resisted the control that Jefferson Davis tried to exercise in order to present a more unified defense of the new nation. Thus, while we love to talk about the tyrant Abraham Lincoln, we want to overlook the cries by some Southerners that Davis was a tyrant. Lincoln had the advantage of defending a strong central government while Davis supposedly fought for states' rights, so we must admit that we cannot call Lincoln a hypocrite as it relates to this subject.

Underlying the military weaknesses as well as some of the internal issues was the Southern economy. They had to pay for a war when they had no money. The states' rights advocates of course wanted to limit the taxation powers of the new federal government. It was difficult to find foreign financiers for a country which had not been recognized by the greatest financial powers of the world such as England and France. Stocks and bonds of a new company will always be more risky than stocks and bonds issued by an existing company that has a good debt history.

THE BORDER STATES

Some claim that the term "border states" is a Northern invention. These are the states which had slavery but according to Mr. Lincoln did not join the Confederacy: Delaware, Maryland, Missouri, Kentucky, and an illegally formed state called West Virginia. The most obvious contradiction about these states is that Lincoln claimed them all as loyal to the Union; however, they all had slavery. West Virginia did agree to end the institution, but it was accepted into the Union with slavery. How could this have been a war to end slavery if states that were still part of the United States had slavery? Many look to the Emancipation Proclamation as a document that ended slavery, but it exempted these states Lincoln considered to be Union states. Slavery was not abolished until the ratification of the Thirteenth Amendment, which happened after the war. Basically, the term border state meant those slaves states which did not join the Confederacy.

In the case of Missouri and Kentucky, the state governments split into factions in which one claimed to be loyal to the Union while the other sought and received admission as a Confederate State. Delaware had very few slaves; however, it is interesting that they voted for Breckinridge in 1860. Many Librev scholars considered a vote for Breckinridge as a pro-Confederate vote. Delaware failed to come up with their quota for the seventy-five thousand troops, which Lincoln had ordered. In their case, they claimed a loophole in which their state had no militia system and therefore did not have the mechanism to come up with their quota.

The most controversial of the so-called border states was Maryland. I have no doubt that Maryland would have voted to follow the lead of Virginia if Lincoln had not taken such giant steps to squash democracy in that state. This point is debatable. Again, there are numerous books which get into the details, but suffice it to say that the Union arrested many Marylanders after Lincoln suspended habeas corpus. Some spent only a few days behind bars while others served until they submitted to the might of the Union. Meanwhile, General Butler occupied one strategic point after another before finally entering the city of Baltimore and establishing a rule that would have left Hitler envious. By the time that the state legislature voted on the issue of secession, the Union army had been established and the legal system dismantled to the point that it was clear that a vote for secession would lead to immediate arrest. I am sure many feared the consequences of such arrest, and this is why they voted down secession. The vote did not come until after Union military might had been well-established.

The Librevs often take the position that Maryland would not have seceded since Lee and the Confederate army twice marched into the state in an attempt to liberate them but failed to find the anticipated support. This could be a valid point, but I firmly believe that by the time Lee arrived, the opportunity had passed. Many of the pro-Confederates had either left, joined the Confederate army elsewhere, or feared the consequences of their actions if they failed in an attempt to overthrow a well-established Union military. A relative stability had been achieved by the time Lee arrived in the state and to upset the cart at that point would have been at great risk to property and family.

THE WAR AND OVERALL STRATEGY

As stated earlier, I will offer here a mere outline of the military aspects of the war. There are countless number of books on the subject and I do not have any new contributions. I present this outline for those who have little or no knowledge of the subject. For those already familiar with the generals and the battles, do not expect to find new material nor any challenges to the topics of debate. The military aspects of the war are not relevant to my objectives with this book. The reason I give at least an outline here is that since there are so many books on the war I feel it is wise to make sure we are all on the same page.

Both sides believed it would be a short war when it started. The original Union enlistments were for ninety days. For the South, victory could be achieved when the North recognized Southern independence. Many in the South believed that the average Northerner would never support Lincoln in his attack on fellow Americans. For the North to win, they had to get the South to abandon their claims of independence. As it turned out, this meant that they had to totally conquer the new nation. The South would win if the North stopped invading them. There were times when this seemed like a good possibility.

After the loss at the Battle of First Manassas, Winfield Scott convinced Lincoln that it would be a long and difficult path to victory. They would continue to travel that long road to Richmond, but in the meanwhile, they would follow Scott's Anaconda Plan. With this, they would strangle the life out of the Confederacy. First, they would form a blockade to limit Southern trade, and second, the Army would follow a plan of divide and conquer with a march down the Mississippi River.

THE TRANS-MISSISSIPPI

The struggle west of the Mississippi began with the attempt to subdue the Confederate government of Missouri. Governor Jackson had led the pro-South faction of the state to the Southwest corner. The Union army tried to defeat them, which led to the battles in that part of Missouri and overflowed into Northwest Arkansas. The climax came with the battle of Elk Horn Tavern and then later at Prairie Grove, both in Arkansas. The Confederates lost and never did get reorganized west of the Mississippi.

The Five Civilized Tribes signed a treaty with the Confederacy, and they became a buffer zone for Texas. They held off the first invasion, but with the second, the Union captured Fort Gibson and the Cherokee capital of Tahlequah. The Yankees took the principal chief, John Ross, to Philadelphia where they operated a puppet government. General Stand Waite led the Confederate faction. By the summer of 1863, the Union had gained control of much of the Cherokee nation, Fort Smith in Arkansas, and by September, Little Rock fell. After that, the war in the West degenerated into guerilla warfare, which resulted in terrible destruction and numerous cases of torture and murder on both sides. At times, it spilled over into Kansas. Some major campaigns occurred in 1864. The Confederate General Sterling Price led a raid into Missouri, and the Union attempted an invasion of Texas going up the Red River.

The Trans-Mississippi is one area where the desertion rate did get very high. The contemporary Librev historiography likes to use this information to paint a picture of the common farmer and soldier as lacking dedication to the Confederate cause. I have done a lot of research on Arkansas since most of my ancestors in the war were from that state. I have not collected statistical data, but I have noticed that the desertion rate of Arkansas soldiers serving on the other side of the Mississippi did not seem any higher than from other states. I believe the desertion rate was higher on the west side of the river because they were being invaded and conquered. I have seen a few Librev accounts in which they admitted that the high desertion was probably due to the fact that the invading army occupied the home and farms of many of the soldiers. It seems like a natural response to feel that your place is with your family at such a time rather than to remain with the army.

THE WEST

When we talk about the western front, we are referring to the war involving the Army of Tennessee rather than the far west. This is where we saw the most direct impact of Scott's Anaconda Plan. U. S. Grant made a name for himself by leading the attacks on forts Henry and Donelson, which defended the Tennessee and Cumberland rivers. Shortly after that, he led his army down the Tennessee River and met the enemy at the Battle of Shiloh in April of 1862. A big turning point was when Vicksburg fell in July of 1863, the same month as the loss in Gettysburg. Some think the biggest price the Confederacy paid was that up until then the British and the French saw a chance for Southern victory. After that it became much more difficult for them to recognize the new country.

From there, the Union army went into Northern Mississippi, over to Chattanooga, and then into North Georgia where they finally took Atlanta in the summer of 1864. There are those who believe that was a major defeat also. Up until then it seemed likely that Lincoln would lose the presidential election to McClellan, and with the change in command a chance that the North would accept Confederate independence. After Atlanta, the Union army went on its rampage through Georgia and up to the Carolinas while the remains of the Confederate army of Tennessee headed back toward Franklin and Nashville where they faced total annihilation.

THE EAST

Robert E. Lee and his Army of Northern Virginia basically defended Richmond for most of the war. Lee did not assume command until 1862. He defended the capital, though he did invade Maryland twice with the assumption that the people of that state were awaiting liberation. I discussed this earlier. This is what some Librevs use to support their belief that Maryland would not have joined the Confederacy even if Lincoln had not disposed of the Constitution and denied the people any voice in their future. Lee reversed his defensive strategy in the summer of 1863 when he led his army into Pennsylvania. He failed to accomplish what he hoped to, but he did make it back to Virginia, where he continued the struggle for another year and a half. Following the siege of Petersburg, the Army of Northern Virginia fought its last battle at Appomattox where Lee surrendered on April 9, 1865.

FINAL DAYS

It is often assumed that the war ended at Appomattox. It did not. After the fall of Richmond, Jefferson Davis attempted to take his government across the Mississippi to Texas where they would continue the struggle for freedom. He did not make it. As stated earlier, the Army of Tennessee was decimated after Franklin and Nashville. The Army of the Trans-Mississippi under Kirby-Smith did not surrender until May of 1865. It was the following month when the conquering Union army occupied Texas and informed the slaves that they were free. This is why we still have the holiday celebrated by black Southerners called Juneteenth.

The Cherokee general Stand Waite was the last Confederate general to surrender in Doaksville, Indian Territory, on June 23, 1865. Some former Confederates could not live in the United Yankee States and so they fled the country. Some eventually came back while others were buried in foreign lands. Edmund Ruffin, for one, preferred death over living in an occupied nation. As we will see in the next chapter, the military aspects of the invasion and defeat of a proud people was over. However, the conquest was not complete. Some have described Reconstruction as being worse than the war.

ETHNIC DIVERSITY

The earlier quote about furling the flag came from the Southern but Librev historian David Goldfield; it is a prime example of the main rationalization for the extermination of our Southern heritage. He called for the furling of the flag "in the interest of reconciliation." Those of us who are old enough to remember America before 1965 realize that it is much different today. Before 1965 we called the nation a "melting pot," but it in no way resembled the land of diversity that is the United States of today. Whereas we grew up in a country that had some Africans, a few surviving Indians, and in some areas a number of those with Mexican background, for the most part, diversity meant being Italian, Jewish, Polish, or some other non-Germanic Europeans. The melting pot was mostly white. At the time of the war the United States had not even really reached the "melting pot" stage, much less the diversity we see today. We had a bunch of Germans and Irish with a smattering of others, but we did not even have the eastern and southern Europeans in the mix until after the war. Let me emphasize here that my comments on diversity are not intended to say whether the changes are good or bad, but simply to make it clear what the country was at the time. I consider this important because I believe much behind the destruction of our heritage which is taking place today is based on the politics of multiculturalism and those who want to make it official US policy.

As I commented on previously, many of those opposed to Confederate symbols today are the multiculturalist liberals who see our heritage as anti-American. They like to believe that diversity is what America is all about, and that it has always been that way. I am not complaining about this change in America; I am simply setting the stage for discussion of the role that diversity plays in the annihilation of our Southern heritage. I am convinced that this is a big part of what is going on with the destruction of our heritage. They have begun attacks on other symbols of American heritage which seem to be contrary to their view of a multicultural world. Columbus is the starting point. Next, they have moved on to other slave owners such as George Washington, Thomas Jefferson, and Andrew Jackson. They want to paint a picture of the America that existed before multiculturalism as a racist society that needs to be erased from the pages of history so that they can have a clean landscape on which to build their new world order.

With the promotion of "diversity" some like to promote the notion that this country has always been about diversity. The new America represents democracy, freedom, opportunity, and "diversity." Even though the Librevs have never been shy about pointing out the faults of the United States, they have gone off in the direction of blaming past racist attitudes on Southerners. I have covered this topic in previous chapters, but it is the most crucial in understanding why the scapegoating that is taking place with Confederate icons is not only unjust but based on misconceptions. It should also be clear that once Confederate history has been erased, or at least recognized as evil, they will then do the same to the heritage of the white, mostly British, who created the nation in the first place.

The fact is that the Confederate army was diverse for the time period in which it existed. It was not diverse in the same way America is today, or even compared to the late nineteenth and early twentieth centuries' melting pot diverse. However, the Confederate States and the Confederate army was more diverse than the United States and the Union army. The Confederate symbols that Dr. Goldfield and his friends wish to sacrifice for the sake of "reconciliation" in fact generated patriotic pride from people of many backgrounds other than the white Anglo-Saxon protestant background that most of those from New England came from. I am not attempting to compete with books which have been written on this topic, but rather I am using them to support this view.

Let me also remind the reader that I am not attempting to paint Southerners as lovers of all mankind. I repeat, most of our Confederate ancestors were racist compared to Americans today. The point is that most Americans were that way until well after World War II. Those minorities who did support the Confederacy did not do so out of any great love or appreciation for the way they were treated, but rather because they saw more hope for a better future by doing so. The bottom line is that they did not see the Confederacy as being about nothing by slavery and racism.

The minorities who chose the Confederacy or the Union did so because they saw their choice as the one that would most benefit their people. Some of different racial and ethnic backgrounds turned to the Union, but others turned to the Confederacy. The main point here is that these ethnic minorities saw greater advantage for them to side with the Confederacy. The Confederate States of America was no less but no more racist than the United States of America. Therefore, it is not valid to attack those symbols of the Confederacy as being any more racist than other symbols of an American past which is contrary to the way people are today.

INDIAN CONFEDERATES

As mentioned previously, the Cherokee general Stand Waite was the last Confederate general to surrender. In the early days of the conflict, the United States Army evacuated the forts in Indian Territory and made no attempt at catering to the Indians. I believe that it was Northern racism that led them to ignore any interest in an alliance with the red man. Albert Pike of the CSA went into the present state of Oklahoma and negotiated an alliance with all five of the Civilized Tribes and also signed treaties with some of the western Indians. Those from the Five Tribes (the forces of political correctness do not like to use the term "civilized tribes" these days, the implication being that the other Indians were not civilized) had reasons to support the North. It is the people of the South who drove the Indians from the lands of their ancestors. Perhaps the most compelling reason to support the Union is that the government of the United States still owed them annuities payable to them from when they agreed to vacate their ancestral homes. Opposition to the Union would probably mean that they would sacrifice these future receipts.

The fact is that the Five Civilized Tribes were Southerners. To a large degree they had assimilated into white culture, but mainly Southern white culture. They had economic bonds to the region which means that they grew cotton and owned slaves as many white Southerners did. By 1860, there was a large population of mixed bloods which had established familial bonds with Southern whites. Not all agreed with the Confederate alliance. For example Opothleyahola led a faction of Creeks and assorted others, including runaway slaves, who fled to Kansas in November of 1861 and became involved in the first Civil War battle in Indian Territory known as Round Mountain.

Annie Heloise Abel, one of the first to study the war in Indian Territory, gave us a good explanation for the reasons why the Indians chose the Confederate States over the United States. This is an old book, but is still generally accepted by professional historians as one of the best on this topic. The Indians promised alliance and, in return, were given political recognition they never received from the old country. The Confederates allowed them representation in the Confederate Congress and promised them the status of statehood. "The Southern white man, embarrassed, conceded much more than he really believed in, more than he ever could or would have conceded, had he not himself been so fearfully hard-pressed." She went on to say that "it was quite otherwise with the Northern white man . . . he, self-confident and self-reliant, negotiated with the Indian in the traditional way, took base advantage of the straits in which he found him."

The Northerners asked the Indians "to help him fight his battles, and, in the selfsame moment, plotted to dispossess him of his lands." She went on, "the very lands that had, less than five and twenty years before, been pledged as an Indian possession 'as long as the grass should grow and the waters run.'"[21]

I persist in claiming that the North was as racist, if not more so, than the South, and this is reflected in their attitude toward the Indians. At first, they did not consider them worth catering to. Then they treated them with the same attitude of racial superiority that they had always used when dealing with nonwhites. After the battles at Elk Horn Tavern and Prairie Grove in Arkansas, the Northern press complained of the savages employed by the Confederate army who had removed scalps from the poor Yankee soldiers they defeated in battle. The Indians were more concerned with their own welfare more than either Northern or Southern whites. In the end, the majority of the Indians believed they would be better off supporting the Confederate States of America. The Confederate symbols represent Southern Indians as well as Southern whites.

JEWISH CONFEDERATES

In 1860 the Jewish population was much smaller than today. About one-third of the Jews living in America in 1860 lived in the South, where recent research claims they were more widely accepted than in the North. Historians are usually handicapped by restricting their comments to what they consider proven facts. As a Southerner, I have an advantage over all of those Yankee Librevs who are writing the "true history" of our people. I was raised by Southerners and know them. Many, and probably most, have their prejudices. They also have the ability to overlook their prejudices for the sake of kindness to someone they see as a good person despite his defect of being black, or Indian, or Jewish. In other words, if "he's still a good ol' boy." When one understands this aspect of the Southern nature then historical facts make more sense. Most of those of the North think of the typical Southerner as a racist bigot who can only express hatred and contempt for those they see as their inferior. I am not the only one to believe this an invalid assumption.

James W. Johnson, an early black activist, said "...that the claim of the Southern whites that they love the Negro better than the Northern whites is in a manner true." He explained "Northern white people love the Negro in a sort of abstract way, as a race; through a sense of justice, charity, and philanthropy, they will liberally assist in his elevation. A number of them have heroically spent their lives in this effort. . . . Yet, generally speaking, they have no particular liking for individuals of the race." In comparison he claimed "Southern white people despise the Negro as a race, and will do nothing to aid in his elevation

---

21. Annie Heloise Abel, *The American Indian as Slaveholder and Secessionist* (Lincoln: University of Nebraska Press, 1992), 18–9.

as such; but for certain individuals they have a strong affection, and are helpful to them in many ways. With these individual members of the race they live on terms of the greatest intimacy; they entrust to them their children, their family treasures, and their family secrets; in trouble they often go to them for comfort and counsel; in sickness they often rely upon their care." I realize this is only anecdotal evidence, but it does offer some credibility to my claim. Johnson insisted, "This affectionate relation between the Southern whites and those blacks who come into close touch with them has not been overdrawn even in fiction."[22]

Most of the Southern Jews immigrated in the 1840s and 1850s from what is today Germany although back then there was no Germany, so they came from places such as Bavaria, Prussia, Alsace, Hesse, Baden, Swabia, or Westphalia. Some came from other areas such as Poland or Russia. "American Jewish experience reached a consensus long ago that the Jews were more accepted in the antebellum South than in the North." Their "loyalty to the Confederacy often was a matter of intense personal gratitude. Nowhere else in America had they experienced such fullness of opportunity or achieved comparable political and social acceptance."[23] It should not be surprising that three of the six Jewish congressmen came from the South, even though the North had twice the Jewish population.

As I have repeatedly stated, I do not deny Southern racism, I'm only pointing out that the North was as bad or worse. The first known Jew in Boston was "warned out" in the 1640s. They flourished in Charleston but were not allowed to live in liberal Boston. The Northern president "John Quincy Adams referred to David Yulee as the 'squeaking Jew delegate from Florida' and Rep. Albert G. Marchand of Pennsylvania as 'a squat little Jew-faced rotundity.'" As the war approached, the *Boston Evening Transcript* "blamed secession on the Southern Jews." *The New York Times* referred to Senators Benjamin and Yulee as "president and vice president of a Southern Jerusalem," and in 1864, "castigated the Democratic Party because its chairman, August Belmont, was 'the agent of foreign jew bankers.'"[24]

---

22. Johnson, J.W., *The Autobiography of an Ex-Colored Man* (Boston, Massachusetts: Sherman, French, and Co., 1912) pp 138-9.

23. Robert N. Rosen, *The Jewish Confederates* (Columbia: University of South Carolina Press, Inc., 2000), 31.

24. Ibid., 35.

"Jewish soldiers . . . fought for the South for many reasons, but the chief reason was to do their duty as they saw it."[25] The Librevs and the haters of our Southern heritage would like us to believe that our part of America bares the sin of American racism. Robert N. Rosen, author of *The Jewish Confederates*, clearly does not buy that thinking. The Jews of the South fought so hard in Tennessee that Grant expelled them. They remained loyal to the cause to the end. According to Rosen, "They had grown accustomed to breathing the free air of Dixie and were determined, like the Jews of Shreveport, to stand by, protect, and honor the flag of the Confederacy." Rabi Korn said, "The Jews of the Confederacy had good reason to be loyal to their section. . . Nowhere else in America - certainly not in the ante-bellum North - had Jews been accorded such an opportunity to be complete equals as in the old South."[26] The Confederate symbols represent Southern Jews as well as Southern whites.

HISPANIC CONFEDERATES

Thousands of Hispanics fought for the Confederacy, many of them documented in books written by John O'Donnell-Rosales, originally of Cuba but later a resident of Alabama. Entire companies were raised of Spanish or Hispanic men. Rosales said, "I must honestly admit that although I love the United States, I have never felt American, but instead I feel Southern." He went on to add "This land is our sacred birthright, each group having earned it by their blood and toil." He spoke of his Confederate ancestor, Pvt. Kelvin (Carlin) Rosales of Louisiana and said, "he was wounded many times and surrendered with the last Confederate units still active in June of 1865."[27] Between 1762 through 1813, Hispanics settled in two pockets. The coastal settlements included New Orleans, St. Bernard Parish, St. Louis, Biloxi, and Ascension, Assumption, and Iberville Parishes of Louisiana. Some other settlements include those in Arizona and New Mexico, St. Augustine, Florida, Saint Elena, South Carolina, and of course, many in Texas. There were also Spanish Jews in New Orleans, Savannah, Charleston, and parts of Virginia. The fact is that Confederate symbols belong to Hispanic Southerners as well as white Southerners.

BLACK CONFEDERATES

There have been numerous recent publications about black participation in the Confederate cause. I will make no attempt here to compete with them but instead will point out that it is a fact regardless of how many Librevs wish to deny

---

25. Ibid., xiii.

26. Ibid., 54.

27. John O'Donnell-Rosales, *Hispanic Confederates* (Baltimore: Clearfield Company, Inc., 1998), v.

it. The undeniable reality exist that if the slaves were prime for a rebellion, such as that imagined by John Brown, then the time would have never been better. It is true that tens of thousands of slaves followed the Union army as it invaded the South; however, hundreds of thousands remained on their plantations. Their labor in the fields allowed many more whites to serve in the army. If they had broken out in rebellion, those same white soldiers would have been needed to quiet said rebellion instead of fighting Yankees. The Confederacy would have fallen in a matter of months, maybe even weeks, if this had been the case.

We may never know the exact numbers of blacks who fought for the South; they did not serve in segregated regiments as in the North. The Confederate army utilized thousands of slaves in the construction of defenses. The first black regiments formed were Confederate regiments, not Northern ones. Some Librevs and South haters will say that many of those who served the Confederacy did so as laborers. They overlook the fact that the same could be said about many of those in the Union army—a policy which continued with the United States Army through World War II. Some blacks had not only gone to the front as servants for the Confederate masters but also participated when the time to fight came. I have seen numerous cases of those who had served as substitutes for their white master. Anyway, the anecdotal evidence is overwhelming supporting the notion that numerous blacks fought for the cause of Southern independence.

The main reason for resistance to this fact is that many cannot believe that a slave would fight for the nation that enslaved them. I cannot blame anyone for questioning this. First of all, I would suggest that maybe they did not see this as a war to free the slaves. Lincoln and most of his general officers denied that on numerous occasions. The second thing I don't understand is how these same liberals can talk about the blacks who fought for American independence. Did they not fight for the country that was enslaving them? In most cases, those in 1861 would have been the grandsons of the slaves who served in 1776, and their masters would have been the grandsons of the masters of the Revolutionary-era slaves.

In 1776 and in 1861, the blacks thought of themselves as Virginians, Carolinians, and Louisianans, not Americans. The free blacks who first joined up would have done so out of a "sense of community responsibility which impelled them to throw their lot with their neighbors." I could give many, many examples, but one of my favorite is the black servant who had been captured along with his master. When questioned by a white Northern officer of why he was fighting he answered, "I had as much right to fight for my native state as you had to fight for your'n, and a blame sight more right than your furriners, what's got no homes."[28]

---

28. Richard Rollins, *Black Southerners in Gray: Essays on Afro-Americans in Confederate Armies* (Murfreesboro, TN: Southern Heritage Press, 1994), 6.

Many Southerners resisted the arming of black troops; no doubt because they realized that to do so would greatly reduce the possibility of returning to slavery. In March of 1865, the Confederate Congress finally passed legislation which called for the conscription of black soldiers. Not long after, Davis sent his secretary of State to Europe with the message that the Confederacy would abolish slavery in exchange for recognition of the new country by France and England. It was too late at that point. The Librevs love to point out that this did not occur until near the end of the war which they interpret as an act of desperation. Perhaps it was, but they over look the fact that the North did not use Africans until January of 1863. The main reason they did not do so sooner is that they knew that many of their white soldiers would not like it. The main reason they did so when they did was to make it difficult for the British to recognize the Confederacy. With the Emancipation Proclamation and the use of black solders they hoped to make it look like a war over slavery. To me this seems to be as much an act of desperation as the actions of those in the South, and in fact many of the British saw it as such also.

The bottom line is that not all but many blacks fought for the Confederate army. Like the white Southerners, I am sure there were many different reasons for why they did. Regardless, Confederate symbols stand for black Confederates as well as white ones.

THE LOSS OF CIVILIAN LIFE

The Librevs underplay or completely ignore the atrocities committed against Southern civilians by their President Lincoln's invading hordes. They do admit to Sherman's march to the sea and render a little more than a footnote account of the destruction in the Shenandoah Valley, but they seem to accept the idea of collateral damage as something justified by the fact that these actions resulted in the greater good of freeing the slaves. The liberals of America love to complain about atrocities committed by the United States Army in other wars but seem to be accepting with this one. I have seen estimates as high as two million total deaths, which would mean well over a million civilians. Most sources I have seen put the number at about fifty thousand. In either case, they almost completely ignore the fact that many of these were the blacks whom they were supposedly there to rescue. The Librevs speak of the thousands of blacks who tagged along after the liberating Yankee Army, but assume that the millions who remained on the plantation did so out of fear. I think it is quite possible that many of them feared the Yankees more that the white Southerners. A great many of the civilian deaths were due to starvation; the invading army was starving the slaves too. The sad thing is that much of the food was intentionally destroyed and not simply consumed by the invaders. There are a number of books that list some of the destruction, none that I am aware of written by the academic historians. I suspect that they would say that it is because such stories are part of the "Lost Cause myth." I tend to think it is because such stories contradict their preconceived ideas about what makes Lincoln so great.

CONCLUSIONS

The Confederate cause probably had a greater racial diversity than the Union cause. The North did have more immigrants—mainly Irish, German, and other Northern Europeans. The South had Indians, Jews, Hispanics, as well as blacks. They too had a number of immigrants. Those who wish to eradicate Confederate symbols claim that they are divisive symbols that should be sacrificed to the gods of diversity for the sake of peace and harmony in the modern United States, the nation they forced upon us. They encourage respect for different cultures; they believe that to be the glory and beauty of diversity. One exception is those of Southern Confederate background. They believe that our ancestors do not deserve to be remembered, much less honored. The absurdity of their whole attitude is that Confederate symbols were important to many of diverse backgrounds. It is only the attitude of the political correctness supported by the Librev historians that prevents many of those from diverse backgrounds in recognizing their Confederate ancestors. There is no better example the President Obama. He is related to Robert E. Lee, as well as many other Confederates. To most he is generally associated with his African ancestors, people who were not even American, rather than his southern kin connected to the founding fathers of the United States as well as the Confederate States. So many Americans have been brainwashed into equating racism with the South. This has led most non-Anglo-Americans to identify with the North. They do not even consider the possibility that their people may have been supporters of the Confederacy since they come from a minority so persecuted by our people. Another good example is Larry David, one of the creators of the Seinfeld TV show. He was surprised to learn that he has Jewish ancestors who not only supported the Confederacy but were slave owners. Fortunately the Sons of Confederate Veterans have some of the descendants of diversity among their membership today. I have seen the white members of the SCV repeatedly demonstrate respect and appreciation to those who are willing to step forward and be recognized. I have little doubt that President Obama and Larry David would be well received by the Sons of Confederate Veterans. The Confederate symbols are meant to honor the Confederate soldiers who sacrificed for the cause of our independence, regardless of racial or ethnic background.

VI: Reconstructing
Reconstruction, 1865–1877

RECONSTRUCTION IS A PIVOTAL POINT in understanding the *Librev* interpretation of Southern history. Those who wish to erase our Southern heritage look at us unreconstructed Southerners as the last believers in what is called the Dunning School interpretation of Southern history. With the help of the *Librev* historians they have relabeled this view the "Lost Cause myth." This era is almost as important as the war in the defense of our heritage.

Dunning School is the interpretation applied in the movies *Gone with the Wind* and *The Birth of A Nation*. Professor Dunning was from Columbia University of New York, and so the *Librevs* do not deny that this view was widely accepted by Americans from the North as well as the South. As stated in the introduction of one college-level history textbook, Southerners viewed the war not "as a lesson in humility, but as an episode in the South's journey to salvation." Some have been kind and try to sound understanding as to why Southerners are so wrong; "The Southern white view of the Civil War was not a deliberate attempt to falsify history, but rather a need to justify and rationalize the devastation and loss of life that accompanied the Confederate defeat." I cannot be so kind in understanding the *Librev* motivation for their point of view. They would like to believe that their motivation is purely academic. To me it seems that their view is more distorted than what they call the Southern "Lost Cause myth." My thesis is based on the fact that most recognize and accept that history is written by the victors. This was expressed by Dan Brown, author of *The Da Vinci Code*, "History is always written by the winners. When two cultures clash, the loser is obliterated, and the winner writes the history books-books which glorify their own cause and disparage the conquered foe. As Napoleon once said, 'What is history, but a fable agreed upon?'"

For generations, the Northern historians have let the South write their own history as they focused on the New England village and other such topics. With the civil rights movement and growing revisionism, they developed more of an interest in black history. This combined with the fact that they have done more histories of New England than there were Puritans, they turned their attention to the South. They were motivated to revise the view of Civil War and

Reconstruction history. With the increased popularity of Confederate bashing, they acquired a new motivation. According to one *Librev* historian, at first, the "Lost Cause myth" manifested itself in the erection of Confederate memorials "erected typically on the most important site in a town, the courthouse square." It also included "commemorations of Confederate Memorial Day, the birthdays of prominent Confederate leaders, and the reunions of veterans." It was created and fostered by organizations, such as the United Daughters of the Confederacy and the Sons of Confederate Veterans, who saw to it that "the white history of the South was implanted into young minds and the legacy carried down through the generations." This "insured that the Lost Cause would not only be an interpretation of the past, but also the basic reality of the present and the foundation for the future."[29] The good news is that they can accept our claims that the "neo-Confederate" is not motivated by racism but that we are simply victims to the brainwashing of our ancestors.

The Yankee arrogance that led to the war in the first place continues to guide the Yankee *Librev* historian of today. They have recruited an army of scalawag historians who know that they had better accept the Harvard and Yale interpretations or abandon all hope of being an academic historian. They can see so clearly neo-Confederate self-interest in history, but they are completely blind to their own. The basic assumption that guides them is that the war was not only justified but also necessary for the elimination of the evil institution of slavery. A Yankee *Librev* historian who is at the vanguard of this thinking is Eric Foner. He has defined Reconstruction as being the story of the new South in which the black is a freedman rather than a slave. For him, Reconstruction included the so-called border states, even the ones who made no attempt at becoming part of the Confederacy. According to him, if they had slavery, they had Reconstruction. He sees the freeing of the slaves as beginning with the Emancipation Proclamation, completely ignoring the fact of which every competent historian is aware —that that document never freed a single slave at the time it was issued, and that it exempted those slave states which remained with the Union. Therefore the Fonerites see Reconstruction as beginning in 1863. This serves to heighten the nobility of the war and Reconstruction in that the North is simply trying to create a better world for black Americans. The South, whether that be the Confederates of the past or the neo-Confederates of today, are evil because they resisted.

Foner thoroughly combed the historical records. I do not criticize his abilities as a researcher, but I do take exception to his conclusion that the history of Reconstruction has now been corrected. In the preface of his book *Reconstruction: America's Unfinished Revolution, 1863–1877*, he claims "no part of the American experience has, in the last twenty-five years [the book is

---

29. Goldfield et al., *The American Journey: A History of the United States*. (New Jersey: Pearson Printice Hall, 2004), 499–500.

copyrighted in 1988 - LT] seen a broadly accepted point of view so completely overturned as Reconstruction." He sees his book as a need to fill the void left by scrapping the Dunning interpretation. As he said, "yet despite this change in consciousness, so to speak, historians have yet to produce a coherent new portrait of the era." I am impressed with his history of the ending of slavery, but I am not convinced that the War to Prevent Southern Independence and the oppression of the Southern people was justified, nor was it necessary to end slavery.

It may be that some of the Yankees had noble intentions, but many of them did not. This does not negate the fact that the Republicans used them as the foundation on which they tried to build their Republican party in the South, giving them hope they would control Washington for years to come. It is true that during this period, Southerners cultivated the image of their efforts as the Lost Cause, but that does not mean that it was a "myth." The fact is that in 1861 the people of the South, like their grandparents did in the late eighteenth century, declared independence. Like them, they were invaded as the forces of centralism attempted to deny them the right to self-government. The difference between the two occasions is that in the latter they were defeated. This does not mean that they were wrong. In the end, the slaves were freed, but this does not mean that the atrocities committed against the South by Yankee imperialism were justified. It may be that after the South took back control of their governments, blacks were reduced to second-class citizenship. But they were already second-class citizens in the North, so it does not prove that America would have produced a better society for all if the North had not abandoned their noble crusade. It may even be that race relations were worsened by the fact that they used the blacks as pawns in their attempts to control and dominate the hearts and minds of the Southern people.

ORIGINS OF THE DUNNING SCHOOL (LOST CAUSE MYTH)

In the early twentieth century, North and South had somewhat of a consensus regarding Reconstruction regardless of any disagreements over the war. William Dunning and John W. Burgess saw Lincoln as trying to achieve sectional reconciliation, which Andrew Johnson tried to follow after he came to the White House. They blamed the radicals of the Republican Party as being responsible for turning Reconstruction into the debacle that failed with the Compromise of 1877. *Librev* historians of today see this as the dominant interpretation in both the South and the North from the late nineteenth century through World War II. They see this as the simplistic views expressed and solidified in the American conscience with films, such as *Gone with the Wind* and *The Birth of a Nation*.

I, for one, see *Gone with the Wind* as a soap opera, both the book and the movie. This movie is still loved by many today thanks to Scarlet's beautiful dresses, the romantic balls and the colorful backdrop. There are others who despise the film today; they see it as portraying the blacks as simple-minded buffoons who speak and behave in the stereotypical ways with which many whites viewed their fellow Americans. I have shown the Reconstruction scenes from the movie to some of the history classes because they were classic Dunning School. Nonetheless, I have the opinion that the movie is better than most Hollywood productions as far as historical accuracy. They may have shown Mammy as being loyal to her white mistress, but the fact is that this was most often the case with house servants, such as the one she portrayed. The field slaves were gone; that is why Scarlet had blisters on her hands. They showed the Ku Klux Klan as simply trying to restore law and order where the carpetbaggers and occupation army had failed. It would not be long before unsavory elements started to use the organization for nefarious purposes. Scarlet, as a symbol of the New South, surrendered her morality to modernization as she greedily pursued wealth at any price. Karl Marx, however, would probably see this as an example of one of the weaknesses in the capitalist system. My greatest objection to the movie is the general portrayal of the South as resisting modernization and the Confederate soldiers as defenders of a feudal society. They saw their way of life as "gone with the wind," and thus the meaning of the title.

It is a movie, and like most movies not a reliable source for history. It is classic Dunning School, but I am not convinced that this alone is the cause for its deficiencies. In the 1930s the author had access to a valuable source for historical information. Margaret Mitchell knew many who had lived through the war and Reconstruction. I have no doubt that she used stories which she had picked up from her family and acquaintances. There were Confederate veterans who attended the premiere of the movie in Atlanta in 1939.

One must be careful with anecdotal history, but that does not mean it should be ignored. It does not mean that it is wrong. The *Librevs* believe that the memories of those who lived through the war and Reconstruction were distorted by the "Lost Cause myth." This is so typical of Yankee, especially Yankee intellectual, arrogance. They believe that they are the only ones wise enough to see the true history of the events which tore apart the United States. They know more with their research than those who were there. I realize that an eye witness may have a more distorted view of reality than someone who has studied several sides of a story, but we cannot simply ignore the eyewitness account when it is contrary to the conclusions of researchers. It may be that one or two eyewitnesses believe they saw something that did not happen the way it appeared. When we are looking at the accounts of the Southern experience during the war, we are talking about thousands of eyewitnesses. It seems unlikely that they are all wrong or deluded.

The racism in *The Birth of a Nation* should be a source of embarrassment for all Americans, Northerners as well as Southerners. Nonetheless, that is the way people were in 1915. The movie itself is of historical significance. When it came out it was the first epic film. It was the first movie shown in the White House, viewed by President Wilson, a Southerner. The silent movie was the story of two families who lived through the war and Reconstruction. The thing to remember is that people in 1915 held different beliefs than people today. At that time racism was generally accepted whereas today it is generally condemned. In the 1930s things had not changed much. When the move *Gone With the Wind* was made, most American schools were segregated, interracial marriage was illegal in most states, and the United States Army was segregated.

We think of Adolph Hitler and his Nazi Reich as an evil empire that had delusions of Aryan superiority. What we try to forget is that the United States, as well as most other European powers, held similar beliefs. In our country, such beliefs were often referred to as Social Darwinism. In the United States, North as well as South, we assumed that those of colonial stock were superior to either the immigrants from Southern and Eastern Europe or those with African ancestors. Those of American Indian, Asian, or Mexican were also inferior, but in most parts of America, they were not numerous enough to be as much of a threat. In the final scenes of *The Birth of a Nation*, a line of Klansmen prevents blacks from casting their votes on election day. This reflects an obvious pride in reestablishing Aryan superiority. In 1915, most Americans clearly saw these Klansmen as heroes who were helping to keep our country pure. The movie also reflected the fears which people had of the time. They believed that black men were obsessed with white women. That is the way many people were in those days, in the North as well as the South, and that is why most US states had laws against blacks and whites getting married. Such racism may embarrass us today, but it was the way that not only Americans but also most of those of Western European culture saw the world before World War II. If there is any good that came from Adolph Hitler it may be that he showed the world how bad this kind of thinking can be.

Through the 1920s, this thinking was prevalent and explains the revival of the Ku Klux Klan, increased activity of nativist organizations, and an increase in violence against the non-Aryan intruders of the United States. This new Klan of the 1920s was as popular in the North as in the South. The largest single chapter was in Chicago. They took over the state legislatures in Oklahoma and Texas, but they did the same in the Northern states of Oregon and Indiana and came close in California. In the North, they were more opposed to the immigrants who were Catholic or Jewish or Communist. In 1924, they passed the first of the quota acts, which seriously limited further entrance of non-Aryans into this country, a law which was refined further and lasted until 1965. Remember, the United States Army which invaded and conquered the Third Reich was segregated.

The Birth of a Nation was clearly a Dunning School interpretation of the war and Reconstruction. It was also clearly a racist point of view. I do not agree with the racist philosophy of our ancestors during the period, nor during the days of slavery, but that is the way people thought back then. I do not wish to disown them because things have changed. That is what history is all about. I repeat once more, my Southern ancestors were no more racist than most in the North, nor in other parts of Northern Europe. Such thinking was not even limited to whites and Europeans. Around the world various people have seen themselves as superior. The Chinese built the Great Wall to keep out inferiors. Racism is how the Aryan nations rationalized their conquest of other peoples. It is wrong to think of the South as bad because they were racist and the North as good because they were not.

The racism evident in this movie is not relevant to the Yankee conquest of the South. It does not mean that they were justified in what they did to the Southern people. It does not mean that Confederates were wrong to declare independence from the North. It does not mean that they went through some sort of mass self-hypnosis where they created a "Lost Cause myth" to rationalize their position. It was not a myth to those who lived it. Colonel John Washington Inzer wrote in a letter to his grandson, "Glad that you were pleased with *The Birth of a Nation*. That part of the show that attempted, or sought, to illustrate the conditions of the South during Reconstruction Days—to your mind—was most horrible, but I am sure that it did not begin to illustrate things as they really occurred in those days." He went on to say "I passed through that period, and I could give you only a faint idea of the occurrences of that time."[30] Am I to believe that this man who served in his country's army was under some kind of mass-induced delusion when he wrote this? The *Librevs* want me to believe that thousands of his contemporaries who recorded similar descriptions were likewise deluded. Perhaps their interpretations were filtered by their view of what the world is. I have little doubt that they were. I also believe that many of the revisionists see the history of the time from their perspective. This is called presentism.

THE SPECIFIC ISSUES

I see seven specific areas in which the *Librevs* believe they have successfully corrected American history. I admit that some adjustments to the Dunning view were needed. There are some aspects of the traditional interpretations of our history which needed to be revised. I disagree with their use of the term "Lost Cause myth," and with their assumption that the "broadly accepted point of view" has been "so completely overturned."[31] The first of these issues is that the *Librevs* are convinced that they have proven that the carpetbaggers and scallywags were not as corrupt as Southerners have claimed they were. Second, they believe that they have shown that they did not leave the Southern people saddled with intolerable debts and taxes. Third, they are convinced that they have shown that the blacks did not run rampant through Southern cities as they

---

30. Mattie Lou Teague Crow, ed., *The Diary of A Confederate Soldier: John Washington Inzer, 1834–1928* (Mattie Lou Teague Crow, 1977), 159.

31. Foner, Eric, *Reconstruction: America's Unfinished Revolution.* (Harper Collins Publishers, Inc. History Club edition, 2005), xix.

seized control of the Reconstruction governments. Fourth, they claim that they have proven that Reconstruction was not merely an attempt by the Republicans to establish control. Fifth, they also say that the South was not occupied by the United States military. Sixth, they think they have shown that not only did the Yankees not commit horrible atrocities against Southerners but also that they even accomplished a number of beneficial reforms. Seventh, some have even begun to attack the near deification of Robert E. Lee as they attempt to show that he is not the man Southerners have painted him to be in their "Lost Cause mythology." I will now go into more detail on these myths. These are the issues I will address in the remainder of this chapter.

FIRST ISSUE

Perhaps the greatest criticism which Southerners have levied on Reconstruction has traditionally been the charges of corruption. The *Librevs* do not try to deny that there are proven examples of this corruption. There are many stories of the Northmen who came and got themselves appointed or elected to public office from which they resigned and took the treasury back North with them. The Dunning view may have been a little exaggerated, perhaps giving the impression that they were all corrupt. I do believe that there were some who had noble intentions; however, I believe that most came South seeking profits and in some cases what could even be described as plunder. Even the famed carpetbagger Albion Tourgee admitted that he did not head South on any kind of crusade but rather because "the South seemed to offer economic opportunities to the man with initiative."[32] He was not about the devil's work; however, he did possess Yankee arrogance, which was demonstrated by the fact that "he shared the hope of other Yankee settlers that the South would be quickly transformed into a duplicate of the North 'by the power of commerce, manufactures, and the incursion of Northern life, thought, capital, industry, enterprise.'"[33]

There have been a number of revisionist histories that have demonstrated that some of these men had good intentions, but like other European and American imperialists around the globe, they end up forcing their improved lifestyle on people who do not necessarily want it. As to those who clearly were corrupt, the *Librev* response is that the Grant administration was noted for corruption, not just in the South. And they accuse us of rationalizing? It amazes me that these liberal types who have consistently been critical of American imperialism as something more than simply spreading truth, justice, and the American way; yet in the case of the conquest of the South, they seem to have swallowed that same type of thinking hook, line, and sinker.

---

32. Albion W. Tourgee, *A Fool's Errand: A Novel of the South during Reconstruction* (New York: Harper Torchbooks, 1961), x.

33. Ibid, x.

SECOND ISSUE

One of the myths that the *Librevs* are satisfied that they have disproven is that of the big debts and high taxes which the Republicans saddled Southerners with. Like the corruption charges, they confess that in some cases the large debts accumulated by the Republican Reconstructed governments were due to the corruption, especially in North and South Carolina and Georgia. Nonetheless they feel that they have still destroyed the Dunning interpretation. In some cases, they have demonstrated that the debts were simply the result of poor decision making. The poor decision making on the part of carpetbaggers, who cheered on as property taxes increased by an average of 400% in the South. This scenario is played out in *Gone With the Wind* when the scallywag overseer offers to buy Tara from Scarlet by paying the new taxes. Others came about following Johnson's plan for Reconstruction, which ended up being spent to develop railroads. These and other needed post war rebuilding expenditures led to more debts than those caused by corruption. The debts led to increased taxation. Somehow they have concluded that by showing that some but not all the increased debt and taxation was the result of things other than corrupt carpetbaggers that they have thus disproven the traditional view of Reconstruction. To me it seems that they have shown that not all the debts and high taxes were due to Republican Reconstruction governments, but many, if not most, were. They may have shown that this aspect of Reconstruction may not be as simplistic as some have considered it, but they certainly have not demonstrated any "Lost Cause myth."

THIRD ISSUE

Another "disproven myth," at least according to the *Librevs*, is the Southern complaints that the Reconstruction South was dominated by incompetent black Republicans. I have no doubt that this has been exaggerated, but it is understandable why they felt this way. Before the war, there were some free blacks. They were a significant population in some areas such as Virginia, Maryland, and Louisiana. There were even some who were well-off financially, including some who owned plantations or businesses worked by slaves. However, compared to the way things were after the war, it must have seemed to the white Southerners that the tables had been turned. It is a fact that in the ten states subject to reconstruction that there were 735,000 black registered voters compared to 635,000 whites in 1867. Most of the whites who were former civic leaders and had served the Confederacy, were not allowed to vote. There is little doubt that this fact inspired fear. Another factor which adds some confusion is the fact that the Radical Republicans were sometimes called Black Republicans, not because of skin colour but because of their dubious proposals.

The *Librevs* are self-satisfied at disproving a Dunning myth. They pointed out that only sixteen blacks served in Congress. They held other high offices throughout the region, but the only state legislature that they dominated was South Carolina. This may not have been as dominating as some have implied over the years, but it is still a radical change compared to the prewar South. Yes, they have demonstrated that the feelings of being overrun were exaggerated; however, I find it completely understandable that some Southerners felt that the blacks had taken control.

They have done some studies which have shown that the black politicians were more competent than it has been claimed by whites. I do not doubt that this is true, and that it is an improvement in our history. I see no error in their conclusions. It is an improvement and should be recognized as such. It does not destroy the overall Southern interpretation of our history and certainly does not justify what the Yankees did to our people. Nor does it justify calling the Southern view of our own history a "Lost Cause myth."

FOURTH AND FIFTH ISSUES

The fourth myth, and most ridiculous claim of *Librevs*, is disputing that a primary objective of the Republican Party during Reconstruction was to build and maintain a strong presence in the South. As far as I am concerned, that was their purpose. That was their main purpose. I will discuss this in greater detail later.

Related to this is the fifth myth concerning the occupation of the South by the United States military. Like the Southern view of black domination, I have little doubt that this was exaggerated in the minds of Southerners. It is understandable why they felt this way. They had lived all of their lives in a nation which was not patrolled by soldiers. Law enforcement was left to civilian authorities. On this particular charge, we have the statistics. Only 18.000 troops remained in the South in 1866 and by 1876 the number dropped to 6,000. These troops were rarely used against the whites. The *Librevs* do point out that those occasions generally involved incidents in which the Southern whites were trying to impose their will on Southern blacks; the implication being that this was a good thing. The fact is that the United States military occupied the land in which such things had been previously unheard of. It may not have been as big a deal as implied by some, but it did happen. There is little else to say about this issue; ten states fell under martial law during Reconstruction. I am sure that if any states today were placed under martial law enforced by a military presence, the liberals would be leading the protest, yet in this case, they do not seem to think it a big deal.

SIXTH ISSUE

The *Librevs* believe they have proven that the Reconstruction Yankees did not commit horrible atrocities. They have admitted that some bad things did happen, but they were not as bad as they could have been. Some wanted to charge Davis with crimes, but they didn't because most experts believed the South had committed no crimes. The military occupation and plunder of what treasures were left could have been even more widespread. I suppose that there is no denying that it could have been worse. Hitler could have gassed two or three million more people than he did. He too could have been worse than he was. Is that a logical justification for the evil he did commit?

It seems to me that some recent research does show that they had some successes in creating a better life, especially for the freedmen. However, recent research also shows that hundreds or even thousands of freedmen died in camps because of federal incompetence after the war. This does not seem to fit their narrative. They did a lot in creating educational opportunities for those people who had generally been denied such. They have also been convinced that many of these advances were lost when they abandoned Reconstruction in 1877.

The *Librevs* feel that they have shattered the Dunning myth of Reconstruction by focusing on some of the accomplishments of the Republican occupation of the South. This is an approach still used by United States occupying forces as did the Romans before them. They may conquer a land and impose their will, but they do offer rewards and eventually will even turn over political control to natives as long as they are friendly to the conquerors. The Freedmen's Bureau spent $1 million on relief for Southern blacks and whites and $5 million on education. Literacy rose impressively among blacks who were enrolled in schools for the first time. Rail systems were restored and expanded by nearly 7,300 miles. There were some improvements made by the conquering United States government. I am not convinced that this justifies killing hundreds of thousands of people, burning their homes and towns, killing their live stock, destroying infrastructure and forcing Yankee morality and lifestyle on them. Again, I must point out that liberals have traditionally not accepted these rationalizations in other examples of American imperialism, yet they believe it was a great good when the North conquered the South.

SEVENTH ISSUE

Of late, there are some *Librevs* that have attacked the image of Robert E. Lee making it the seventh issue in what they call the "Lost Cause myth." Not only has he been the father figure of the South, displacing George Washington in the minds of many Southerners, but he has also been the object of respect for many others around the world. This is why they feel it necessary to make him more myth than reality. The fact is that he was a man who deserves respect.

He is the only man in history to be offered command of opposing armies. He is the only man to have changed the course of the Mississippi River with his plan to save the city of St. Louis. He began his career by graduating West Point without a single demerit and tried to live his life with the same kind of discipline and integrity. It is no wonder that they feel compelled to cut the man down; he was indeed a giant. He was a man and no doubt was not as perfect as some imagine him to have been, but people need to have someone to look up to and admire. I cannot think of anyone who has come any closer to being a true hero, and it seems to me that those who attack him have only demonstrated how mean-spirited and deficient in character they are. The deeds of heroes are often exaggerated in the minds of admirers, but there are usually reasons that they have been given so much respect.

Lee was not only admired by Southerners, but from others around the world. This included those who won World War II. Sir Winston Churchill once remarked, "Lee was the noblest American who had ever lived and one of the greatest commanders known to the annals of war." The following is a letter from Dwight D. Eisenhower:

> August 9, 1960
>
> Dear Dr. Scott:
>
> Respecting your August 1 inquiry calling attention to my often expressed admiration for General Robert E. Lee, I would say, first, that we need to understand that at the time of the War between the States the issue of secession had remained unresolved for more than 70 years. Men of probity, character, public standing and unquestioned loyalty, both North and South, had disagreed over this issue as a matter of principle from the day our Constitution was adopted.
>
> General Robert E. Lee was, in my estimation, one of the supremely gifted men produced by our Nation. He believed unswervingly in the Constitutional validity of his cause which until 1865 was still an arguable question in America; he was a poised and inspiring leader, true to the high trust reposed in him by millions of his fellow citizens; he was thoughtful yet demanding of his officers and men, forbearing with captured enemies but ingenious, unrelenting and personally courageous in battle, and never disheartened by a reverse or obstacle. Through all his many trials, he remained selfless almost to

a fault and unfailing in his faith in God. Taken altogether, he was noble as a leader and as a man, and unsullied as I read the pages of our history.

From deep conviction, I simply say this: a nation of men of Lee's caliber would be unconquerable in spirit and soul. Indeed, to the degree that present-day American youth will strive to emulate his rare qualities, including his devotion to this land as revealed in his painstaking efforts to help heal the Nation's wounds once the bitter struggle was over, we, in our own time of danger in a divided world, will be strengthened and our love of freedom sustained.

Such are the reasons that I proudly display the picture of this great American on my office wall.

Sincerely,

Dwight D. Eisenhower

REPUBLICAN DOMINATION OF THE SOUTH

I cannot call it "proven" but I believe that the actions of the Republicans during Reconstruction were primarily motivated by politics. This is an expansion on the fourth issue mentioned above. My thesis about the Northern motivations behind Reconstruction rests on the same basic assumption that Adam Smith made in his *Wealth of Nations*; people operate out of self-interest. Despite the *Librev* claims that they have disproven the importance of Republican ambition, common sense seems to dictate to the contrary. There are a two other assumptions that I make in reaching my conclusion. First, political parties are organized to accomplish what the members feel is in their best interest. Second, I also believe that the members of political parties become so obsessed with their objectives that at times they function to the detriment of those not in their party. This is why George Washington warned about political parties in his farewell address. If these assumptions are accepted then it is easy to see what concerned Republicans. The Republicans were a minority party that got elected because of a split in the majority Democrat Party. If the Union was reconstructed without slavery then the differences that divided the majority Democrat Party would be gone; therefore the Republicans would have to do something to survive. In other words, the basic objective of the United States government during Reconstruction reflected the self-interest of the dominant Republican Party. They worked out a plan where they could try to build Republican support and cut Democrat voters.

The South had become Democrat by 1860 and after their military defeat by a Republican president could not be expected to change their party loyalties. The fact is that for a century after the war, the South was solid Democrat, which should be no surprise. There were numerous measures taken by the Republican Reconstruction establishment to limit the return of Southern Democrats to positions of power and to even limit their voting abilities.

One priority for a minority party would be to increase their numbers. The source for new Republicans was obvious—the newly freed slaves who made up about 40 percent of the Southern population. I think it is safe to assume that the majority of slaves were ecstatic to be free. It would be an easy sale for the Republican conquerors to point out to the freedmen that Abraham Lincoln and his Republican Party are the ones that freed them. If the Republicans could make certain that the freedmen could vote, then their numbers combined with the white Unionists would at least come close to a majority vote. This thesis is supported by the fact that up until the election of Franklin D. Roosevelt the blacks who voted did vote Republican. It could still be close in some areas, so it would be necessary to limit the voting of Confederate Democrats. This thesis is supported by the fact that they did go to great lengths to limit the white voting and to assure black *voting*.

The *Librevs* like to talk about the "Lost Cause myth," but I can point out a "Won Cause myth." Lincoln often denied that he was fighting the war to free the slaves. Professional historians know that this is true. However, when the war was over it was obvious that the days of slavery were over and it would be easy to pass an amendment to the Constitution making it so. Motivated by a need to recruit Republican voters it should be obvious why they would want to change the cause from "Union" to "Abolition." There were those, such as Frederick Douglass, who saw the war as opportunity to end slavery, but that was not the stated objective. Abolition of slavery not only served as a tool to recruit freedmen voters, but it also helped to make the war seem a noble cause. There were many Northern whites who did not think that preserving the Union alone was worth fighting for, especially those who had no economic interest in the war or in forcing the South back into the Union. Abolition of slavery would not only sound better to these whites, at least now that it was a done deal, but could also sound better to those in other countries. Thus we have the birth of the "Won Cause myth."

My thesis works in explaining motivation for Republican Reconstruction policies, and it is supported by many of the events that unfolded during the period. They did pass laws, including the Fourteenth Amendment, designed to weaken the Southern Democrat ruling class. They passed laws to insure the voting rights of freedmen. Southern whites countered this strategy by trying to limit the voting of blacks. They even turned to terrorism with groups such as the Ku Klux Klan which not only attacked blacks but also carpetbaggers and scallywags. It even explains the Republican desertion of blacks after 1877.

If one accepts the *Librev* claims about Reconstruction then they have a problem explaining why Republicans abandoned the Freedmen with the Compromise of 1877. My thesis makes this quite understandable. It fits. By that time, they had built their party and found a constituency based on the businessmen of the Industrial Revolution. At the same time, they were losing votes as the Northern racist found appeal in Democrat politicians who preached against racial equality. I see no problem in understanding why the Republicans abandoned the blacks after 1877. They found Republican support elsewhere and saw that continued preoccupation with the blacks could lose them votes among the majority of the American population who were racist. This includes the more numerous Northern voters. This is also another example of what I have often repeated, I do not claim that Southerners were not racist, only that they were no more so than Northerners.

I will concede that some of the *Librev* criticisms of traditional Dunning interpretation are valid. I am sure that there were some who went South with the desire to give help to the freedmen on moral grounds. I have no doubt that they were prepared to sacrifice their time to help the people they felt empathy for. Likewise, I am equally confident that there were many who simply saw an opportunity to make money. This is a characteristic of capitalism which many have criticized. I also believe there are those who supported the Republican Party and its legislation with the conviction that they were doing the right thing. Nonetheless, I believe the greatest force behind events that transpired was Republican self-interest.

THE LOST CAUSE IS NO MYTH

When looking at Southerners, the *Librevs* seem to be overlooking a common human feeling—no one likes someone else telling them what to do. It is no wonder that *Librevs* ignore this since they have the delusion that Southern identity is a myth that did not come about until shortly before the war or even after. Because of my own personal experiences, I cannot accept their nonsense. No arrogant intellectual Yankee is going to make me believe that my Southern identity is a myth and not real.

When the *Librevs* talk about the "Lost Cause myth," they should understand that national identity is an emotional thing and not intellectual; that is why I will now submit to an emotional outburst. That is also why I know that their thesis is nonsense. It is common that those of us who spent a significant part of our lives outside of the South are quite often the most patriotic. I am a California Okie. I was raised by parents that never spoke of evil Yankees. I graduated high school and even college with an identity of being a Californian. I knew of my Confederate ancestors, but I had to learn to hate Yankees by myself. I was aware that we ate different food than most of my California friends (beans and cornbread) and that we went to a different church (Southern Christian) and that my parents listened to different music (country and gospel). My parents even spoke a different language (Southern English).

I learned to speak from them and so that was my first language, but since I was a child I learned to talk like my friends. I was like the children of immigrants who grew up speaking a different language but since they were children they learned to speak English without a foreign accent. I should say that I was ridiculed into talking like my friends and classmates. Hillbilly was my native language. In time, I learned that most of the people I disliked the most because they were arrogant, self-righteous, pretentious, and at times downright mean had something in common; they or their families came from the North. I started doing genealogy at an early age, and I eventually realized that I was Southern. It all came together for me—the food, the music, the religion, the Confederate ancestors; I am Southern. I may have been raised in California, but that is not my ethnic background. Most of my friends in California had hyphenated ethnic identities, and I began to realize that I had one too. I am Southern-American. I also began to realize that I had lost much of my culture and began to embrace what remained. I now value that culture as part of my identity. For me these were conclusions I reached on my own, not because I was brainwashed by any "Lost Cause myth."

I also became aware of the fact that there are many people who hate Southerners. This is nothing new. I repeat a quote from Isaac Trimble which I used in chapter 4 when I discussed the growing hatred toward Southerners, "Your bigatry [sic] & hatred of every thing Southern drove us from you-the Union was at variance with our feelings, tastes, pursuits, honorable aims & religion and time instead of removing these, has strengthened them, untill [sic] on the great principles of self preservation and self respect, the Union has been sundered forever."

Growing up in California I often heard how those of Southern roots are bigots. I used to believe what they said. Now I realize how many of those who would say that are the real bigots. Many of them hate Southerners. They hate our hillbilly music, the way we talk, our fundamentalist religion, our fried food, and just about everything else Southern. They do like our sunshine, but when they move South to retire they call it the Sunbelt, not the South. We are a different people, ask them. They know that Southerners, black and white, walk slow, talk slow, and are slow-witted. Our Southern identity is not a delusion that our people developed to rationalize the war that we lost. Our Southern identity is what we are. I, for one, will not allow arrogant Yankees to take it from me, no matter from what uppity school they got their Ph. D.

The Yankees conquered us, but this does not mean that we liked it. The story of Reconstruction from the Southern perspective is that our people did all that they could do to preserve what self-respect they had after accepting the reality of military defeat. They were told by the lying, thieving Yankees that they would be accepted back into the Union with forgiving arms, but when they tried to rebuild their lives, they found that there were many more restrictions than they anticipated. We could not fight anymore, but that did not mean that we believed that we had been wrong. You cannot beat your beliefs into someone. Even the famous carpetbagger Albion W. Tourgee understood; thus, he emphasized the fact that in the years immediately following the Civil War, the former Confederates had control of their own state and government. It was during this period "that they clearly demonstrated their unwillingness or inability to face up to the implications of surrender at Appomattox."

The South had put down their guns but did not comprehend what this meant. Some fled the country rather than to live under Yankee rule. A few, such as Edmond Ruffin, chose death. Most faced the humiliation and focused on what was left of their homes and families. They had all lost loved ones and many lost limbs. No doubt their self-esteem suffered considerably. They made these sacrifices for a cause they believed in, but they did not suddenly experience a change of heart. They still had their cherished beliefs. Like Governor Stockdale of Texas said, "but they have none of the spaniel in their composition. No, sir, they are not in the least like the dog that seeks to lick the hand of the man that kicked him." They did what they had to do. "They know that they resisted the federal government as long as any means of resistance was left, and that any attempt at resistance now must be in vain, and they have no means, and would only make bad worse."[34]

The charges that Northern cruelties were nothing but the delusions of Southerners who wanted to rationalize their unjust war is arrogant and absurd. The *Librevs* love to quote Lee about furling the Confederate flag, but they ignore what he told Governor Stockdale: "if I had foreseen the use those people designed to make of their victory, there would have been no surrender at Appomattox Courthouse; no, sir, not by me." He went on to add, "Had I foreseen these results of subjugation, I would have preferred to die at Appomattox with my brave men, my sword in this right hand."[35]

The following words of "I'm a Good Old Rebel" were not delusions: (said to have been written by Major James Randolph, a Virginian and member of General J.E.B. Stuart's staff)

---

34. James R. Kennedy and Walter D Kennedy, *The South Was Right* (Baton Rouge, LA: Land and Land, 1991), 23.

35. Ibid., 24.

Oh, I'm a good old Rebel,
Now that's just what I am;
For this 'fair land of Freedom:
I do not give a damn.
I'm glad I fit against it'
I only wish we'd won.
And I don't want no pardon
for anything I've done.

I hates the constitution,
This great Republic too;
I hates the Freedmen's Buro,
In uniforms of blue.
I hates the nasty eagle,
With all his braggs and fuss;
The lyin' thievin' Yankees
I hates'em wuss and wuss

I hates the Yankee nation
And everything they do,
I hates the Declaration
of Independence, too;
I hates the glorious Union
Tis drippin' with our blood
I hates their striped banner,
I fit it all I could.

I followed Ol' Marse Robert
for four years, nearabout,
got wounded in three places
and starved at Pint Lookout:
I cotch the rheumatism
a' campin: in the snow;
but I killed a chance o'Yankees,
I'd like to kill some mo'.

Three hundred thousand Yankees
Is still in Southern dust;
We killed three hundred thousand
befo' they conquered us.
They died of Southern fever
And Southern steel and shot;
 I wish they was three million
Instead of what we got.

I can't take up my musket
And fight' em now no mo',
But I ain't a-goin' to love 'em,
Now that is sartin sure;
And I don't want no pardon
For what I was and am;
And I won't be reconstructed,
And I do not give a damn.

FREEING THE SLAVES (BEGINNING RECONSTRUCTION)

The latest thinking by the wise and all-knowing *Librev* historians is that Reconstruction began with the freeing of the slaves, based on the book by Eric Foner. Foner is a famous historian and I am simply one who could only find work as an adjunct professor, so I know that most will see Foner's interpretation as better than mine. Nonetheless, I will attempt to make my case. The *Librevs* know the numerous quotes from Lincoln and his friends in which they stated that they were not fighting to free the slaves, yet the *Librevs* keep insisting that the war was a war to free the slaves. Since they accept Foner's thesis that Reconstruction was really about the abolition of slavery, then the biggest problem I see are those states they call "border states." There were five slave states which Lincoln and his government insisted were still in the Union. If that were the case, then why would they need to be Reconstructed? As far as I am concerned, these "border states" are part of the South. If the term is used simply to distinguish them from the "Deep South," I would much prefer the term "upper South."

Good or bad, as far as I am concerned, the definition of the South is those states that still had slavery as of 1860. I will first talk about those which were definitely not part of the Confederacy: Maryland and Delaware. I will then cover the two states which had Union and Confederate governments: Kentucky and Missouri. The *Librevs* generally refer to the latter two as remaining with the Union and generally ignore Confederate claims and the two extra stars on the battle flag which represent the Confederate states of Missouri and Kentucky. I will then conclude by discussing West Virginia.

MARYLAND AND DELAWARE

Maryland continued to have a divided population even after Yankee occupation. I have already discussed the question of Maryland secession and how I believe that they would have been Confederate if allowed the right to democratic process. Now I will look at abolition of slavery since that is what Foner and the *Librevs* say we must do. They had about 87,000 slaves, mostly in the Southern part of the state. They had a long tradition of antislavery sentiment and, as a result, had the largest free black population. Naturally they added to the abolitionist fire. The slave owners accepted the inevitability of abolition but attempted to gain compensation. The 1863 elections called for a constitutional convention to reconstruct a state that supposedly remained part of the Union. Foner did offer a quote from one Maryland Unionist after the constitution passed:

> [It] must be a source of mortification that emancipation
> has . . . not been from high principle, . . . but party spirit,
> vengeful feeling against disloyal slaveholders, and regard
> for material interest. There has been no expression, at least

in this community, of regard for the negro - for human rights, but . . . many expressive of the great prosperity to result to the state by a change of the system of labor.[36]

Lincoln did carry the state in 1864, but the whole thing has the same stink about it that it did in April of 1861. They clearly tried to exclude those who had not only served the Confederate cause but were also known to have expressed any sympathy for the Confederacy. Occupying military forces were used to guard the polls to insure only 'qualified' voters cast votes. This, of course, is in addition to those who had fled Maryland after Yankee occupation. I do see evidence for my oft repeated claim that Southerners were no more racist than Northerners. The Yankeefied Marylanders did not give blacks the vote.

Delaware was a collection of inconsistencies, which may explain why Foner did not delve into that state. Most people do not think of Delaware as the South, and I must confess I have a hard time accepting it as such despite the fact that it meets my simple definition of the region—those states which had slavery in 1860. It also meets the requirement of being south of the Mason-Dixon. The fact is that the history of the state was different from the others. It was closely connected to Pennsylvania and its Quakers, and so that suggests an antislavery outlook. Though introduced earlier, the institution did not take serious root until Dutch involvement as in New York. (Remember, the first slave ship in Virginia was a Dutch ship.) With the Enlightenment and Quaker influences, Delaware discussed the end of slavery during the early days of the United States and the Constitutional Convention. This was common in other states too, including Virginia. One of the biggest barriers in Delaware, as in the country as a whole, was American racism. Even many who did not approve of slavery did not want free blacks living among them.

Nonetheless, the freeing of slaves continued so that by 1810, 78 percent of the blacks in that state were free. After Nat Turner's Rebellion in 1831, they began to pass "black codes" to control the inferior population. Soon Delaware was "the least hospitable place in the Union for freedmen prior to the Civil War."[37] This unique background accounts for the inconsistency of the state's voting on slavery issues. They opposed the extension of slavery during the days of the Missouri Compromise and passed resolutions against the annexation of Texas and the spread of slavery into the territories after the Mexican War. In 1860, they voted for Breckinridge thus fitting the *Librev* definition of those places that would have supported Southern secession. Despite attempts by Lincoln to talk them into abolishing the institution during the war, not only did they fail to do so, but they also did not ratify the Thirteenth Amendment until 1901. It

---

36. Foner, 41.

37. William H. Williams, *Slavery and Freedom in Delaware, 1639–1865* (Wilmington, DE: Scholarly Resources, 1996), 171.

is interesting that Lincoln offered the state compensation at the average rate of about $500 per slave if they voted for abolition. No doubt the confusion in trying to explain Delaware is due to its diversity. Some talked of states' rights, some may simply have reacted to Lincoln and his telling people how to live their lives, and some, if not most, had the racist fears of an uncontrollable free black population which was a dominant feeling in America, North and South. Delaware, in any event, had to await Maryland's decision, as its secession was impossible without Maryland's secession because of its geographic location.

MISSOURI AND KENTUCKY

These two states share the fact that not only did they have factions which supported the Union and the Confederacy, but each also had factions which claimed to be the real government of the state. Most *Librev* historians seem to ignore the Confederate states of Kentucky and Missouri. Not only did both states have factions that claimed they were Confederate, but both also provided armed regiments to each side. The inconsistency of the Yankee and *Librev* perspective is evident when looking at these two states. How can states need reconstructing if they never left the Union? The *Librevs* need Foner's thesis that the abolition of slavery constitutes Reconstruction to explain the need for Reconstruction of states which they say never left the Union.

Kentucky had the largest number of slave-owning families among the "border states," and at the end of the war still had 65,000 slaves. It is commonly believed that Kentucky chose to stay with the Union because, like many others in the South, they saw greater opportunity to keep their slaves by doing so. If this is true, then it worked, they still had their slaves at the end of the war. They denounced the Emancipation Proclamation as unconstitutional, but of course, it did not apply to them anyway. The slaves in that state were freed by the Thirteenth Amendment. This is what it would have taken to end slavery, since the Constitution did not authorize the president to emancipate slaves. The Thirteenth Amendment was not ratified until after the war's end.

The pro-Confederate faction of Missouri fled to the Southwest corner of the state, and the Union's attempts to bring them under their control led to the first major battles in the far west. The region near the borders of Missouri, Kansas, Indian Territory, and Arkansas experienced long and painful years of guerilla war and bushwhacking. Both sides committed great atrocities, each claiming revenge as justification for their actions. Foner used the term "internal reconstruction" to describe those states like Missouri, which were not reconstructed because of conquest but rather to free the slaves. In 1864, Union Missouri required loyalty oaths for voters which helped to get Radical Thomas C. Fletcher elected governor and to call a convention to devise a plan of emancipation. They gathered in January 1865. They passed the new constitution utilizing the Republican strategy of recruiting black voters and barring "rebels" from voting and holding office. They also barred the "disloyal" from acting as teachers, lawyers, and ministers. They failed to pass proposals to confiscate the lands of the planters to compensate loyalists for their wartime losses.

WEST VIRGINIA

The best example of Yankee logic is the creation of the state of West Virginia. The unionists usually claimed that secession was unconstitutional, yet they accepted the secession of numerous counties from Virginia to form an unconstitutional state. Neither the Yankees of yore nor the *Librevs* of today seem worried about Section 3 of Article IV of the constitution: "nor any state formed by the Junction of two or more States, or parts of States, without the Consent of the Legislatures of the States concerned as well as the Congress." The decision for these counties to form their own state was made at the two conventions in Wheeling, not by general convention for the state of Virginia. Those who took this action claimed that Virginia was treasonous to secede from the United States; however, the official position of the United States was that it was not constitutional for them to secede. If the Union is denying the right of states to secede then there should only be one state legislature. I see no provision in the Constitution for any state whose legislature claimed to have seceded while the federal government says that such claims are not legal. West Virginia was accepted into the Union in 1863 as the last slave state, though eighteen months later they abolished slavery.

LOUISIANA

The situation in Louisiana is the best example of how the *Librevs* stretch their imaginations so that they can defend their view of Lincoln as a noble man who defended the poor slaves rather than as a typical sly politician who would do almost anything to accomplish his objectives. Louisiana was a Confederate state in which he attempted pre-Appomattox reconstruction. New Orleans especially was unique, but I do not see this had as much to do with the situation as the political motivation.

Foner pointed out that the city of New Orleans had strong business connections with the North and Europe; however, so did the other economic centers of the South. I will discuss this under a separate topic in the next chapter. Foner mentioned the large free black population of the Crescent City but ignored the fact that they formed the first black regiment, and this regiment was committed to the Confederacy. Lincoln endorsed a program for the Free State Association and urged General Nathaniel P. Banks to organize a constitutional convention that would abolish slavery in Louisiana. By January of 1864, Lincoln endorsed the enrollment of freeborn blacks as voters in Louisiana.

The *Librev* Lincolnists embrace the notion that the 10 percent reconstruction plan of Lincoln's is an example of what a caring empathetic man he was. They say that he just wanted to make it easier for the Southerners to rejoin the Union. Occam's Razor and the nature of politicians support my interpretation of the situation in Louisiana. As November, 1864 approached, Lincoln became more and more convinced that he could lose the upcoming election. The fact is that 45 percent of the Northern population voted against him. I think most of the *Librevs* would agree that if Atlanta had not fallen in the summer of 1864, that most likely would have been the case. Lincoln needed to get electoral votes. The Republicans in Congress would have interest in seeing their party retain power, but they did not have to worry about electoral votes. Lincoln did need the votes. I believe this is why he got Nevada admitted to the Union in 1864 and why he pushed to get Louisiana readmitted. I understand that I cannot prove that this is the case, but it does seem to make more sense than the typical *Librev* interpretations. They claim that Lincoln was simply kind-hearted. Ninety percent of the people in Louisiana could be wearing grey uniforms and shooting at Union soldiers, but he wanted to readmit the state? That sounds more like the desperate act of a politician than someone who was simply a kind man.

LINCOLN'S RECONSTRUCTION

So, the *Librev* Lincoln worshipers see the former president as a kind and gentle man who wanted to make it easy for Southerners to rejoin the Union. I see him as a typical politician who had plans on how to win the election of 1864. Neither one of us can prove our beliefs. He did seem to have some concern about the slaves; however, he was a believer in the colonization effort. He was a disciplinarian at times, but at other times, he was merciful. Motivation is a hard thing to prove, but the fact remains that by the time of the Lincoln presidency, democracy had become prevalent enough that the greatest skill that a politician needed to be successful was the ability to get votes.

Congress did not agree with presidential Reconstruction. The Republican congressmen did not have the same interest. The survival and future of their party was of primary importance. During his years in the White House Lincoln had usurped many of the powers that belonged to the legislative branch of government. No doubt, some allowed this as long as the outcome of the war was unclear. As it drew to a close and victory became certain, Republican congressmen were in a better position to defend their self-interest. Lincoln never got a chance to implement his plan at war's end since he was killed shortly after Appomattox.

In July of 1864, Congress challenged the president with the Wade–Davis Bill. They were more interested in creating state governments that would truly be part of the Union. They required that at least half of the voters take a loyalty oath. This does seem much more logical than Lincoln's plan. How could anyone consider a former "rebel" state as reconstructed if up to 90 percent of the men are still shooting at Union soldiers? They provided for some protection of black Southerners, but at first they did not give them the vote. They needed the blacks to build their Party, so they were only interested in getting the Southern blacks to vote, not all black Americans. They recognized the inconsistency of not allowing Northern blacks to vote too. I submit this as evidence of what I have stated many times, the South was racist but so was the North. They knew that many of their white voters did not want Northern blacks to vote. One of the questions *Librevs* debate is why did the North abandon the Freedmen in 1877? My answer is that by 1877 they realized that they did not need this strategy for the postwar Republican Party to thrive. They were losing some Northern voters who were racist, so this is why they "abandoned" the black Republicans of the South.

JOHNSON'S RECONSTRUCTION

Andrew Johnson had interests different from either Lincoln or the Republican Congress. He was among those of the South who opposed secession, so much so that he remained in the Union. He was still a Southerner, and as such, he did not hate Southerners. He felt empathy for the majority of the Southern population. His problem was with those of the planter class and so he wanted to restrict them from regaining control. He was still a racist, as most Americans were, and as such he did not favor the plans that involved giving the freedmen the vote. His policies and actions pleased the defeated Southerners as much as possible under the circumstances. He proved to be contrary to the ambitions of the Republican Congress, especially the radical portions.

THE UPPITY SOUTH

In the spirit of Johnson's plans, Southerners began to feel that they could come back into the United States and carry on business as usual. Their lives had been shattered by the tragedy of war—homes burned; livestock gone; many of the men dead or crippled; railroads destroyed ; and a heavily disrupted market economy. They suffered the humiliation of defeat at the hands of the Union army, but their sense of self-esteem had not been totally subdued.. They may have lost, but they did not think they had been wrong. As they rebuilt their land, they would not have slavery, which for many was just as well. Most of them never owned a slave before the war, and many of those who did regretted the system they had inherited from their ancestors.

The majority of the South had fought for the Confederate cause, regardless of whether or not they quit fighting before Robert E. Lee did. The *Librevs* love to point to the high desertion rate as proof that most did not really support the new nation in the first place. I think this is utter nonsense. The degree of loyalty to the Southern cause varied considerably; however, I see the main reason for the desertion to be the results of giving priority to family. As their land was invaded and occupied by foreigners, more and more men felt a need to be home rather than to remain in the army. I could produce numerous letters to support this interpretation as others could produce their anecdotal evidence to support the contrary. Neither side could "prove" their case. The fact is that the Confederate army fought long and hard and did a pretty good job for people who were outnumbered two to one. They did not act like a people who did not really believe in what they were fighting for. Why would the North have such a problem with uppity Southerners if they did not really believe in their cause in the first place? The *Librev* response would be that this is why they created the "Lost Cause myth." Bull!

I am not sure if they believe the lower-class and middle-class Southerners to be smart or dumb. On one hand, they want us to believe that they were smart and never fell under the spell of the planters, and thus did not really support the Confederacy. On the other hand, they paint these people as mindless dupes who are manipulated into believing the "Lost Cause myth." Which is it?

The first reports by Union officers who occupied the South indicate that the people did not act like a people who had done wrong, and most did not seem all that eager to embrace the Union flag nor Reconstruction laws. Mississippi and Texas refused to ratify the Thirteenth Amendment. Mississippi and South Carolina would not repudiate state debts. Several of the state constitutional conventions would not fly the Union flag. The newly elected Southern congressmen included seven Confederate cabinet officers, nine ex-Confederate congressmen, four generals, four colonels, and from Georgia, the former vice president Alexander Stephens. It would seem that this "Lost Cause myth" appeared immediately at war's end.

Overall, they had met Johnson's demands for reconstruction. Most accepted emancipation, granted some civil rights to the freedmen, swore allegiance to the Union, and formed new state governments. The Radical Republicans led the crusade that would attempt to remove Johnson from office with the first impeachment of a president. They proceeded to subjugate the South to their rule. The *Librevs* believe that they have disproven the Dunning view of Reconstruction by writing about the New England schoolmarms who worked in the freedmen schools and the nobility, in their warped minds, of such Radical Republican leaders as Thaddeus Stevens. This is what Stevens had to say about Reconstruction: "Hang the leaders—crush the South—arm the Negroes— confiscate the land . . . Our generals have a sword in one hand and shackles in the other . . . The South must be punished under the rules of war, its land confiscated . . . These offending States were out of the Union and in the role of belligerent nation to be dealt with by the laws of war and conquest."[38] This

---

38 Kennedy, 105.

attitude would explain the previous quote from Lee in which he said he would have preferred to die at Appomattox. I am not a smart Harvard graduate, but it seems to me that the Reconstruction Yankee government was not so noble.

CONGRESSIONAL RECONSTRUCTION

How could we possibly prove the motivations behind Congressional Reconstruction? On one hand, the *Librevs* are right about some of the issues. There were some who moved South and honestly wanted to help the freedmen. Some Southerners worked to restrict the social equality of black Southerners. Not all the corruption and economic problems of the postwar South were due to carpetbaggers. On the other hand, the Dunning-type interpretations are partially true. Many men did move into the region from the North like the barbarians into Rome. They were conquerors who saw the opportunity to loot and pillage. Some did want revenge and foamed with a genuine hatred of not only slavery but also the Southern people, white and black, and just about every aspect of their culture.

Congress had a need to not only establish domination over the South but also to recoup some of the power they had lost to the executive branch of the government. In December of 1865, when Congress reconvened, they refused to seat the newly elected Southerners in the House or the Senate. In the election of 1866, the Republicans gained a three to one majority in Congress. With Johnson subdued by impeachment, Congress had no trouble gaining control. In 1868 they got Grant elected to the presidency, and under him, things pretty much proceeded as Congress wanted.

They began to pass legislation intended to restrict the Southern ruling class and to empower the freedmen. The Thirteenth Amendment solved the slavery question once and for all. They continued the Freedman's Bureau, which was established to aid the former slaves. After the impeachment of Johnson, they were able to pass their laws restricting the black codes, at least in the South. Northern black codes were of no concern to them. Nonetheless, many of the Republicans and most of the Northern Democrats did not endorse a philosophy of racial equality. If they believed such things, we would have never had a need for a revolutionary civil rights movement in the 1950s and 1960s, which involved the North as well as the South. The reality is that most Americans were racist up to the end of World War II and even beyond.

The *Librevs* like to think that they have disproven the Dunning view of military occupation, but the Republican Congress did pass the Fourteenth Amendment. The *Librevs* like to praise this amendment as the grounds for civil rights cases in this country until the civil rights movement. They seem to think this was the main reason for the amendment. It does offer some rights for the black people; however, I have no doubt that the intent was to promote the growth of the Republican Party more than to help blacks.

Clearly it enforced the voting rights of the freedmen. Entire books have been written about the 14th Amendment, so it is clearly controversial. I cannot prove that the Amendment was not altruistically motivated, but if one accepts my interpretation of it being politically motivated, then it would be more consistent with Section 3 of the Amendment. This forbid those from taking office who had "engaged in insurrection or rebellion" against the United States government. It would also be consistent with Section 4, which repudiated Confederate debt. Section 5 guaranteed that "Congress shall have the power to enforce, by appropriate legislation, the provisions of this article." I won't even go into the legalities of the passage and ratification of this amendment. The New Jersey legislature said, "the origin and objects of said proposed amendments were unseemly and unjust . . . "[39]

NEW ORLEANS, MEMPHIS, AND THE QUESTION OF RACE

The riots in Memphis are examples of how white Southerners were not about to recognize the equality of black Southerners; however, the riots can also be explained by Party politics. Southern whites had to give up their slaves, but they were not all were ready to accept them as equals. Northerners were not prepared to accept racial political equality, but it was a more important issue in the South because the South had many more blacks. This means that they had more reason to be aggressive in maintaining the traditional racial domination. The situation in Memphis was more the product of the frustration which accompanied the surrender, whereas the New Orleans case was more political.

The riots in Memphis began in the spring of 1866 and appear to have been aimed at the unionists as well as the freedmen. Following the collision of two carriages, one driven by a white man and the other by a black man, rioting broke out involving blacks, former Confederates, and Irish immigrants. Such violence only fueled Northern Republican anger and not only their desires for revenge but also fears that the Democrats would regain control in the South. If reunited, the Democrat Party would dominate in the United States government as it would have in 1860 had it not divided into Northern and Southern factions.

The New Orleans situation made it clear that the Democrats intended to control the South and that the political struggle would center on the prospect of the new black voters. The resulting violence produced thirty-eight fatalities which included thirty-four blacks, three white Republicans, and one white Democrat. The Louisiana Democrat Party had declared the government as one of white people, "made and to be perpetuated for the exclusive benefit of the white race. . . ," and that there would not be "any equality between the white and other races." Similar situations occurred in Chattanooga, Louisville, and Vicksburg. This is the kind of fuel the liberals love to use to prove the offensive

---

39. Kennedy, 192.

nature of Confederate symbols. The North responded with the passage of the Fourteenth Amendment and subsequent legislation to protect black voters; however, I do not see that they did so out of any sense of racial justice rather than the utilization of the freedmen as political pawns.

As mentioned above, the Librevs struggle with weak explanations for why the noble Republicans deserted the cause of racial equality in 1877, but I do not have the same problem with my interpretation of the events. The way I see it, by 1877, the Republicans concluded that they did not need to depend on black Republicans for survival. They could surrender the South to the Democrats. They began to realize that with the enlistment of blacks in their party that they gave fuel for the racist Northern Democrats, who frequently campaigned against what many considered a repulsive platform of racial equality. There were some Republicans who genuinely believed in racial equality, and worked to achieve that goal. There were others who were racist and had joined the party because they did not approve of the expansion of slavery into the territories. These were the ones who would be willing to abandon the Republican Party in favor of the Democratic Party which did not hesitate to speak about their racist platform.

The Radical Republican Senator Charles Sumner proposed legislation to prohibit racial segregation in public schools, in selection of juries, on all forms of public transportation, and in public accommodations. The Southern Republicans endorsed it, but Congress had reservations as to the constitutionality of it and feared the reaction of their voters. After Sumner's death in 1874, they did push through the Civil Rights Act in 1875, but the Supreme Court threw it out in 1883. I repeat once more, it was not just Southerners who were racist but the majority of Americans. The way I see it, the Republicans gave up on the Southern blacks because they no longer needed them and were losing support among the white Northern voters.

RECONSTRUCTION IN INDIAN TERRITORY

Having roots in Indian Territory, I have always resented the way historians have ignored their sufferings during Reconstruction. I also see it as a good example of how the Republican policies were designed to serve their dual purposes of revenge and the promotion of their political agenda. In September of 1865, Washington officials summoned the tribes to a conference in Fort Smith. They were told that they had made unprovoked war on the United States and that they had forfeited all of their annuities and lands. Then they were informed that the president would forgive them "of their great crime." The Indians pointed out that some of their people supported the Union and that the United States had abandoned their nations to the Confederacy.

The final treaty had some points which support the noble purposes claimed by the Librevs. The Indians agreed to abolish slavery and give their freed slaves citizenship and property rights. Other changes indicate that the government was not so altruistic. They had to accept one north–south and one east–west railroad through their lands. They did not have to submit to a territorial government, but they did consent to an intertribal council.

One reason I resent the ignoring of Indian Territory in Reconstruction is that they, in fact, were the only Southern state or territory which lost land because of the war; that is unless one wants to consider the creation of a new state out of Virginia. It is clear that the reason for taking away the western lands was to provide a place to which they could remove the plains' Indians as the United States government opened the western lands for white settlement. The great liberating United States apparently had no problem with forcing the Indians into submission to the white men. The Seminoles had to sell their old lands to the U.S. government for fifteen cents an acre and then pay that same government fifty cents an acre for land which they had purchased from the Creeks for thirty cents an acre. The facts seem to indicate that the main purpose of the new treaties was to allow for the advancement of the white Americans, more specifically the Northern white Republicans.

Ku Klux Klan

The existence of the Klan is probably the greatest source for the liberal revulsion of all things Confederate, if not Southern, and one of the first images they conjure related to the Confederate battle flag. I certainly make no attempt to justify the freaks who call themselves the Klan today, and for that matter, I do not take any pride in the racist attitude which was part of what they stood for in the beginning. The main thing that we need to understand about the original Klan is that the racism was only part of what they did. They were more comparable to terrorist groups we see in Iraq today rather than the racist odd balls in sheets who appear on the Jerry Springer show. Terrorist groups are not something we want to admire, but they come about as a way to resist a more powerful overlord. The primary objective of the KKK was to resist occupation of the South by United States military. Books have been written about the Klan, so I will make no attempt at an in-depth analysis. My view of this original Klan is in agreement with Albion Tourgee who said that the Invisible Empire was "fundamentally a political organization aimed at frustrating the Negro voter and blocking the federal government in its efforts to transform the South."[40] These are the words of one of the most famous Reconstruction Republicans. One who was there. I know that there are those who would disagree with this interpretation, but for the sake of brevity this makes sense to me.

---

40. Tourgee, xiii.

The Southerners were racist. Many of the activities that involved the Klan or similar groups involved attempts to force the blacks into a subservient role as well as the political motives, but even some of those in the North understood why this happened and the role that the conqueror played:

> After having forced a proud people to yield what they had for more than two centuries considered a right, - the right to hold the African race in bondage, - they proceeded to outrage a feeling as deep and fervent as the zeal of Islam or the exclusiveness of the Hindoo caste, by giving the ignorant, the unskilled, and dependent race - a race which could not have lived a week without the support or charity of the dominant one - equality of political right! Not content with this, they went farther, and by erecting the rebellious territory into self-regulating and sovereign States, they abandoned these parties like cocks in a pit to fight out the question of predominance without the possibility of national interference. They said to the colored man . . . "Root, hog, or die!"[41]

The resulting violence against black Southerners was partially due to the whites' desire to maintain dominance over them but was primarily a political conflict because the Republican used the blacks as pawns. I am not trying to justify what the whites did to the blacks, and this is not the part of our Southern heritage I am interested in preserving. I know that based on the standards of today much of this sounds disgusting. We must avoid presentism. We must be able to avoid judging those of the past and focus on understanding them. My discussion here is simply to point out why it happened. Violent change, by definition, produces violence. Perhaps if the change had not come so rapidly or been forced on them by outsiders, the results would have been better for the blacks too. It is one of those things we will never know for sure.

THE REDEEMERS

"Redeemers" is the name given to those who regained control of the South for Southerners. They are considered to have accomplished this with the Compromise of 1877. Although I attempt to include Southern blacks in my study of the South, in this particular subject I am talking about white Southerners only. Redeemers were white Southerners who gained control of their respective states for white Southerners. In doing so, they established the South as a solid

---

41. *National Anti-Slavery Standard*, October 19, 1867.

Democratic region which would remain as such until late in the twentieth century. Those black Southerners who could still vote remained predominantly Republican.

Even the *Librevs* have difficulty defining the Redeemers. Most of them were former planters. Some were supporters of the New South, others were not. There are those who have tried to define them as defenders of the feudal South and thus those who rejected modernization, but this is not true. They did hope to preserve as much of the Old South as possible, but they accepted the reality of military defeat and knew that talk of secession was dead. They were the perpetrators of the Lost Cause, though I firmly disagree with the *Librev*'s declaration that this was a myth.

Though I reject the notion that Southern identity evolved with the "Lost Cause myth," I do realize that Reconstruction Southerners begin to refer to the war as a Lost Cause. Whereas *Librevs* insist on calling it a myth, I see it as a refusal to admit that our people did anything wrong. Southerners simply believed they were trying to save the republic of the Founders. This is the same reason I call myself "unreconstructed." First, the Confederacy was founded on a correct constitutional principle. Second, the South lost because they were outnumbered. It was not due to lackluster support of the poor, but rather they were overwhelmed by superior strength with men and materials. Third, though I do not see the hand of God in the outcome, I do believe that the Southern people were and still are religious. The South is more of a Christian society. I am not saying that there are not religious people in the North. The North, on the other hand, is more into money-making. This is not to say there are not those in the South who seek the rewards of capitalism. I do believe that more Southerners are fundamentalist Christians and that they are the same ones who went political by supporting the Republicans in 2000 and 2004. I doubt there are many *Librevs* who would deny that the South is the Bible belt. I also believe the stereotype that Northerners are more money grubbing. They would probably not acknowledge this as easily, but I would not be surprised if many agreed with my claim.

The unique situation in Virginia offers a glimpse into the less-talked-about South, the division between the rich and the poor, or what some would call the planters and the rednecks. I am referring again to the application of self-interest across class lines. Virginia did have some unity, which, combined with the fact that they had a smaller black population than many of the conquered states, enabled them to resist occupation by Radical Republicans. Thus, they did not have the same need for Redemption and thus no need for Redeemers. After gaining enough solidarity to block Radical takeover, they ended up splitting over the issue of state debt. The more conservative wanted to pay all debt despite the extreme burden on the state treasury. It has not been proven, but it seems that self-interest may have been as much a part of their desire to pay the bonds rather than simply the matter of doing the most honorable thing. The Readjusters, under the leadership of William Mahone, wanted to reduce the interest and

OLD TIMES THERE SHOULD NOT BE FORGOTTEN

the payment. Mahone did win a lot of support from the working people. When the dust settled, Virginia came out looking similar to the other Southern states, even though they did not have the same need to oust Republicans. In the end Virginia too was a state where the whites were Democrats and dominated over the blacks who had little political power.

THE COMPROMISE OF 1877

With the Compromise of 1877 the official occupation of the South was ended. This is considered to be the end of Reconstruction. Southerners surrendered control of the federal government to the Yankees, but under the leadership of the Redeemers, they regained control of the local communities and states. The abbreviated story is that following the election of 1876, the Republicans rejected the Democrat victory of Samuel Tilden. Though Tilden clearly defeated Rutherford B. Hayes, they insisted that the elections in Louisiana, South Carolina, and Florida were not fair because of terrorist-type actions that kept black Republicans from the polls. After a long drawn-out contest, Hayes's representatives engaged in negotiations with the Southern Democrats and struck a bargain in which the Yankees got their president, and the South got what they wanted. First, federal troops would be removed from the South. Second, the Republicans would no longer prop up their governments in South Carolina and Louisiana. Third, Hayes agreed to appoint a Southerner to the cabinet and give some patronage to moderate Southern Democrats. Fourth, Hayes claimed to support the idea of federal funds for more internal improvements in the South, mainly railroads.

The *Librevs* have proclaimed that the North won the war, but the South won Reconstruction. I really have no problem with this claim. The basic idea is that before the war, the Southern economy and politics were controlled by the planters. They returned to power after Reconstruction despite being briefly deposed by the Fourteenth Amendment and other such Republican legislation. Slavery was dead, but the planters still owned their plantations, and by 1877, most of the blacks were back in the fields picking cotton. In a way, the planters profited from the change to sharecropping; they now added poor whites as a source for cheap labor. They may have taken a hit on the balance sheet with the loss of "personal property," the category in which the slaves fell in on the census records, but soon after the violence of Reconstruction had settled, the income statements looked the same or, for some, even better.

Socially, the foundations for the new American society and the Dunning School had been laid with the Compromise of 1877. The *Librevs* like to focus on black subservience in the South and their so-called "Lost Cause myth," but the reality is that it established apartheid America, which included the North and the South. I have a belief that one of the main reasons that the Northern population found the terms of the Compromise acceptable is that the majority of them disapproved of the notion of racial equality. I can accept that a few of the carpetbaggers believed in the racial equality which they tried to establish in the South, but I also believe that most simply saw it as a strategy to increase the strength of their party. The fact is that the North failed to achieve racial equality too. The *Librevs* boast of the achievements of Massachusetts; however, I see that as due to the fact that very few blacks lived in that state.

The assumption I make in my claim is that one of the main reasons for hatred is fear. This is true for race hatred also. Whether it be economic competition or feelings that the presence of foreign elements will weaken the social fabric, it is fear. Many people fear the presence of strangers, especially when they appear in large numbers. Blacks were rare in Massachusetts, whereas they were a majority in many parts of the South. Therefore Southerners viewed blacks as more of a threat than the people of Massachusetts did. A lot of the hatred of immigrants came from the North, starting with the Know Nothing Party. In the North the immigrants were more numerous and thus generated the same fears Southern whites felt toward blacks.

The Compromise of 1877 did bring about a social and economic system that would leave black Southerners, as well as all black Americans, as second-class citizens. Most Americans believed in the intellectual and moral superiority of white people and, in fact, of the Aryan race. The American belief system was not a whole lot different from Germany where the Nazis rose to power with their theories of Aryan superiority. There is nothing Southern or American about this belief; it seems to have been the dominant philosophy among most people of Northern European background. French and British history is full of examples of this philosophy. It is not even something limited to Europeans. Throughout world history those living in powerful empires have viewed themselves superior to outsiders. I can see no reason why Confederate or Southern symbols should be singled out as emblems of racism.

BLACK SOUTHERNERS

We need to be careful in defending our Southern heritage to not fall back on the defense that our ancestors used. When the *Librevs* complain about the Dunning School, they are thinking in terms of the old belief that the "darkies" were happy with the way things were. Some do not see slavery as whips and chains but rather as a time when the happy-go-lucky "darkies" would gather and sing songs and dance when not busy in the cotton fields. This thinking was probably a carryover of the old belief system that Africans needed to go through slavery to achieve the intellectual growth that would allow them to adapt to the superior European civilization. No one in the old days thought in terms of civilizations as simply being different. The Europeans were the ones conquering the world; it is natural that most of them felt that they were superior over those they dominated. Again, this was nothing uniquely Southern. The fact is, as stated above, black Southerners would be second-class citizens. Still, they did make some gains which have been acknowledged by the *Librevs*.

OLD TIMES THERE SHOULD NOT BE FORGOTTEN

The negatives were plenty and obvious. The majority of black Southerners did not have jobs as good as whites, and even if they did the same work, they rarely received equivalent pay. As a result, they did not have as much money and all that money buys in a capitalist society: food, housing, clothes, entertainment, and political clout. After the Compromise of 1877, their political power began to diminish so that by the next century most would not even be able to vote, much less hold public office. More blacks would be lynched by vigilantes; imprisoned for longer terms; and less likely to receive justice in the courts. Black women would be less safe from sexual harassment, and black men would be more likely to face complications when simply trying to defend themselves and their families against aggressive white citizens. Life for black Southerners was not as good as it was for those with white skin. It would be nonsense to dispute that.

Nonetheless, there were some improvements for black people. They were not slaves. This meant that they no longer feared the unexpected breakup of family units that sometimes came with the selling of slaves. Violence, rape, and other such aggressive behavior would be less likely to happen since the perpetrators would face the possibility of being arrested, even though they would probably not receive the same kind of protection that whites would. They did have the sense of working for themselves, even if someone else actually owned the land. They would have more freedom to live and socialize in black communities and worship in their own black churches.

Though we should be careful about describing the life of black Southerners as contented, either under slavery or shortly after, I do think that there existed a relationship between black and white Southerners. Black Southerners are different in many ways, but there are many characteristics which black and white Southerners share. As stated earlier, most blacks still identify with being Southerners. I repeat the words of Ann Moody, "I got a feeling that there existed some kind of sympathetic relationship between the older Negroes and whites that the younger people didn't quite get or understand."[42]

CONCLUSIONS

At this point, I think the situation of Reconstruction can best be summed up by one of those who took part in the attempt to capture Southern hearts and minds as well as their country and homes. This is from a man who was not the product of the so called "Lost Cause myth." The following was stated by Tourgee, one of the most famous carpetbaggers. He is one who was there, and one who admitted going South with an attitude of superiority. It sounds to me like he might agree with my interpretation of Southern identity and disagree with the Librev notion that it came about as some sort of "Lost Cause myth." It is also clear that he would accept my claim that Northerners have thought of

---

42. Anne Moody, *Coming of Age in Mississippi* (New York: Dell, 1968), 109.

themselves as superiors to Southerners. I believe this is an attitude which is still with us today and accounts for the attitude toward our heritage which so many possess.

> Undoubtedly. The North and the South are simply convenient names for two distinct, hostile, and irreconcilable ideas, - two civilizations they are sometimes called, especially at the South. At the North there is somewhat more of intellectual arrogance; and we are apt to speak of the one as civilization, and of the other as species of barbarism. These two must always be in conflict until the one prevails, and the other falls. To uproot the one, and plant the other in its stead, is not the work of a moment or a day. That was our mistake. We tried to superimpose the civilization, the idea of the North, upon the South at a moment's warning. We presumed, that, by the suppression of rebellion, the Southern white man had become identical with the Caucasian of the North in thought and sentiment; and that the slave, by emancipation, had become a saint and a Solomon at once. So we tried to build up communities there which should be identical in thought, sentiment, growth, and development, with those of the North. It was A Fool's Errand.[43]

---

43. Tourgee, 381.

VII: THE NEW SOUTH, REDNECKS, AND JIM CROW, 1877–1920

A FTER WINNING RECONSTRUCTION, Southern patriotism began a period of decline. This is one of the main reasons we are losing our heritage. There are fewer Southerners willing to fight for it. There are a number of reasons for this decline of Southern patriotism. As each year passed, the number of veterans of the Yankee invasion, both military and civilian, declined while the population of those born after the war increased. The children and then grandchildren grew up hearing the tales of great battles and Yankee atrocities, but with each passing year, such tales slid into the realm of legends and history. During Reconstruction, the concerns of the Southern people were part of the political system and, in effect, was the ironing out of the final details of surrender. After the compromise, it is not that the people changed in their thinking about who was right and who was wrong, but new issues gained priority. They started down the path to becoming Americans again, and by the late twentieth century, not only were they once again American, but I believe that even most Liberals would agree that it became the most patriotic region in the United States.

There were three main changes that diverted the attention of our people during the period between 1877 and 1920. First, the middle classes and wealthy became absorbed with the notion of the "New South." The *Librevs* will be the first to point out the new mantra. The South lost the war because the North was more industrialized and had a more diverse economy. The South must follow in their footsteps. Second, the American dream of the family farm progressed down the same road to extinction that the Confederacy had gone down. We all know about the Industrial Revolution and the growth of big business in America, but we don't usually think of what this means to the small businessman. In addition, we rarely think about the small farmer as being one of these small businessmen. After the war, they had to compete with the freedmen and the planters. The economies of scale that gave the manufacture an advantage would also give agribusiness an advantage. Third, the rise of the new kind of imperialism which would send the United States Army across the seas would end up increasing American patriotism. At first, the average Southerner would display little interest in such things, but as time passed and the United States became involved in one war after another, Southerners would end up fighting the wars. That is at a greater rate than other regions. As a result more and more were coming home more American rather than Southern.

Two other negative developments came along during the period this chapter covers which would contribute to the decline of Southern patriotism. I emphasize the distinction between Southern patriotism and American patriotism. It is difficult to serve two masters. As Southerners became more American, they became less Southern. The first problem, and the one most relevant for those of us who take pride in the display of our Confederate heritage, is the rise of the Jim Crow South. Black Southerners may have been slaves before the war, but they were not segregated. How could they be? Black and white Southerners lived together and worked together. One was master and the other slave—an established order which the whites worked hard at maintaining. What most Americans do not realize is that the Jim Crow system which Martin Luther King fought against did not come into being until the late nineteenth century. This of course is what many claim to be the main reason to ban the Confederate flag. They say it represents the system of segregation and racism. That is what Jim Crow was all about.

The second negative thing to occur by the end of the nineteenth century is decay of the Southern economy and a resulting Southern Diaspora. Southern industry grew in both quantity and diversity, but apparently, the prosperity remained in the hands of the few while the working class and poor, both black and white, became more and more entrenched in Southern poverty. The *Librevs* have focused on the black exodus from the South, and in the true liberal fashion, have explained it as the product of black resistance to Jim Crow. Since Jim Crow originated in the North and was brought South by carpetbaggers, that makes no sense. I see it as primarily an economic problem which affected all the lower classes regardless of color. I open discussion of the Southern Diaspora in this chapter, but I will not go into detail until the next chapter. It began by 1920, but most of those who left did so later, and so I will cover this issue in greater detail in the next chapter.

THE ECONOMY AFTER THE WAR

When the war ended, the Southern land lay in ruin. Many of the men in their prime were dead or wounded. Even more lost their homes, farms, plantations, businesses, and had to face the humiliation of defeat. I certainly don't mean to defend the institution of slavery; however, abolition did mark the end of an economic system and thus it required major adjustments. The freedmen faced their own economic and legal hardships. Most felt giddy with freedom but sobered up to the reality that they now had to support themselves. They no longer feared being separated from their families, but they had the new worry of providing for them. The white Southerners were determined to keep them in the cotton fields and to keep them in a subservient social status. From chaos all Southerners, black and white as well as a mixture of Hispanic and Indian, needed to restore order. They all served a new master—the Union.

I have already pointed out the error of looking at the South as resistors to modernity. The business and economic leaders understood that they trailed the North in most respects, but they were on the road to modernization. They did remain entrenched in agriculture, but the production of cotton and other cash crops was their way of participating in the world-market economy. Their greatest sin had been the lack of diversity. The former Southern Whigs would lead the way in correcting that error with the battle cry of "the New South."

SOUTHERN POVERTY

The South had lagged behind the nation as a whole since 1840. After the war, they dropped to their lowest point with the average per capita income of only 51 percent of the national average. It would be the 1950s before the region as a whole would approach the level it had been before the war, but that would still be three quarters of the national level. The western part of the South actually exceeded the national average before the war. They too paid for the sin of joining the Confederacy though they still did better than the region as a whole. The fact is that poverty became part of being Southern and would lead to one of the greatest mass exoduses in world history where almost twenty-nine million would leave the South in search of better economic opportunity.[44]

The division between the planters and the poor had been there since the early days of the South, and it would only get worse during the century that followed the war. Before the unpleasantness, there were the planters who fancied themselves as American aristocracy. They had slaves to work their manors while they raced their horses, hunted, and danced the night away at their balls. After the war, the poorest of the whites would be reduced to the new social class of redneck. There were a few wealthy people who prospered while the majority went shoeless and lived on beans and cornbread. The planters not only had the blacks picking their cotton but now also had white sharecroppers. They could play the poor blacks and whites against each other while they achieved the economic diversity they sought for the new South.

THE NEW SOUTH

The merchants joined the planters in becoming the leaders of the New South. Planter or merchant, they were probably Whigs before the political polarization of the 1850s, which gave birth to the Republican Party and the divided Democrat

---

44. Richard A. Easterlin, "The Regional Income Trends, 1840–1950," in Seymour E. Harris, ed., *American Economic History* (New York" McGraw-Hill, 1961), 28.

Party. Many of the *Librevs* see this period as one where the merchants seized control of Southern communities. I am not convinced that this is the case. Before the war, the merchants and larger agribusiness planters helped each other in the popular American pastime of accumulating wealth. This is what I have been saying all along; the South did not resist modernization. They did not advance as rapidly as those in the North, and that is one of their big disadvantages when the war came, but they were still building railroads and had some big cities, such as New Orleans, Memphis, and Charleston. I believe that the most important aspect of the concept of the New South is the push for economic diversity. A number of new industries blossomed in the late nineteenth and early twentieth century.

SHARECROPPING

A few brief words are needed about sharecropping. The *Librevs* rightfully see one of the main reasons for the black codes which followed the war was a way to put the freedmen back in the cotton fields. I do not have a problem with this point of view. It is important for us to understand the basic idea if we are going to understand the turn of the century South. It is also an important reason for that mass exodus from the South through much of the twentieth century. Quite simply put, the small farmer worked the planters land for a portion of the crop. On the surface, it seemed like a reasonable capitalistic business arrangement. Unlike forced servitude, the worker benefited from increased efficiency and hard work. Apparently the system had some appeal to working people as many whites also became involved with the tenant system.

The *Librevs* accuse the planters of recreating the slavery system as the tenant became chained to the land by debt. The debt was usually to the local merchants where they purchased seed, tools, work boots, and other supplies on credit. Much of their share of the crops went to pay their tab to the local merchant. Many times the planters had connections to the merchants or may have even owned the mercantile themselves. The *Librevs* often look at the high-interest rates charged for the credit as an additional link in the chain of bondage, but there were rational reasons for this situation. First of all, interest rates do traditionally represent risk for the lender. Generally speaking, a tenant farmer will be a greater risk than a property owner. Second, the national financial policies dictated by the Yankees produced high-interest rates which the Southern merchant or planter had no control over.

BANKING AND FINANCE

There are a number of financial reasons that the South struggled for the next century after the war. First of all, most of the wealthy suffered great financial losses. The great loss for many would be their slaves, a major asset on the balance sheet. It was common for the value of their slaves to exceed that of their real estate. Much of their cash had been invested in Confederate notes and bonds, both of which were worthless. They suffered major losses to buildings, draft animals, stock animals, and equipment as a result of the ravages of total war; any cash they did have access to would be used for needed repairs. In addition, there were few banks in the South. Another problem was that the North won in the struggle for a tight monetary policy which worked to their advantage but was a problem for the Southerners.

The South trailed in banking prior to the national conflict, and it got worse after. In 1863, Congress passed a Banking Act that increased the reserves required to charter a bank. This made it more difficult for the New South to open new banks. By 1900, the former eleven Confederate states had only 252 of the 1,737 banks in the United States, with only $26 million of the $417.6 million. New York alone had 252 banks with $75.9 million. The banking regulations of the time did not allow for the easy transfer of funds from one region to another so that little could be done to meet the increased demand in the South for capital. The increase in demand with low supply resulted in high-interest rates. The North at no time showed any interest in policies to help the South, though the South continued to pay high taxes, as before the war, to benefit the North.

In addition, the United States had policies which created deflation. The Resumption Act of 1875 halted the green backers and silverites who wanted to increase the money supply. The deflation cut the cost of cotton but Republican protectionism increased the cost of manufactured goods. The Gold Standard Act of 1898 and low federal spending further aggravated the situation. By the 1890s, the leading demand for the Populist Party would be the increased demand for the minting of silver, which would increase the money supply and thus stimulate inflation. The small farmers of America, mostly in the West and the South, hoped to pay back their mortgages with cheaper inflated dollars.

RETURN TO COTTON ON A CONFEDERATE GRAVE

As soon as the veterans returned from the war, they planted cotton. The following statistics are from the *Encyclopedia of Southern Culture*. In 1850, the South produced 2,469,000 bales of cotton which increased to 5,385,000 by 1860. Production dropped in 1870, but at 3,011,000 bales, it still exceeded the 1850 levels. By 1880 they topped the 1860 production with 5,709,000 bales. Likewise they returned to other favorite crops in other parts of the South, such as tobacco in Kentucky and sugar in Louisiana. Nonetheless, the business leaders of the region developed other industries. Among the numerous journalists singing the praises of the New South, none had greater influence than Henry Grady, editor of the *Atlanta Constitution*. With the rise of the new South, they began to cut away at Southern patriotism. He said, "There was a South of slavery and secession—that South, thank God, is dead. There is a South of union and freedom—that South, thank God, is living, breathing, growing, every hour." Grady praised Abraham Lincoln whom he called "the first typical American" who had "within himself the strength and gentleness of this republic . . . the sum of Puritan and Cavalier." This attitude conflicted with the redeemers as far as generating Southern patriotism.

RAILROADS & OTHER INDUSTRIES

The existence of railroads in the South alone challenges the notion of resistance to modernization. The 9,000 miles of track which the region had in 1860 was not that deficient compared to 11,000 in the Northeast and 11,000 in the Middle West. Of course, Sherman and his friends greatly reduced the mileage in the1860s. By 1880, the region had more than doubled the prewar mileage with 19,430. They saw railroads a key to the New South. Every Southern state created their own railroad commission, and Southerners played a key role in the passage of the Interstate Commerce Act of 1887.

By 1900 lumbering was the largest industry in the region. Congress opened federally owned lands in the South without restriction, which gave an already growing industry a boost. Much of the land originally intended for former slaves was sold, almost 5.7 million acres by 1888. Northerners as well as English investors profited with help from the railroads, which built lines to haul the Southern pine. Poor whites and blacks found an alternative to working a tenant's share of cotton. Hardwoods also came in demand for furniture making. Rich men, mostly Northern, of all backgrounds got richer on the sweat of those who lived on beans and cornbread. The supply of cheap labor is what made the South attractive to some industrialists.

The South had no shortage of minerals. The proximity of coal and iron gave a boost to an Alabama city which would carry the same moniker as a steel-making center in England— Birmingham. Yankees and rich Southerners reaped the profits while the poor, black and white, risked their lives in the mines. The western regions of the South benefited from oil discoveries in Oklahoma, Texas, and Louisiana. The ranks of the wealthy picked up some new recruits from the lucky wildcatters who struck it rich, which even included a few of the Indians from eastern Oklahoma. Today some of the wealthiest families in the western part of the South made their fortunes in oil. They rarely came from aristocratic tidewater families but rather from those who happened to have been lucky enough to own a farm with oil under the fields.

Medicines and elixirs became popular, and to this day, fortunes ride on those remedies that became soft drinks. The most famous was the product of Asa Candler. The man purchased the rights to a headache remedy in Atlanta and turned it into Coca-Cola. By 1892, he sold 35,000 gallons of the carbonated drink compared to only 25 gallons in 1886. Coca-Cola utilized the power of advertising, which became their key to success.

In addition to the growing of tobacco, which has been in the South since the first colonies, there were developments in the manufacturing of cigarettes. By 1880, tobacco production approximated the 1860 level, nearly doubled it by 1900 and doubled it again by 1920 and continued to grow until 1980. During the war, soldiers were introduced to the tobacco grown in the Durham, North Carolina area. The former Union and Confederate troops loved it. Bull Durham led the way in production. To challenge the highly successful company, Washington Duke and his sons became the first company to use the Bonsack cigarette machine in 1881. Within two years Duke cigarette production increased by 600 percent. In the later part of the decade they boosted sales further with the use of advertising and gimmicks. In 1890 Duke and four other competitors formed the American Tobacco Company. They created another industry that made the capitalist wealthy and provided jobs for those less fortunate.

Before the war, most of the cotton went to mills in the North or in Europe. Between 1880 and 1905, the South increased the number of mills turning the Southern staple into cloth. There is an assortment of statistics which show the increased production. Spindles increased from 11,898 to 110,000 which helped to increase the production of raw cotton seven times between 1880 and 1900. The value of Southern cotton mills increased from $11.1 million to $124.6 million, and the number of workers went from 16,714 to 97,494. Compared to 22,423 workers in the steel industry, we can see the advantage textiles had was due to the much lower requirement for start-up capital. Like the other industries in the South, the wealthy benefitted from the lower cost of labor, both black and white, and thus widening the gap between rich and poor.

URBANIZATION, WORKING CLASS & SUCH

The increase in Southern manufacturing, whether it be in minerals, steel, tobacco, or textiles, had an effect on the region by increasing the number of working class and the growth of cities. Railroads probably did the most to increase the number of cities from 119 in 1880 to 320 in 1900. Steel helped Birmingham, oil helped Dallas and Tulsa, but even though many of the textiles mills had their own "mill towns," the increased agricultural production contributed to the development of urban centers. We are not talking about large cities, 80 percent of these towns had populations of less than 10,000. Nonetheless, this still means that more people in the South had moved off the land and into working-class jobs.

Librevs and the unreconstructed alike have a tendency to look at the South as being a land of planters, poor blacks, and farm families. This started before the war and continued to some extent until the last half of the twentieth century, but the New South increased those who found other lifestyles. Some of the needed cash for development came from Northern businessmen, but the majority of the new manufactures were Southerners. They profited most from the low cost of labor. Southern attitudes helped to limit the popularity of labor unions though there were some exceptions. Men like Huey Long in Louisiana preached "sharing the wealth," and in Oklahoma, the Socialist Party had more success than any other state in the Union. This is why Woody Guthrie and some of his fellow Okies were feared when they went to California during the days of growing anticommunism. Many of them were labor organizers.

Through the years there have been those who have proposed the notion that the wealthy encouraged racism as a way to keep the working class from uniting. Such theories have been used to explain the lack of appeal that socialism and communism had throughout the United States and not just the South. I can see why some have been drawn to this thesis; however, I am skeptical of the conspiratorial nature of the charges. I do believe that the ethnic and racial diversity of the laborers made it more difficult for the workers of the United States to unite. Whether it be the Italian immigrants in New York or the blacks in Alabama, the numerous ethnic communities would naturally look after their own interest and thus look at the others as competition. I am sure that there were times when management took advantage of these divisions, but racism was more the rule than the exception in those days. Americans of the North or the South were racist, just like the Aryans of Germany, France, and England; and thus, racial and ethnic disunion should be expected. It did not take a conspiracy to create it.

This is what I have been saying all along and will continue to say throughout this book; racism is not a Southern thing. The white workers may have realized that the blacks were working people like themselves and that their sweat was helping to make the capitalist wealthy, but they still believed that white people were superior. Likewise, the white owners and management may have realized the advantage they had in keeping the working people divided; however, they too believed in racial superiority. Those in the North had an even more complicated situation because of the larger and more diverse immigrant population. I have spoken about how the South was more diverse before the war, but after the war there was a big increase in the number of immigrants from eastern and southern Europe. Those of Aryan background also believed themselves to be superior to some other whites. They did not look at some of the other Europeans as white. The Italians, Greeks, and others from eastern and Southern Europe tended to be darker in complexion, and were Catholic, Jewish and Orthodox. The native white American population of Germanic Protestant extraction considered the darker-complexioned Europeans to be inferior. This is why Italians were called Guineas, a name that is derived from an African nation. To the Anglo-Americans, the Italians were no better than blacks.

FROM YEOMAN TO POPULIST

I cannot prove it, but I firmly believe the main explanation for the delayed economic development of the South during the century following the war had nothing to do with either the Southern resistance to modernization or the evil carpetbaggers. The *Librevs* like to blame racism, the Southern lack of respect for education, the twisted code of honor, disease, the long hot summers, and overall Southern backwardness for the extreme poverty which plagued the region. Many Southerners, especially the unreconstructed, like to blame Yankee imperialism. To them, it is the greed and corruption of Reconstruction which laid the foundation and the powerful Northern Republican businessmen who profited from the continued oppression. Perhaps all of these variables contributed; however, I believe that the key is the fact that not only did the region continue to be predominantly agricultural, but they also depended on the traditional American mechanism of agriculture, the family farm. Though many, if not most, of the crops grown were commodities, such as cotton, much of it was still produced on the small family farm. Agriculture was becoming agribusiness, but most farmers worked on family farms. The South retained the impression of being a land of small farmers since so many were sharecroppers. They did not own the land, but they worked it as a family unit, black and white alike.

The main reason for the success of the sharecropping system is that it allowed for more of the poor farmers, especially the freedmen, to assume the role of the traditional American farmer who continued to be the majority of the American population until the 1920s. They may not have owned the land, but like the majority of white men, they worked the land and reaped the profits of their labor. This may have been more theory than reality according to the *Librevs*. I do not consider these charges to be as important as the fact that it left agricultural production to families, and thus, the agricultural industry could not benefit from the lower cost associated with the returns to scale found in manufacturing during the Industrial Revolution.

Today the vast majority of agricultural production in America is agribusiness. They use machines much more than labor. Between 1865 and the late twentieth century, the small family farm advanced down the road toward extinction because it could not compete with agribusiness. The people continued to work on the land, but only because they did so often for little reward. Between 1865 and 1900, the pain of the small farmer was expressed with the development of the Populist movement. This happened in the West too, but dominated in the South.

My intent is not to give a detailed analysis of Populism but rather simply an outline. The small farmers of America blamed their problems on the railroads for their high rates, the bankers for their high interest, and the Republican capitalist for their adherence to the gold standard, which produced deflation. There is no doubt that these are the more direct and obvious causes for the decline of the family farm, but it was not the main cause. The more inclusive cause for the problems suffered by the American farmers is modernization. Economic survival under industrialization depended on cutting cost. This would allow the successful to bury the competitors who could not control cost. This included agricultural goods too. The cost of goods produced on the family farms were higher than those produced on the larger tracts of land owned by the agribusiness. This was just as true for those who operated as sharecroppers as those who owned the land they worked.

The first attempt by the farmers to attack what they saw as the enemy was the Grange. This was more of a social club than a political movement. The Grange became replaced by the Alliance movement. When Kansas and both of the Dakotas joined the Southern Farmers Alliance, they formed the National Farmers Alliance. In 1890, they met in Ocala, Florida, and drafted the demands that identify for us what their main concerns were. Top of the list was the free minting of silver. This they hoped would increase the money supply, which would create inflation, which would benefit the small farmer who could get a rise in prices and allow them to pay mortgage debt with cheaper dollars. They also wanted to abolish national banks; surrender railroad lands not actually needed for the operation of their business; lower tariffs; and implement a subtreasury plan. Some of their goals were downright socialistic, such as graduated income tax and government control or even ownership of the public means of communication and transportation.

In the 1890s, they formed the Populist Party. The depression of 1893 no doubt contributed greatly to the demise of the political party which experienced rapid growth and some success before its equally rapid decline. Historians point out how many of the demands became implemented under the Progressives, which they usually dismiss to the lack of political sophistication of the Populists. I believe that the real significance of the failure of the Populist movement is that it could not do anything about the main reason for the problems in the first place. The family farm could not compete with agribusiness and the sharecropper who had maintained a delusion of independence became replaced by machines.

FROM POPULIST TO REDNECK

With the changes that came after the War of Southern Independence, the most significant has been the decline of the small Southern farm. Before 1860, farmers were not only the majority of the Southern population, but they were also still the majority of the American population. The American dream since the founding of the first colonies was for the average farmer to own his land. This is why most crossed the ocean, killed the Indians, and struggled against nature or any other perceived enemy. The *Librevs* love the book by Edmond S. Morgan, *American Slavery, American Freedom*, in which he put forth the notion that democracy grew in the South because of slavery. The black slaves occupied the lower rungs of the social ladder, which lifted even the poor whites to a level of equality that fostered the spirit of democracy, at least among whites. In other words, the white population who owned their own farm, no matter how modest, had feelings of equality to even the wealthy planters. The end of slavery, the decline of the family farm, and the industrialization that did occur in the South created a new Southern elite who began to look at the poor whites as "rednecks." The magic of being white in the South began to disappear, which may at least partly account for the rise of Jim Crow.

THE BIGGEST ENEMY OF OUR CONFEDERATE HERITAGE

The greatest problem we have defending our Southern heritage is due to the use of the symbols of the fallen country, mainly the Confederate battle flag, by racist. Images of Jim Crow and our Southern kin who waved the Southern banner in defense of segregation and the destruction of American apartheid are what give us the most grief. Most of America was segregated prior to World War II; however, in the South legislation made it official. In the case of Oklahoma, which became a state in 1907, it was even part of the state constitution. Most who want to extinguish the symbols of the Old South see them as representing "white only" signs, lynchings, and voting restrictions, etc. Blacks in the North suffered the same kind of discrimination, but it is easier to put the burden of American racism on the shoulders of the South. Since more blacks lived in the South, there were more laws limiting black freedom. It was the federal courts; however, which opened the door for the Jim Crow laws in the first place.

In 1883, shortly after the Compromise of 1877, the Supreme Court ruled the Civil Rights Act of 1875 unconstitutional. All the indications are that it was more than an abandonment of the freedmen when the North allowed the white Southerners to establish domination over black Southerners. I have no doubt that most of those to the North did not accept the liberal notion that the two races were equal. If the Republicans of Reconstruction succeeded in forcing equality on the people of the South then it would be logical to expect the same in the North. In the nineteenth century, few white people, especially Aryans, doubted the superiority of their race. When the Supreme Court upheld "separate but equal" with the Plessey v. Ferguson decision of 1896, it opened the floodgates of Jim Crow.

More important in politically castrating blacks was the virtual elimination of voting rights. During Reconstruction, not only did blacks vote but many were also elected to public office. There are those who argue that the real attacks came in the 1890s in an attempt to limit the Populist white voters as well. Most of the laws followed the example of the Mississippi Plan of 1890. This legal mechanism circumvented the Fourteenth and Fifteenth amendments. The new state constitution required voters to have resided in the state for at least two years and in their election districts for one, to have paid all their taxes for two years before registering, and to pay their two-dollar poll tax. In addition, they had to prove that they could comprehend any part of the constitution when it was read to them. The traditional accusation is that the examiner could control who passed and who failed. It has been claimed by some that this type of law had also been used to limit the power of the Populists.

It has not been firmly established what the role of lynching has been in the establishment of the Jim Crow South. The liberals of America have assumed that it served to establish control over the black population. Between 1882 and 1951, 4,900 people were lynched in the United States. More than 80 percent were black, and 80 percent of the cases took place in the South. The most gruesome involved torture or mutilation. Many began with accusations of relations between black men and white women, and a good many involved making certain that the blacks accepted their status as second-class citizens. Some were criminals who inspired the ire of the local population to the extent that they simply could not wait for a trial. On one hand, the evidence is that many such group crimes were racially motivated. On the other hand, this is an average of about seventy per year with less than sixty in the South, some of which were not racially motivated. I am not convinced that these numbers prove the importance of lynching in the Jim Crow era. I am sure that it had some impact, but I am not sure it is that much of a deviation from the American tradition of violence. New York City, for example, has at least that many murders in a year. Race riots occurred in many other parts of the country, with hundreds of blacks killed. This should always be considered when looking at this period. The violence against blacks was not limited to the South, and as we have seen, Jim Crow originated in the North. Therefore, there seems to be reason to single out the South for criticism when all sections of the country were guilty. These actions certainly do not compare to the violence against the Jews in Nazi Germany.

THE ATLANTA COMPROMISE

The Atlanta Compromise tells us a lot about the attitudes of blacks and whites during the founding of the Jim Crow South. Booker T. Washington made a speech at the Cotton States and International Exposition in Atlanta in which he advised his fellow blacks to work hard, educate themselves, and be patient in advancing in white America. The predominantly white crowd applauded him. Some blacks were glad to have one of their own praised by the whites, but others objected to the comments. W. E. B. DuBois began to challenge Washington for leadership of black rights. DuBois would later be involved in the founding of the NAACP. The first black to earn a PhD, he felt that the blacks should not have to wait any longer.

What I see from this incident and the events following is that white people had an attitude of racial superiority, and that blacks were still divided on the best way to improve their lives. On one hand, it reflects that most of those whites present did not hate black folks. On the other hand, they clearly did not see them as equals. They reflected the same attitude that had been used to justify slavery for generations; blacks were not equal, but with white guidance and time, they could be. Some blacks were pleased with the advances they had made. In 1895, there were many who remembered slavery. I suspect that there were those who accepted what they had always been told and believed themselves to be inferior to whites. When people are raised from infancy with the idea that they are inferior, I am sure that it is easy to accept that philosophy as fact. That is called self esteem. Others understood that the education that Washington provided for blacks was the best way to achieve equality with the dominant race. The reaction by DuBois tells us that some blacks already believed themselves to be equal. This, after all, was the claim of Thomas Jefferson when he said all men were created equal.

DuBois is admired by the *Librevs*, and in my opinion, he had a good grasp of the situation during the turn of the century. The following quote is revealing in its description of black/white relations and also distinguishes between the lower and upper classes of Southern white society. I wish that some of those among us today could accept his comment, "to inveigh indiscriminately against 'the South' is unjust."

> To-day even the attitude of the Southern whites toward the blacks is not, as so many assume, in all cases the same; the ignorant Southerner hates the Negro, the workingmen fear his competition, the money-makers wish to see him as a laborer, some of the educated see a menace in his upward development, while others - usually the sons of the masters - wish to help him to rise. National opinion has enabled this last class to maintain the Negro common schools, and to protect the Negro partially in property, life, and limb. Through the pressure of the money-makers, the Negro is in danger of being reduced to semi-slavery, especially in the country districts; the workingmen, and those of the educated who fear the Negro, have united to disfranchise him, and some have urged his deportation; while the passions of the ignorant are easily aroused to lynch and abuse any black man. To praise this intricate whirl of thought and prejudice is nonsense; to inveigh indiscriminately against "the South" is unjust; but to use the same breath in praising Governor Aycock, exposing Senator Morgan, arguing with Mr. Thomas Nelson Page, and denouncing Senator Ben Tillman, is not only sane, but the imperative duty of thinking black men.[45]

---

45. W. E. B. DuBois, *The Souls of Black Folk* (New York: Dover Publications, 1994), 33–34.

SOME GAINS, SOME LOSSES

During the period between 1877 and the end of World War I, blacks had made some gains and then suffered some losses. Whereas only a small minority had been free in 1860, by 1877, all had gained their freedom. They no longer had to take orders, at least in theory; they no longer had to allow their women to be victims of white passions; they no longer had to see their families split up because the master decided to sell them. With Reconstruction (carpetbag government and military occupation) and the Republican Party, they had gained the right to vote, and they listened to promises of land and a mule. By 1920, most had lost their voting rights, most had been reduced to the quasi-servitude status of sharecropper, and they were forced to accept second-class citizenship in the country that they and their ancestors had lived in since 1619. The bottom line is that they were still better off than they were in 1860. They were still free, and they had established their independent community identity. They may have had limited power in the white-dominated world, but they had their own corner of that world and they had their own leaders.

IMPERIALISM, ANOTHER ISSUE IN SOUTHERN IDENTITY

First of all, let me make sure that everyone realizes that the United States is an imperialist power. This is a repeat of material I have already covered, but so many Americans deny that we are imperialist that I feel compelled to repeat it. Any nation, which started with thirteen states and ended up with fifty states spanning a continent, put down a self-government movement with barbaric violence, as well as acquiring numerous possessions, military bases and interests around the globe, is imperialist. The techniques utilized by this country are not signs that they are different from European imperialist but rather that they are employing the modern imperialist strategy. The Europeans do not use the old style imperialism as they too have converted to the new.

The new style is what Americans later called Mahanism. Alfred Thayer Mahan is the author of late nineteenth-century American imperialism. His two books on the benefits of a strong navy laid out the plan. First, industrialization leads to surpluses. Second, surpluses lead to the need to enter the world markets. Third, world market competition requires a merchant marine. Fourth, a merchant marine needs a navy to protect it. Fifth, the merchant marine and navy need fueling stations. Sixth, fueling stations mean colonies. The key difference between the old imperialism is that the fueling stations mean only minimal occupation of foreign lands. Remember, the main objective of imperialism, old or new, is to make money. The modern imperialist have realized that the fewer colonial possessions require fewer expenditures to support the empire and therefore produce more profits. They have also realized that global expansion can be for the distribution of goods as well as the acquisition of raw materials.

The new imperialism is for the advantage of the industrialist. In the United States, that means those with money in the Northeast. Some Southern merchants, manufacturers, and other businessmen also benefited from this new imperialism; however, most people in the South between 1877 and 1920 were farmers, not merchants. They too were part of the world-market economy, but their struggles, which were many at the time, revolved around domestic issues. They had more interest in limiting the power of Northern railroads and bankers rather than in helping them.

During the late nineteenth century and early twentieth century, the South offered little support for the rise of modern American Imperialism; however, in the end it would eat away at the number of unreconstructed Southerners. Politicians, with the support of Southern Democrats such as Grover Cleveland and Williams Jennings Bryan, as well as Southern authors such as Mark Twain, were members of the anti-Imperialist League. I would guess that the majority of Southerners were at best indifferent concerning the rise of America in the international imperial competition. Most were Populists or Populist sympathizers who were more concerned about the state of the American farm family than in the quest of Northern businessmen as they competed with the other great powers.

There is one side affect that helped to eat away at Southern patriotism, and that is the growth of American patriotism in the South. Some were glad from the start to be back in the United States, the land of their birth. Others resisted being conquered and occupied by the imperialist American military. This was part of the struggle of Reconstruction. After the Compromise of 1877, most Southerners were satisfied with the fact that they controlled their local governments; they went back to planting cotton, and the blacks were back to picking it. Whereas I object to the term "Lost Cause myth" it is true that most Southerners spoke highly of the Lost Cause and the glory and bravery of the Confederate soldier. In 1898, the United States sent troops, at least on a large scale, overseas for the first time. The proportion of Southerners serving in the foreign wars was higher than expected based on the ratio of Southerners to the total population. Many Southerners like to think that this was due to our patriotic enthusiasm. I tend to think it was more due to economic consequences. The poorer classes tend to fill the ranks of enlisted men in wars. This is true for the American military as it has been for others throughout the ages. The South was worse off economically during this period, and I believe that it is the main reason they served at a higher ratio.

Regardless of the reason, the more that Southerners served in the military, the more veterans they produced. The veterans came back and supported their kind. As the numbers of American veterans increased, including those from the South, so did American patriotism. The increase in American patriotism decreases Southern patriotism; as I said earlier, it is hard to serve two masters. There are still many people in the South who continue to speak highly of the Confederate soldier and the Confederate cause of states' rights, but most today place their American patriotism on a higher pedestal. As far as I am concerned, a truly unreconstructed Southerner feels greater pride in being Southern, which was the original American, rather than the current imperialist American, which the Founders would find abhorrent; that is our nationalism.

CONCLUSIONS

The period 1877 to 1920 has produced a number of variables that has led to a decrease in the number of our people who can be called unreconstructed Southerners. The changes were primarily economic. The wealthy and middle classes profited from being part of the American empire again and what they enthusiastically labeled the New South. The lower middle-class farmers and white sharecroppers struggled for survival so that their money worries overshadowed any interest in the Lost Cause. Black Southerners became convinced that the conquest of the South and the wonderful deeds of Abraham Lincoln is what set them free. I have not done an exact count, but I would say that more than 90 percent of those in the *Slave Narratives* looked at Abraham Lincoln as their liberator. I am sure that this was largely due to Reconstruction propaganda, but nonetheless, that is what they believed, and that is what they taught their children and grandchildren to believe. Meanwhile, more and more Southerners became involved in American empire building by serving in the military. This has produced an ever-increasing number who considered themselves Americans first, Southerners second. During this period, there were many who abandoned their heritage, and their children and grandchildren would find it even easier to do. By the time we get to the late twentieth century, most Southerners seem to be willing to leave their Confederate past in the dust as they cling to their American patriotism. This will be the trend which I will discuss in the next two chapters. By the beginning of the twenty-first century, many more Southerners will adorn their cars and pickups with "United We Stand" bumper stickers, which display the Stars and Stripes while fewer will brandish the Stars and Bars. All of this contributes to the loss of our heritage. Fewer and fewer white Southerners are prepared to fight to preserve it.

VIII: THE FALL OF THE SOUTH, 1920–1970

I HAVE TITLED THIS CHAPTER "The Fall of the South" because I see it as a time of the fall of the Old South. By the end of this time period there is a New South, but not in the same way as the term has been traditionally used by the likes of Henry Grady. This period of change can be subdivided into two main periods. The first is that time between the two world wars. The second is that period after World War II to 1970. It was during this second period that the South went through a racial crisis so that by 1970 the stage was cleared and all was set for the rise of a truly new South. There were many good things that came out of these changes, but we also lost a lot of our Southerness.

Remember that one of the objectives of my analysis in this book is to explain the decline in the number of unreconstructed Southerners. I want to make it clear that I am not saying that the old ways were better, it is only that with the changes we lost much of our regional identity. This is why we are losing so much of our culture. There are many ways in which the Old South was demolished to create vacant ground which allowed for the rise of a truly new South. Many of those changes have been good. What is sad is that we have lost much more than was needed to make way for improvements. It is a classic case of throwing the baby out with the bathwater. When we lose our heritage we lose our culture, and then we lose our identity.

The most obvious change is that by 1970 the South was no longer a land of farmers. The New South of Henry Grady was more of an adjustment to a new labor system that went from slavery to sharecropping. There was some increase in economic diversity, but in the end they still had a culture where the majority depended on the traditional American family farm. There is still a lot of agriculture in the South, but fewer people depend on that industry for their livelihoods. The most important impact on the common people of our land was the demise of the family farm. In 1970 there were many in the region who still remembered our agricultural past, which is why we liked *Hee Haw* at a time when much of the country was watching *Laugh-In*. What many did not think about at the time is that those days were gone. The children of the South would no longer share this common culture. As time goes on we are not the nation of farmers that we once were, Fewer people in the South have picked cotton.

One thing I want to focus on in this chapter is how the unreconstructed became the minority. I emphasize again that I am not making a statement on values but simply describing what happened. That first phase, the interwar period, began a great diaspora that resulted from a defective economy. This great exodus contributed greatly in diminishing the self-esteem of Southerners. The depression took a toll on all Americans, but the scars seemed greater for the millions from the South who fled their homes, families, and way of life as they headed toward the great cities of the North and West.

This is the main cause for change, but there were other variables which also contributed to the decline of our regional identity. As previously pointed out, many Southerners served in the two world wars. They were veterans of the United States Army. This helped to make them patriotic Americans and, as a result, they became a little less Southern. This was also a time of political changes. Black Southerners shifted their loyalties from the Republican Party to the Democratic Party. I recall an interview I heard on a radio show once where one elderly black lady said that she can explain the change in one word: "Roosevelt." She also pointed out that this happened at a time when the Democrats of the South were the main enemies of black equality. It was also a time when white Southerners started to become dissatisfied with the Democrat Party. This change was just beginning in 1970, but the white Southerners began to move to the Republican Party.

THE GREATEST CHANGE

Since the beginning of the colonies, people came to America for the opportunity to own their own farm and to obtain the status and independence which came with being land owners. At the end of the War of Southern Independence most Americans, even most Northerners, still dreamed of the family farm. By the end of the American Industrial Revolution, most in the North had made the transition to some alternative. It may not have been good, but the majority no longer depended on the land for their living The change came to the North first so that by 1920 most Americans lived in urban areas. Southerners, black and white, still clung to the dream of the family farm. By 1945 it was clear that the dream was over in the South too. Only then could the economic diversity dreamed of by Henry Grady be realized.

The transition was brutal for many people. Perhaps it was the conservative nature of the Southern people that made it so that they had to be forced off the land. More likely it was because they had to learn the hard way that they would have to find some other way to make a living. The South today is still the leader in many agricultural products, but the producers depend more on machines and less on labor. There are a few in the South and West who cling to the concept of the family farm. These are the ones who need Willie Nelson and Farm Aid to help them out. When we get to the next chapter, we will see a greater diversity in the Southern economy which produced a reversal in the Diaspora.

THE KING IS DEAD (COTTON)

Cotton did not become king in the South until the early nineteenth century. It has become a classic symbol of the antebellum South, that South which is also known as the "Old South." It has been so much a symbol of the old South that some of those out to destroy our heritage have even objected to cotton plants as if they were the same as Confederate monuments. It is an exaggeration to proclaim the king dead; the reality is that production in terms of bales of cotton was close to 13 percent higher in 1950 than in 1920. What I really mean by this proclamation is that the labor system that produced the cotton has died, and thus, a much smaller percentage of the population depends on cotton production for their living.

Cotton production was among the first agribusiness. Small farmers produced cotton too, but the planters were the big producers. The large producers changed from using slave labor to sharecroppers and then to machines. The latter meant they no longer needed people. These people were the lower or working classes. The middle-class family farm producer also had a harder time competing so that they too searched for a new way to make a living. For the most part, all but the great planters would be forced off the land. Between 1920 and 1930, the number of farm owners in the South declined by 350,000. There were others affected by these changes too. Approximately 60 percent of the Southern farm operators worked someone else's land.

There were other forces which helped to rob the Southern families of their land. The boll weevil came up from Mexico and added to the problems. California became more of an economic threat with its agribusiness. Foreign competition took its toll as did the manufacture of synthetics. After so many turned to sharecropping as an alternative to starvation, economic forces began to dismantle the sharecropping system. The Agricultural Adjustment Act paid farmers not to plant crops; this money did not go to the tenants, and thus, they no longer had a job. The sharecroppers lost their jobs and homes in one blow. During the Second World War, the cotton-picking machine would remove the remaining families from their jobs and homes.

There were not enough other jobs in the South to provide for those forced off the land. This led to the great exodus to the North. The *Librevs* like to reinforce the myth that sharecroppers were black and that the Southern exodus, which they call the "great migration," was mostly blacks. The fact is that in the early twentieth century there were 5.5 million white tenants, sharecroppers, and laborers in the United States and only 3 million blacks. Historically, whites made up two-thirds of the farm hands in Tennessee. In Mississippi, 36 percent of whites were not private farmers while 60 percent of the blacks fit in this category. Blacks may have suffered more during this period as was most often the case in American history; however, many whites also paid the price for the transition to machine-powered agribusiness. In the South, the changes in cotton production had the greatest impact, but almost all Southern agriculture went through similar changes.

THE SOUTHERN ECONOMY IN GENERAL

Immediately following World War I, there were some good times in the South. At first, the demand for cotton decreased because of the war, so that by 1920, the prices had risen from five cents a pound to twenty-seven cents. Even the black tenants were reported to have "come to town with their pockets stuffed with paper money" to pay off their bills. Other Southern industries prospered during the war years, including chemicals, timber, and oil. Cigarette smoking became more acceptable, which helped the South's tobacco farmers.

Cities represent merchant economy; the growth of Southern cities during this time suggest that there was some development in the nonagricultural segments of the economy. New Orleans remained the largest city in the South in 1930, but Houston was closing in and Dallas was not far behind. Urban growth spread across the South and included cities, such as Louisville, Atlanta, Birmingham, Memphis, San Antonio, Richmond, Oklahoma City, Fort Worth, Nashville, Tulsa, Jacksonville, and Norfolk. Cities divided the Southern people between the sophisticated urbanites who had electricity, more store-bought goods, more automobiles, and more education from those who remained in the rural areas and who heated with wood-burning stoves, read by oil lamps, and had less education. The cities became governed by civic elites who cared less and less about the Old South and the Lost Cause.

The South suffered during the Depression as did the rest of the nation. On one hand they had some advantages since so many more lived on the land. Those who were able to hold on to their land at least could grow food. On the other hand, this is the time when the sharecroppers were hurled out onto the roads and highways as the government paid the landowners to not grow crops. This was when John Steinbeck burned the image of the dust bowl into the minds and hearts of Americans. In reality it was the demise of the sharecropping system that pushed most of the Okies off the land. Those Steinbeck described included more than just the Okies. Many of those who Californians called Okies came from Texas, or Arkansas, or even Kansas as well as Oklahoma. Anyone arriving in California in a dilapidated car with only a few dollars in their pocket and spoke with a Southern accent was an "Okie." The dust bowl itself was centered in the high plains of the panhandles of Texas and Oklahoma. Severe erosion was a price paid for the generations of land abuse throughout the West and South. The images of the Joads became part of the great Diaspora, but the migration taking place involved more than Oklahoma and those who went to California. People fled the South in general in the 1930s. It was more than just the Depression era too. This continued and even escalated during the war and shortly after as black and white Southerners searched for jobs in the Northern cities. In the western part of the South they went to California or other points on the west coast; in the central parts they went to Chicago, Detroit, or Ohio; and in the east they went to New York, Washington D.C., and Boston.

As part of the New Deal, Roosevelt implemented the Tennessee Valley Authority. This project brought jobs, flood control, but most importantly, rural electrification. With the electricity produced by the TVA and other such projects, the majority of the Southern population who still resided in rural areas had greater access to radio, and later, television. This brought the South closer to the rest of the nation and helped considerably in making its people American. Southern identity remained strong during this period, but with the ties to national networks and the president's fireside chats, the spirit of being American grew at the expense of being less Southern.

World War II brought more rapid change to the South than they had experienced since the War of Southern Independence and Reconstruction. The economy of 1945 differed considerably from that of 1940, which in turn sparked considerable social and political change. Cotton, segregation, and one-party politics were weakened so that in the years after the war, these would no longer be characteristics of the region.

The South received a disproportionate share of military bases. The climate played a part in this policy, especially with the increase in air power. Airplanes have a greater dependence on good weather so that their takeoffs and landings are not limited. Roosevelt played a bigger role. He recognized the South as being the most impoverished region in the nation, and he saw the military installations as one way of helping to solve that problem. The federal government invested more than $7 billion on the bases and industrial plants. Many of these bases were expanded and made permanent after the war, and even some of the post-1970 population growth came from retired military personnel who remained in the region. Industrial capacity of the region grew 40 percent from 1939 to 1947. The number of production workers increased from 1.3 million to 2 million. Personal income rose from $13.6 billion to $32.1 billion, bringing the South from 59 percent of the national average to 69 percent.

Despite the economic growth, the greatest exodus from the South occurred after 1940. More than 4 million served in the armed forces; however, many more fled to the war-related jobs on the coasts or in Northern cities. The *Librevs* focus on the blacks who left, and even though they admit that economic factors played a big part, they prefer to emphasize Southern racism as a major reason, if not the major reason, for "the great migration." I have a problem accepting that as the explanation. Didn't they experience racism before the great migration?

THE GREAT MIGRATION MYTH

Most of the United States textbooks these days have a topic called "the great migration." This is not to be confused with other such periods in American history, such as the puritans who went to New England in the early seventeenth century. When I call this a myth I do not mean to say that it did not happen, but rather to say that I do not agree with the way is has been interpreted. I believe this to be largely due to the error of trying to separate the story of black Southerners from white Southerners.

The main thing I object to is the claim that the main reason it happened was because of Southern racism. Using this logic, Northern racism would have caused an immediate reversal. Historians often use the terms "push" and "pull." With "pull" they recognized the economic reasons. With the "push," they talk about "the poverty, indebtedness, racism, and violence most blacks experienced in the South."[46] I believe that the pull was more significant, in other words, I believe that the blacks of the South left for the same reason the whites did, to find jobs. The main reason I believe the push variables to be less significant than do the *Librevs* is that nothing changed in this regard, blacks were never treated as equals.

To summarize, the main reason I call this a myth is not because there was no great exodus of blacks from the South, but rather because they talk of the black population only. This is typical of ways in which they focus on and emphasize racism in the South. When they cover this topic, they admit that the blacks moved into a segregated North also and that they did not get as good jobs as the whites and that they lacked in education and so forth, but the *Librevs* imply that blacks were still much better off than in the South. Later I will give some statistics showing ways in which the North was as bad as the South.

It is a fact that some of the blacks themselves promoted the North as being a better place. The black-oriented newspaper *Chicago Defender* wrote in the early 1900s: "To die from the bite of frost is far more glorious than at the hands of a mob. I beg you, my brother, to leave the benighted land." However, I can recall a number of songs from that time period, such as the one by Louis Armstrong, in which he longed for the sunny South. The bottom line is that the *Defender* may have influenced some in their decision to move north, but the fact is that it was an exodus of all Southerners, not just blacks. To me this fact indicates that it was primarily for economic reasons. Of the more than 28 million Southerners who left the region, only 28 percent were black, 68 percent were white, and 4 percent Hispanic.

---

46. Alan Brinkley, *A Survey: American History* (New York: McGraw-Hill, 2007), 623.

The *Librevs* did not create the term "great migration." It is the Northern white media that first begin to write of the increase in the black population among them. I am sure that it was not because they were boasting of the greater opportunities for people of color in the North but more in the same way California press wrote about the Okies in their state in the 1930s. They were writing about a topic of distress, not praise. By the 1940s, they were using the term "great migration."

The blacks who went to Chicago before World War I, when the *Defender* started publication, did find jobs. However, they were replaced by white immigrants so that the black weekly journal complained about the fact that they had taken the jobs previously filled by blacks. When Martin Luther King, Jr. took the civil rights movement north, and after a night of rioting in Chicago, he claimed that he had never seen so much hatred, not even in Selma, Alabama. They may have lived in segregated neighborhoods and communities in the South, but they likewise moved into segregated neighborhoods and communities when they moved north.

As far as I am concerned, this entire subject is a perfect example of why I try to include both black and white Southerners in my study of our history, they were both part of the regional event called the Southern Diaspora. The black and white Southerners who moved North during the twentieth century had a major cultural impact on that region. Southern Baptist churches appeared in communities where they had never existed before. They both helped to change the North as Blacks would later be elected in Northern communities for the first time, and Southern whites would help in building the political careers of men like Ronald Reagan. The South suffered a loss of population, but the Southern people influenced the nation as a whole in ways they had never done before.

The sad thing to me is that this Diaspora had a negative influence on our Southern identity. Some would consider this a good thing since it means that we as a people were becoming more American. There are advantages to assimilation, but I personally regret the loss of our unique cultural identity. As we will see in the next chapter, this became a two-edged sword beginning in the 1970s when the Diaspora reversed itself. During World War II, even though many moved out, there were 6 million outsiders who moved into the South. After 1970, we see a trend where more people are moving into the region than out. Some are returned Southerners such as myself; however, most were not. In recent years, as in the United States in total, many have been foreign born. Since World War II, America has become more Southern because of the Diaspora; however, the South has become more American. The cultural border between North and South is not as well-defined as it was before World War II, and it seems to be getting more and more difficult to recognize the regional differences. There have always been people in the upper parts of the South who did not identify with the region; however, the surveys done by John Shelton Reed and his friends at the University of North Carolina have shown the number in decline. I will repeat once more, my objective is not to make a value judgment. I feel sad at the loss of

Southern identity, but there is no doubt that some of the change has been good. The best thing out of it all is the end of a society where black Southerners did not have the same rights as those who were white. My main objective here is to account for the decline in numbers of those of us who are unreconstructed and the resulting decline in those who would defend our heritage.

THE TRASHING OF THE SOUTH BY SOUTHERNERS

Starting in the 1920s, a number of writers emerged from the South who the *Librevs* like to describe as being "critical." It seems to be the rule that artists, especially writers, are contrary to the general population whether it is a French artist writing about French culture, English writing about English culture, or Japanese writing about Japanese culture. There are conservative artists and there are conservative writers, but it seems that the most famous are the ones who are critical of their homeland, its people, and its culture. They quite often are critical of the entire human race. I have no problem accepting that many of the Southern writers who came along during the 1920s were critical of our Southern ways. I do not even have any objection to the fact that we have plenty of habits for the writers to be critical of—the treatment of black Southerners is the most obvious example. What I resent is the way this topic is presented in most of the textbooks today. The implication is that the Southern writers were critical of the South in a way that implies we should be following the example set by the great and wise Northerners. Unfortunately, that is what some of them did.

I understand this experience since I myself yielded to Northern domination in believing their ways to be superior to ours. Since I was one of those California Okies who was intimidated into adopting their language, I could easily pass for one of them. I have always identified with the lines in the Don Williams song, "I was smarter than most and I could choose, learned to talk like the man on the six o'clock news." I did not think of myself as Southern like I do now. Today I can see that our ways are far from perfect. Every culture has its faults; however, I much prefer the ways of my Southern people over the self-righteous and arrogant ways of Yankeedom.

Perhaps the most famous of these writers was H. L. Mencken, and his most famous attitudinal essay was "The Sahara of the Bozart." Mencken was born in Baltimore in 1880. Some might argue that he was not a real Southerner since he was from Maryland, but I personally have no problem accepting those from that state as fellow Southerners. In his famous essay, he wrote, "Virginia is the best of the South today, and Georgia is perhaps the worst. The one is simply senile; the other is crass, gross, vulgar, and obnoxious. Between lies a vast plain of mediocrity, stupidity, lethargy, almost of dead silence." Mencken was a cranky old man who seemed to hate everything American, but he said, "The North, of course, there is also grossness, crassness, vulgarity. The North, in its way, is also stupid and obnoxious." He went on to say that at least in the North they are trying to improve themselves. Where I take exception to his criticism is that he measures these advances by looking at the American imitations of European culture, such as orchestras or little theater.

What I love about the South is that the people have their own culture, and most of it is uniquely American, or more specifically, uniquely Southern. Today, most of the Southern cities do have orchestras who play the classical European music, but we also have Nashville, Memphis, and New Orleans where the music of the South flows from the homes and clubs into the streets. We have created a music that the entire world admires and some imitate. We have some of the best food in America. We do not copy French "haute cuisine" but rather have jambalaya, or catfish and hush puppies, or chicken fried steak and okra, and of course every state in the South claims that they have the best bar-b-que. We have rodeo, we have our own style of clothes, and we have our own literature. Since the days of Mencken, we do more copying of European culture, which is what Yankees think of as culture. What is more important is that we have developed our own culture. It is that culture that I am proud to be part of.

Second to Mencken in importance is Wilbur J. Cash. Coming from South Carolina, twenty years later than Mencken, he was indisputably Southern. He grew up in small towns in North and South Carolina, and in his youth never questioned his culture. He became a journalist and freelance writer when he wrote articles for Mencken's *American Mercury*. One was titled "The Mind of the South," which attracted so much attention from publisher Blanche Knopf that he received a contract to expand the essay into a full book. It took him ten years to accomplish the task. In 1941, the book was published. He criticized the South's bigotry, violence, and anti-intellectualism and influenced historians in that direction since. The scalawag schools like the University of North Carolina or LSU have followed the lead of their Yankee academic heroes and accepted this attitude as the true way to approach Southern history. They see it as the opposite of the "Lost Cause myth."

I must make it clear that my objective is not to ignore the fact that our Southern culture is not perfect, but I simply resent the implication that we are any less perfect than any other culture. I especially resent the notion that our culture is inferior to that of those Americans to the North. As a historian, I like to study our history as a means to better understand what we are by understanding where we came from. I try to be objective but realize that I cannot be, no more so than the Yankee *Librevs*. This is the land where I personally come from and where my parents and grandparents before me and so on came from. I resent those who imply that my predecessors are inferior beings, as I am sure that black Southerners have resented being told the same thing about their people for so many years. Some of my ancestors were the ones who told the black people that they were inferior, and some even owned black slaves. I realize that my ancestors were wrong. Black people are not inferior, but neither are my people. They lived in a different time and place when people lived by different rules than those which we live by today. All of us have ancestors that did things that we consider wrong or even barbaric today. I deny that my Southern ancestors were anymore barbaric than those who came from the North.

THE SOUTHERN LITERARY RENAISSANCE

The South had writers in the half century following the War of Southern independence; however, in the 1920s, they seemed to flower in a way that they received greater respect from those in others places, especially the North. The most important writers of this time were John Crowe Ransom, Allen Tate, Robert Penn Warren, Donald Davidson, Andrew Lytle, Caroline Gordon, Thomas Wolfe, William Faulkner, Cleanth Brooks, Katherine Anne Porter, Carson McCullers, Eudora Welty, Flannery O'Connor, and Tennessee Williams. They did tend to reject the ways of their homeland, which included the New South as well as the Old South. Some leaned in the direction of Mencken and Cash, but others saw a greater curse in the materialism of the New South.

In 1930, Ransom, Tate, Warren, and others wrote *I'll Take My Stand: The South and Agrarian Tradition*. This is known as agrarianism, and the twelve writers involved in the project have become known as the Southern agrarians. These writers actually objected to Mencken and praised traditional Southern values. They did not invent agrarianism; men like Thomas Jefferson could be put in that category even though they lived generations before the coining of the term. The philosophy sees the good in the cultivation of the soil, which provides direct contact with nature and God. The farmer has a sense of identity and historical and religious tradition as well as a feeling of belonging to a family, place, and region. Farming offers total independence and self-sufficiency. The modern urban life, capitalism, and technology destroy our independence and dignity while fostering vice and weakness. Most of us unreconstructed Southerners are proud of the fact that our ancestors were attached to the land. If you recall, the name of the plantation in *Gone with the Wind* was "Tara," which means land. I confess to leaning in this direction myself and do firmly believe that we pay a price for conveniences that come with modern technology.

I do believe we have lost something, and I have little doubt that identity crisis is behind much of the drug and alcohol abuse that pervades the land today. Having admitted that, I also realize that this kind of thinking is why many see us as backwards. We may live in big cities like Atlanta and Dallas today, but many of us have an uncontrollable sentiment for the land and the ways of our predecessors who were attached to the land. This does not mean that we are wrong or inferior. There have been plenty of those in the North land who held the same beliefs, from Emerson and Thoreau to the hippies of the 1960s.

CONSERVATISM OF THE 1920S

We often think of the "roaring" twenties as a time of advances in the modernization process which included the flappers, booming economy, birth of many technological gadgets and urban fads, but there was also a conservative backlash to the rapidly changing decade. Some of the conservatism took place in the North as well as the South, but more of it has stuck on our people since it fits the negative stereotypes that many prefer to see as Southern backwardness. The revival of the Ku Klux Klan during this period is associated with the South even though the largest single chapter was in Chicago. It makes sense to them that the Klan took over the state governments in Oklahoma and Texas, but they overlook the fact that they did the same in Oregon and Indiana. Tennessee had the famous Scopes Monkey Trial in reaction to the modern teaching of evolution in the schools, but they ignore thriving revivalism that swept the North at the same time, fueled in part by what those people saw as a threat to their religious beliefs.

The KKK of the 1920s was much different than what we think of today when we see the collection of freaks rounded up for the *Jerry Springer Show*. Likewise, it was different than the first Klan that came about to resist Yankee occupation during Reconstruction. The birth of the new Klan took place on Stone Mountain in Georgia and was inspired by the popularity of the movie *The Birth of a Nation*. In the South it targeted mostly Blacks; however, the clan also grew and prospered around the country. In the North it was aimed more at the great influx of foreigners, especially Catholics and Jews, who had infiltrated the country in the late nineteenth and early twentieth century. Some *Librev* historians accept the fact that the organization was as successful in the North, but some have tried to claim that it was largely due to the increase in Southerners living in the North because of the Diaspora. To me this is just another example of their determination to pin racism on Southerners. It is the government of the United States which passed the quota laws in 1924 to limit the non-Aryans from coming into the United States, and Southerners were a minority in that legislature.

There is no denying the fact that the majority of the people of the South are religious; however, let us not ignore the fact that there are plenty of those in the North who are also religious. The Scopes Monkey Trial took place in the South, but it could have taken place in the North also. Mencken and the liberal types saw the trial as evidence of the absurdity of the ignorant religious masses, and he even proclaimed fundamentalism dead as a result of the trial. The importance of this segment of the population in recent elections suggests that he may have been wrong.

FUNDAMENTALISM 1920–1945

The South is the Bible Belt; some are proud to proclaim this while others see it as an example of why Mencken called the region a cultural Sahara. I firmly believe that the greatest fight we have to preserve our Southern culture is not with the NAACP or such anti-flag groups but against our own people, the political fundamentalists that have been created since the 1970s. In the minds of many, they fail to make an important distinction between the religious Southerner who has always been considered to be a big part or our culture, and the politically active today that helped to propel George W. Bush into the White House. Most of the change that I am speaking of came about after World War II, and so I will pursue this topic in much greater detail in the next chapter. Because of the Scopes Monkey Trial, many associate the South with fundamentalism in the 1920s, so I feel compelled to address the subject to some degree now.

Even the definition of fundamentalism can be controversial. I have used it to describe those who believe in a literal interpretation of the Bible. Wikipedia says "The term 'fundamentalism' was originally coined to describe a narrowly defined set of beliefs that developed into a movement within the US Protestant community in the early part of the 20th century. These religious principles stood in opposition to the modernist movement and espoused the strict adherence to and faith in religious 'fundamentals.'" In recent years, with help from the media, the term has been used to describe any group that clings to a set of beliefs whether they be Christian, Muslim, Jewish, or just about any other religion.

The fact is that the historical movement did not begin in the South but began among conservative Presbyterian academics and theologians at Princeton Theological Seminary in the first decade of the twentieth century. After World War I, the movement was more associated with Northern Protestants. Largely because of the Monkey Trial in Tennessee and the popular view of the South as being the "Bible Belt," most people think of our region as the center. According to the religious historian Sam Hill, "In the South, Protestant Evangelicalism has long been the largest Christian tradition, it's most prominent and dominant religious form." He went on to say, "But Fundamentalism was rare before the 1970s."[47] He referred to the Churches of Christ, which have been in the South since the late antebellum period, and he said the Bob Jones element began in the 1920s. In the 1920s and 1930s, they were generally separatist. If they could not remove modernist from the Church, they could remove the Church from the modernist. As one raised in the Church of Christ, I can remember only one time when politics was openly discussed in Church; that was in 1960 when a Catholic ran for President. The fear and hatred of Catholicism seems to be great among fundamentalists. Generally speaking, they removed themselves from politics

---

47. Sam Hill, "Fundamentalism in Recent Southern Culture: Has it Done What the Civil Rights Movement Couldn't Do?" *The Journal of Southern Religion*, Vol. 1, No. 1 (1998).

and America as well as the South. I will end this discussion for now but will take it up in the next chapter when they began to play a very important role in the termination of our Southern culture.

Patriotism Begins To Take Its Toll

I have discussed this before, although I am generally a believer in the Celtic fringe theory I do take exception to the part of the theory that claims that the Southern people are warriors by birth. I realize that this is the main part of the thesis, but what I really like about the Celtic fringe thesis is the part about Southern identity and how the South is predominantly a Celtic culture while the North is Anglo-Saxon. In the great nurture versus nature debate, I believe that each plays a role and that there are many aspects of human behavior which are difficult to reach a conclusion on, probably because it is the result of a combination of these forces. I do not believe that one group of humans is more genetically disposed toward warfare than any other. I do believe in Maslow's hierarchy of needs of which the third level says that we all need to have a feeling of belonging to a community. I also believe in his second level, which says that we need to have a sense of safety. Warfare has traditionally been a situation in which a community feels threatened by another. It is true, as stated in the Celtic fringe thesis, that the Scottish people had a tradition of warfare against the English that spanned generations. Where I disagree is that the history of the world has many other examples of a tradition of warfare between rival cultures. I do not believe that there is anything unique about the Scottish situation.

The *Librevs* seem to accept this military tradition of the South because it helps them in looking down on Southerners. Those of the North have a tradition of hatred toward those of the South. They value education, thus, they look at the Southern anti-intellectualism as proof of their ignorance. They don't realize that the South has a richer tradition of education than the North. Victory gave the North the opportunity to write their prejudices on the South as enlightened thought. The tradition of Southern violence is part of the militarism, which has convinced the Northerners that we are savages. Their claims to having liberated the Southern slaves has further demonstrated to them that we are morally inferior.

There has been an increase in American patriotism in the South at the expense of Southern patriotism. Even though there has been a lack of respect from their fellow countrymen to the North, and that the Union was forced on our people, in recent generations they have once again embraced their American identity. They have not only become patriotic Americans once again, but most would agree that they have become the most patriotic people in the land. They remember the legacy of the Lost Cause, whether you want to call it a myth or not, and thus, they still honor their Confederate ancestors; however, with the return of American patriotism, the Lost Cause has declined in importance.

Many Southerners like to imagine themselves as possessing this martial tradition, and out of self-defense, many Northerners have given them credit for this manly characteristic whether it's true or not. You see, by accepting this as true they have an excuse for why it took them four years to conquer a nation that they outnumbered by two to one. Those in the South and the West have favored a strong army throughout much of American history, but it is more out of self-interest than any military tradition. They have been the ones who kept pushing the frontier westward, and thus, they are the ones who needed an army for protection. For the same reason those in the Northeast have turned their attention to the navy. Their risk for attack by foreign aggressors would be more likely to come from the sea. They had a tradition of fishing and trade on the high seas while the agricultural Southerners and Westerners learned how to ride horses and use their muskets and rifles. This is my theory for why one region has been more inclined toward the navy while the other would be better served by a strong army.

There were many in the South who favored a strong army, but in the early to mid-twentieth century there were also many who rejected American militarism and imperialism. Let us not forget the Populists. Most of the aggressive members of the Anti-Imperialist League were from the North. They rejected the Populist anti-imperialist William Jennings Bryan. This was not because they disagreed with him over U.S. foreign policy but rather because of his favoring the silver standard

Many see American patriotism in the South as evidence of a military tradition; I do not see it as being so simply explained. By the time we get to the late twentieth century, about half of the male population of America are veterans. This makes them sympathetic to those who are serving their country at any given time, which in turn makes them sympathetic to the American military. One of the big issues in the Sons of Confederate Veterans these days is the fact that some do not want to include the Pledge of Allegiance to the American flag in their meetings. Since so many of the members are veterans, there have been a great many that resent the lack of respect for the flag they have served under. Even though many of the common people of the South opposed American aggression in the first half of the twentieth century, the fact is that many ended up serving in both world wars. I do not believe that this is due to patriotism but more because of Southern poverty. The lower classes are less able to resist the draft and the resulting military service. For many of them it offered job opportunities that might seem more attractive than they would appear to those of the upper classes. After the world wars, Southerners served in Korea, Vietnam, and ended up stationed in numerous bases during the half-century long cold war.

Regardless of whether it was due to a military tradition or simply Southern poverty or a combination of the two—the fact is that many in the South have served in the American military, and thus are Veterans, and therefore possess patriotic feelings toward America. They have managed to reconcile this with the pride they still feel for their Confederate ancestors. However, in recent years, such feelings have made it easier for them to abandon their interest in the Confederate flag or other such symbols when they are told that it is in the interest of national unity. This seems superficial on the surface, as many carried Confederate flags into battle in every war of the 20th Century, with seemingly no loss of unity. They may have some resentment for the sacrifice of their heritage, but the fact is that there are more and more pickup trucks out there with "United We Stand" or "God Bless America" bumper stickers, and fewer that have Confederate flags. Even as the military restricts the display of the Confederate battle flag many Southerners accept this as a cost for American Unity. In this way, the growth of American patriotism has contributed to the diminishing of our Southern identity.

FOUNDATIONS OF THE CIVIL RIGHTS MOVEMENT

One of the most important developments of the period between 1920 and 1945 is the rejection by more and more black Americans of their second-class citizenship. There are numerous reasons for the changes in the early twentieth century that lay the foundation for the greater racial equality that would be achieved in the middle part of the century.

Many Southern blacks served in the American military just like Southern whites. As a result, they began to question why they should not be treated as full citizens since they were called on to defend the nation. With military service they saw more of the world. In addition, many migrated north, or moved around more in the South. As a result of the migration and military service, more blacks saw more of the world, and this probably contributed to more questioning of the status which they had accepted up to that time.

I repeat, I do not reject the fact that white Southerners mistreated black Southerners. I do reject the notion that the discrimination that I am referring to was strictly a Southern thing. For that matter, the belief in Aryan superiority that such an attitude was based on, was not even uniquely an American thing during the early twentieth century. Obviously, that was the basic assumption made by the Germans who followed Hitler. The British may have fought the Nazis in World War II, but it was not because they rejected the belief that white people were superior to those with darker skins. They certainly displayed this belief in Africa and India. Americans liberated German extermination camps, but the United States displayed numerous examples of their belief in Aryan superiority. The army that invaded Germany was segregated. The Ku Klux Klan of the 1920s was only an example of the groups that pushed into law the legislation that would restrict future immigration by limiting those who did not come from the Germanic Northern European population.

In June of 1949, George S. Schuyler published an article in *American Mercury* called "'All Over the Country': 1949 Jim Crow in the North." He looked at various aspects of discrimination against blacks and pointed out that conditions were not much better in the Northern states than in the South. He looked at housing, schools, public facilities, and transportation. He found some exceptions but mainly in those parts of the country which had a very small black population. I have already pointed out that hatred is most often based on fear; in the case of racial hatred, some perceive one group or another as a threat to their way of life. For example, Schuyler not only pointed out that twenty-nine states (sixteen of them outside the South) had illegalized mixed marriages, but that those in the North had the strictest punishment. Georgia had a maximum of one year in jail, and Tennessee and Texas had a limit of five years; but Indiana, North Dakota, and South Dakota put it at ten years. I could go on, but I do not feel it necessary to provide any more evidence that all of America treated blacks as second-class citizens in the early twentieth century.

I see the first stages of change as having come from the decreasing acceptance among the black population. This is reflected in the growth of the NAACP. Shortly after World War I, the organization grew from twenty chapters (one in the South) to three hundred chapters (more than half in the South). Between 1940 and 1946, they grew from 355 chapters to 1,073 with 450,000 members. This no doubt contributed to the beginnings of change among the white population. It began with the courts. In Oklahoma, for example, they managed to get the grandfather clause declared unconstitutional by the courts. In other ways, the courts showed signs of rejecting an American tradition of segregation that, of course, would lead to even greater change in the 1950s and 1960s. The Roosevelts made their contributions toward a change in attitude. One famous example is when Eleanor gave up her membership in the Daughters of the American Revolution after they cancelled the contract with the black opera singer Marion Anderson. The First Lady also supported the Tuskegee Airmen when she showed her belief that they were smart enough to fly airplanes by allowing one to fly her around.

We can also see this time period as one revealing the defiance that would come from many of the Southern white population. The once-solid Democrat South began to crack as Roosevelt and the Democrat Party gave support to the birth of the civil rights movement. Those who did not like this change had no idea where to turn. They still despised Republicans, not as in the past because it was the party of Reconstruction, but more because it was the party of rich Yankees. The Republicans would not launch their Southern strategy until the 1970s.

CONCLUSIONS

The period between 1920 and 1945 was an era of great change in the South, and these changes took a great toll on Southern identity. The greatest change was brought about by the continued decline in the economy. Much of that, of course, was the Great Depression that hit all of America. In some ways, this was easier on those who still lived on the land because they could at least grow food. In the long term, this period in history had a greater effect on the South. There are some who like to blame the poverty on Southern conservatism and their stubborn resistance to modernization. Others see it as a continuation of punishment for losing the war against the North, and therefore all of our problems were due to the evil Yankees. As a historian, I see it as part of the trend that has existed since the dawn of the modern age. Modernization has meant that more and more people leave the land because they are forced off by technology. They then turn to the market economy, which later included manufacturing, as a way to make their living. Since the markets are in cities, this means that they move from the country to the city. I believe that the main reason Southerners clung to their agricultural economy is that they found products, such as cotton, tobacco, rice, and sugar for which there existed a great demand in the world-market economy. What changed in the early twentieth century is that new methods of producing these products put a greater dependency on machines and less on people. This made it more costly to compete in the marketplace, which made it more difficult for the small farmer to compete. To be a successful farmer, one had to be able to invest in expensive equipment. We could blame Roosevelt and his Agricultural Adjustment Act; however, all this did was speed up the process of mechanization. The family-run farm, whether that be run by sharecroppers or small land owners, was in decline because they could not compete with agribusiness. The late-nineteenth-century preachers of New South diversity could not lead the people in the direction they wanted to go because the profits in agriculture were still there for those who could compete. They are still there, and these products are still produced in the South. It would not be until the late twentieth century that the South would achieve a more diverse economy. This was not because of better advocates but because technology would force the population off the land and into other endeavors.

The greatest impact of these changes was to send 28 million Southerners fleeing the land of their ancestors; this included black, white, Indian, and Hispanic Southerners. Many of them and their descendants would adopt the identity of their new homeland—the North. This of course would drain much of the Southern pride that our identity lives on. On the positive side, this northbound and westbound migration made America more Southern. I do not think it a coincidence that much of the music of the 1960s came from the same land that received the greatest influx of Southern migrants. California pop music was greatly influenced by the Southern country and blues sounds of those who went there from Oklahoma, Texas, Arkansas, and Missouri. Likewise, Detroit and New York music was influenced by the Southerners who went to those parts of the country.

More and more Southerners, both those who left and those who stayed, became critical of their heritage. Men like H. L. Mencken and Wilbur Cash not only became critical of our culture, but did so in a way that emphasized the superiority of Northern culture. Meanwhile, the conservative side of Southern society became negative symbols of Southern backwardness to those in the North. Even though the KKK prospered in the North, in the minds of most, they became associated with the South. Even though fundamentalist of the North resisted modern theories such as evolution also, the Scopes Monkey Trial helped to convince the progressive Americans of all regions that religious conservatism was a Southern thing.

At the same time America would move toward greater participation in global competition which brought them into an imperialistic contest. In other words, they had a larger military in which Southerners participated. As a result, more and more Southerners were veterans of the United States Army, the same army they despised during the War of Southern Independence and Reconstruction. This had the result of moving more and more of our people toward an American identity. They still came up with clever sayings, such as "American by birth, Southern by the grace of God," but the reality is that dual identity is difficult to maintain. As our people became more American, they became less Southern. They became reconstructed so they were now part of the United States, only this time the nation had been reconstituted in the image of Abraham Lincoln.

This period laid the foundation for change in the relationship between black and white Southerners. The greatest impact would not come until after World War II, but we can see change in the air. The nature of those changes will be covered in greater detail in the next chapter.

All of these together served to diminish our Southern identity and thus the uniqueness of our culture. As World War II ended, many Southerners, if not most, would waive the Confederate battle flag with pride. I can remember growing up in California and even there Southern Memorial Day and the birthday of Robert E. Lee were still marked on the calendar. Those changes mentioned in this chapter were only the beginning. The greatest blows to our culture would come after World War II, and that will be the subject of the next chapter. I would say that in 1945, most in the South thought of themselves as Southern. By the year 2000 the majority would be willing to sacrifice our sacred symbols of identity, and those of us who are unreconstructed would become a minority. We would even become a source of embarrassment to many of our fellow Southerners. I do not like this, but unfortunately it is true.

IX: The Real New South, Since 1970

I N THE POST–WORLD WAR II period, the South finally became the "New South." Henry Grady and his allies tried to establish a new South in the last part of the nineteenth century, and there are some who still look at that time as the New South. When it appears as a chapter title in textbooks the authors are covering the time of Grady. I disagree with calling the late nineteenth century the New South for two main reasons.

First, the assumption is one in which the South is seen as resisting modernization until after they lose their bid for independence. It is then that Southerners realize that the North was right and so they too want to accept progress. As discussed in earlier chapters, I see the South as having been part of modernization prior to the War, it is just that they did not progress as rapidly as the North.

The second reason I do not consider the traditional New South as the real New South is that I believe that prior to 1945 the majority of the population were proud to be Southern. They resisted being totally absorbed into the American identity. I am talking about what the *Librevs* call the "Lost Cause myth." Even though I disagree with them on their basic idea, I agree with them that most Southerners did cling to their uniqueness during this time period, and that is part of what they meant when they spoke of the Lost Cause. After World War II this began to change, and by 1970 the old South was all but dead. The South turned into the "Sun Belt."

REASONS FOR THE CHANGE

While the Southern economy was growing the North turned into the "Rust Belt." In many ways, if not most, the South turned into the most prosperous region in the United States by the beginning of the twenty-first century. The West grew also, but the Northeast declined. In the process, and no doubt partly because of this first change, the South became the true New South. There are many, and perhaps even most, in the South who are proud of their Confederate past, but the reality is that most of them have stood by while Confederate flags, statues, monuments, mascots, place names, and even more subtle symbols of the Old South have been removed. The process was gradual as the South changed from a conquered people who did not celebrate July 4 into that part of the United States which is the most patriotic. One can still be proud of their region, state, or city and be a patriotic American; however, the key to what I am trying to express is that the people in the South changed from being Southern first to being American first. This is why they have allowed the symbols of the Old South to be destroyed. I regret that in another generation The South that I have known will be all but dead. Many became convinced that it was for the good of the United States. There are three main reasons that this change came about.

The first reason is the influence of massive migration, first out of the South and then into it. This has probably been the greatest agent of change. It began with the Southern Diaspora, when millions of Southerners left their ancestral homes. This began before World War II. In the previous chapter I spoke of the Okies going to California, and of the great migration when millions of Southern blacks moved into Northern cities after World War I. This is part of the greater movement called the Southern Diaspora. What most do not realize is that the greatest numbers of Southerners, both black and white, left during World War II and shortly after. After 1970, the trend reversed so that more people entered the South than exited it. Many of the immigrants into the South were those who left and then returned, or the children of those who left and returned to the land of their ancestors. However, it also included millions of people moving into the region who had no past familial ties, some descended from old Yankee stock. Some descended from the new Americans whose ancestors had come from Southern and Eastern Europe in the late nineteenth and early twentieth century. Some are part of the tide of immigrants who have entered the United States since the 1965 reversal of the National Origins Quota Act. The end result of all of this migration and immigration is that America became more Southern and the South became more American.

The second reason is something which I think most of us would agree is a good thing. The South changed dramatically as far as racial relations. Though the whites resisted desegregation, it became a reality. Some have argued that the most important aspect was the Voting Rights Act of 1965, which gave blacks the political clout which was needed to end the discrimination which had held them down for so long. I feel that the most important thing is that white Southerners changed socially and accepted the reality of the situation. If this had not come about, the region would still be a political battleground where the two segments of Southern society fight over every inch of ground, the way they did at the beginning of the civil rights movement. If they had not accepted these changes the region would probably not have achieved the financial growth it has attained. A sad footnote is that blacks and whites in Antebellum times had better relations than after the war. Yankee carpetbaggers, Reconstruction, and corruption drove a wedge between the races in the South to help sustain the Republican Party, which was a minority party before and after the war.

The third reason is the fact that white Southerners shifted toward the Republican Party. It began because of the civil rights movement, but there is more to it than that now. The black Southerners had already changed their allegiance from the Republican Party to the Democrat Party during the Roosevelt years, which I discussed in the previous chapter. In this chapter, I will cover the details of change as white Southerners abandoned their loyalty to the Democrat Party. During Reconstruction, white Southerners were solid Democrat and black Southerners were Republican. Today a large number, if not most, white Southerners vote Republican, at least in presidential elections, and the vast majority of black Southerners are Democrats.

THE SOUTHERN DIASPORA AND CHANGE

I began discussion of this phenomena in the last chapter and will continue the topic in this chapter. James N. Gregory wrote a book called *The Southern Diaspora*. I am trying to avoid simply presenting a synopsis of his book. I am more interested in the causes of this change and the social effects upon the South, whereas Gregory was more interested in the ways in which this migration changed the rest of the country or, in other words, ways in which America became more Southern.

As I stated in the last chapter, the basic economic force that caused the exodus from the South was the change from a primarily agricultural economy to nonagricultural. This does not mean a decrease in agriculture but rather in the percentage of the population which is economically tied to that industry. The South, like the rest of the United States, is still a major producer of agricultural products; however, a much smaller number of people is needed to produce those goods. The sad thing is that the transition from an economy made up of predominantly agricultural workers to one where less that 6 percent of the population makes their living that way is a very painful process. The change resulted in much suffering and even death. Many reached the point of literally starving to death because they failed to find an alternative source of income. The free-market economy can be quite ruthless as markets shift in supply and demand, especially when we are talking about the supply and demand variables of the labor market. Those who had depended on agriculture for their livelihood have been tossed about as they looked for some new way to make a living. No doubt the greatest problem for most of them is that they needed little education to be a farmer, whereas the technology of industrialization demanded people with more formal education.

This painful transition began before World War II, but it continued after the war. As of 1940, there were still 15.6 million Southerners, more than 40 percent of the population, who farmed. By 1980, the number dropped 1.6 million which was much closer to the national average with only 6 percent or less working in that industry. Technology produced the machines that replaced the people, but the cost of these machines made it difficult for the small farmer to compete.

The number of farms declined from 2.9 million to 949,000. This change affected black and white Southerners alike, though the whites did have a little more money than the black ones, which made it a little easier for them to make the needed move in the search for new jobs.

The difficulty and pain of this kind of change comes from the lag in income as the displaced workers move into another job. Many turned to the big cities of the North in their search for work, and thus, we have the Southern Diaspora. Roosevelt was aware of the fact that the South was even more economically strapped, and even though the entire nation was in a depression, he saw to it that more military bases and defense plants were put in the South. This may have slowed the mass exodus, but more jobs were available in the port cities on either coast or in the manufacturing centers to the North so that displaced Southern farm workers continued to move out in search of work.

Other industries developed in the South, but it would be a while before the new industries could provide enough jobs for the displaced agricultural workers, thus making it unnecessary to leave the region to find work. This trend continued for almost a generation after World War II ended. Gradually, the North would begin an economic decline that would end with the once-booming industrial center of the nation being called the Rust Belt, while the South continued to become more diverse. By the 1970s, the situation reversed itself so that more people migrated into the South for the same economic reasons they had left in the first place—to make a living and support their families.

There are two other changes in the South that contributed to the increased migration into the region. First, air conditioning which I will show to have a social as well as an economic impact. Second, the calming of the racial storm which I mentioned above. This left the land a much better place to live than it had been before the changes. Even though they fought integration, in the end this was as great a change for whites as it was for blacks since the end of apartheid helped to open the way for an improved economy. Before World War II, the South lagged behind the rest of the nation. In recent times the economy is as good or better than the nation as a whole. There are still a number of Southern states that are below the national average, but to counter this, the cost of living is also lower, so that the overall lifestyle is better than in some parts of the country where people make a lot more money.

THE MAGIC OF AIR-CONDITIONING

One of the most overlooked technological innovations has been air-conditioning. History books have dedicated many pages to discussions of canals, railroads, the steel-tipped plow, and the telegraph, but they rarely mention the economic impact of air-conditioning. We all know that the North has more cold and snow. This is why the snowbirds head South in the wintertime. It has always been colder in the North; so why is it only in recent decades that so many have moved to the South?

Miami started becoming a refugee camp for escaping Yankees in the early twentieth century, but what we have now is more people who are actually moving to the South and calling it home. More importantly, they are not just the retired but younger people with families. We Southerners have grown accustomed to the heat and humidity, but many of those from the North hate and detest the long, hot, Southern summer heat, more than the snow and cold they are accustomed to. Air-conditioning has changed all of this. They can now stay in their cool houses or public buildings when the heat is unbearable just like they used to stay indoors when the Northern cold became unbearable.

There are some historians who have explored the ways that air-conditioning has changed the South. The homes do not need the architectural features, such as big porches, large eves, or the large windows designed to maximize ventilation. It also means that Southerners do not live on their front porches during the long hot summers like they used to. This has taken a toll on the feeling of community which our ancestors experienced. Rascal Flatts explored this sense of community in their song Mayberry, paying tribute to those small towns like the fictional home of Sheriff Andy. All of this is fascinating to think about, but I am more interested in the ways this change has affected the Southern identity.

This innovation has brought foreigners into our region in such large numbers that much of the South is less Southern because many of the people who live there today have no Southern roots. They came from up North or from lands where people are even more foreign than the Yankees. When journalists poll a city to see what they think about the removal of a Confederate flag, or monuments to Confederate heroes, many of those who live in the South now have no opinion. Some may even have the same negative attitude as their friends and neighbors up North. They live in the Sun Belt, not the South. Many think that concerns about such things are quaint at best, while others may still possess a hatred for what they call the slavocracy of the past. They consider the South as a place where the people are uneducated, provincial, backwards, racist, and generally culturally and intellectually inferior to the people of the North land. They hang around with fellow Yankees or those modern Scallywags who agree that the traditional ways of the Old South do not belong in our New South.

I have been making the point all along that the main reasons for the massive migration, first out of the South and then later into the South, have been economic, and so now I wish to discuss some of the other ways in which air-conditioning has impacted the Southern economy. There have always been those who have argued that warm climates have produced civilizations which are much less productive. Back in 1915, geographer Ellsworth Huntington argued that the tropics had a "dull, unprogressive population." One of his followers argued that cities like Washington, New York, and Los Angeles were doomed. No telling what they would have to say about Atlanta, Miami, or Houston.

There were some technical difficulties with the non-air-conditioned South. Before the controlled climate, cotton threads broke; cigarette machines jammed; bread grew mold; film attracted dust; pasta lost its shape; and chocolate turned gray with the fluctuation of temperature and humidity. In the late twentieth century, controlled climate became even more important as we dealt with products, such as computer chips, CDs, or the high-tech manufacturing of modern medicine.

The bottom line is that air-conditioning, whose development parallels the period I am discussing in this chapter, has contributed to changing the economy which has helped to bring in new carpetbaggers, which has helped in the decline in Southern distinctiveness. Air-conditioning was invented prior to World War II, but it was not until after the war that it became accessible to the common man. No doubt it was a major variable in creating the New South.

OUR BIGGEST BLACK EYE

The frequent display of the Confederate battle flag as a symbol to the resistance to desegregation is probably the biggest barrier we have in the preservation of that flag and other symbols of our heritage. There are those who speak of slavery and the general mistreatment of black Southerners, but the images from the civil rights movement are not merely history. For many living today, it is part of our personal recollections. On television, in newspapers, and magazines, we saw the peaceful protesters taunted by angry faces waving Confederate flags. I will make no attempt to write a history of the civil rights movement since that is a subject which many before me have covered. A thorough coverage of the topic cannot be done with less than a book. I am simply addressing the ways in which this has contributed to the loss of the old Southern culture. Like in the chapter on the War, I will discuss the topic to the extent necessary to make sure we are on the same page and to address ways in which this change has contributed to the decline of our Southern identity.

BLACK SOUTHERNERS AND THE NEW SOUTH

The most important thing for white Southerners is to understand and accept that black Southerners look at our land in a different way than we do. This, of course, is a major part of the controversy I am dealing with. John Shelton Read and his friends at the University of North Carolina in Chapel Hill have done numerous surveys in which it is clear that despite these differences that the majority of blacks do have a strong Southern identity. This is true even after the great migration. What we need to understand is that their Southern identity is not associated with Miss Scarlet, the Confederate flag, or the grand Greek revival antebellum mansions. They do share with us memories of good food, good music, and a kind of social grace that most of the time extends beyond color lines. They may have gone to churches where most of the congregation was black, but they sang many of the same songs; prayed to the same Lord; and most believed that we were all brothers in Christ. Black or white, I firmly believe that most know and understand that we have many things in common, which makes us all Southern.

The number one thing we white Southerners need to accept is that the blacks were either slaves or second-class citizens through most of our history and that we cannot expect them to accept that with any more glee than we would. At this point, I hope I have made it clear that blacks did not find any more equality in the North than they did in the South, but nonetheless, we must be careful to avoid denial of the fact that they have much to be unhappy about in their Southern past. This is the key to why many object to what we consider to be symbols of our heritage. I believe that a large number, if not a majority, of blacks understand that today the Confederate flag, clearly the most contentious symbol, merely represents our heritage. Our goal should be to convince the rest that this is true. The reality is that this symbol has been used in negative ways in the not-too-distant past, and that is why there are still some who see it that way today. However, though *Librevs* fail to point it out, the United States flag has been misused just as much as the Confederate flag. We should follow the example of Martin Luther King, Jr., and have patience and faith that the truth shall set us free. When King first started, he was greeted with jail and violence. He even lost his life as a victim of that violence. Yet he was not a destroyer of Confederate heritage. In the end, after a relatively brief era, white Southerners realized that he was right, and they were wrong. I have hope that the blacks and those whites possessed with white guilt will realize that they are wrong to deny us our heritage.

The Supreme Court decision of Brown v. Topeka Board of Education, Rosa Parks and Central High in Little Rock sparked a savage era in the South in which many whites reacted with anger, frustration, and even hatred. After all of the rock throwing, church bombings, cross burnings, and other such acts of terrorism, who would have believed that within a generation, most white Southerners would not only accept defeat but also even feel an element of shame and regret at our behavior during these tumultuous days. Many blacks have graciously accepted our apologies, but we must realize that there are some scars.

We are far from being one big happy family. On one hand, today there are blacks who feel they have not yet achieved true equality. The fact is that the black population still has an average income below that of the whites; they are still lacking in housing, education, and in many careers they are still underrepresented. On the other hand, there are whites who have complaints with the way things are now. Some are victims of reverse discrimination as jobs, scholarships and benefits are awarded to people because of the color of their skin. They cannot understand the double standard which says it is okay to have a black Miss America contest and not a white Miss America contest, or that it is OK to have black pride but not white pride. It is clear that the issue of race has not gone away. However, things are much different today than they were at the end of World War II. Just as it was before the world war, these problems are an American problem, not just Southern problems.

One way in which blacks have achieved equality is that they have political leaders who profit from the race card. George Wallace claimed that he tried to campaign on other issues, but it is the segregation issue which the public wanted to hear about, and so that is the one which propelled his political career. I have little doubt that black leaders today are using the Confederate flag as a battleground for their personal political advancement in much the same way that George Wallace used segregation. I, for one, hope that black leaders today will demonstrate the same courage Wallace did when he stood before the public and admitted that he was wrong and that those who struggled for civil rights were right. The preservation of our Southern white heritage is also a civil right.

There are two main variables which have helped to make the South of today much different than it was in 1945 when it comes to race relations. No doubt the greatest advance was the Voting Rights Act of 1965 in which blacks achieved equality at the ballot box. The second was capitalism. The businessmen of the South finally understood that the money of black people could buy just as much as the money of white people. They also realized that a South in which race riots, segregation, and racial discord ruled would be a land with a large handicap when it comes to competition in the world market. By the 1970s, as whites began to return to the South, black Southerners joined them.

THE RETURN TO THE SOUTH

Between 1940 and 1970, while so many people fled the South to find work, others stayed and tried to restructure the economy. It began before World War II, but it would take a generation before the migration into the South exceeded migration out of the South. After 1940, the number of nonagricultural jobs in the South more than tripled, from about 7.8 million to 25.9 million in the 1980s. This of course means urban growth, which is evident across the region. Dallas/ Fort Worth went from 473,000 in 1940 to 2.4 million in 1970 to over 4 million in 1990. Atlanta went from 302,000 to 2 million to almost 3 million in the same years. Nashville went from 167,000 to 700,000 to almost a million by 1990. Several cities across the region experienced the same basic growth pattern.

This growth in nonagricultural industries is also reflected in the development of education that would be needed as the people went from being farmers to professional and skilled workers. In the 1930s, only seven universities had departments that offered doctoral degrees and only forty-two such departments of the 661 that existed throughout the United States. Likewise, primary and secondary education lagged behind the nation. They began to catch up by the 1970s. The new workers in the South would need more education and so they became more like the North in this respect.

As of 1990, there has been a trend to divide the South into what is called the inner South, middle South, and outer South. Those in the inner South remain substantially below the national average income. Most are about 70–80 percent of the national average. This includes Arkansas, Mississippi, Alabama, Tennessee, and Kentucky. Out of this group, Tennessee is the only one that exceeds 80 percent of the national average at 85 percent, mainly because of Nashville. The middle South is North and South Carolina, Georgia, and Louisiana. The latter is the only one below 80 percent of the national average. The outer South includes Virginia (the Chesapeake area), Florida, Texas, and Oklahoma. The first two are actually above the national average, and the latter two are in the 80 percent category. However, the low cost of living goes far in offsetting the lower income.

Above, I spoke of the decline in agricultural jobs which caused the great exodus from the South in the first place; by 1990 the South exceeded the North in many nonagricultural jobs. In 1963, the East North Central region (primarily Michigan and Illinois) produced 30 percent of the nation's manufacturing while the much more numerous states of the South produced only 21 percent. By 1990, the South had grown to 29 percent while the East North Central states declined to 15 percent. Since 1990, there are indications that the South even began to exceed the West, which has also prospered since World War II. Their wages are still higher but so is their cost of living, mainly housing. As a result, many of those in California would join the parade back to the land of their ancestors.

BLACKS AND OTHER MINORITIES ALSO RETURN

It is difficult evaluate the role that racism played in the black portion of the Southern Diaspora, and that remains true when evaluating the reversal of that exodus too. The *Librevs* love to talk about race and assume that all the suffering the South went through during the war and the century after was deserved. They assume that the South is much more racist than the rest of America, and therefore they believe that Jim Crow and the large number of lynchings in the early twentieth century was a major factor in what they call the Great Migration. As mentioned in the last chapter, I fail to see that race problems were any worse after World War I than before. I pointed out that a large number of blacks did flee north, but so did a large number of whites as well as Hispanics and Indians. It is a fact that the migration back to the South includes blacks as well as the other minority groups. What makes the whole thing difficult to evaluate when trying to determine the role that racism played is the fact that as the economy got better in the South, so did race relations. It is very difficult to determine how much of the migration patterns resulted from racial issues. I may not be able to prove that the major variable in both the exodus and the return was economic, but I do not see that the *Librevs* have proven otherwise.

I have not found any statistics on Hispanic or Indian movements since 1970, but by personal experience, I am aware that at least some have. I know people of Mexican background, who went to school with me in California, and have returned to Texas in recent years. I also remember when I met Wilma Mankiller, the first woman principal chief of the Cherokee Nation, that she had something in common with me other that our Cherokee ancestry. She is about my age and her family moved to California about the same time as mine; and she returned to Oklahoma about the same time as I. I know that this proves nothing, but I do feel it is more than coincidence. I will never forget something she said in our meeting. "San Francisco is a beautiful place"—the same area where I spent most of my California years—"but it was never home," she added. That expresses my feelings on the subject too.

The events that happen in history such as the migration out of and then back into the South are facts. The reason for such historical events is the material of discussion and debate for historians. We are left with what is called anecdotal evidence, such as the personal recollections I mentioned in the preceding paragraph. For more recent events, we do have access to the results of various polls which lend support to one position or another. However, it cannot really be considered "proof." There is still a bottom line result that blacks make up a smaller percentage of the Southern population than they did before. In 1940, only 23 percent of blacks lived outside the South, but by 1970, that figure rose to 47 percent. However, there is another variable which has entered the picture; there are now a lot of blacks living in the United States who have immigrated from other countries, mainly Africa or the Caribbean.

Nonetheless, the numbers of those returning to the South has increased. Do not forget, as in the case with white Southerners, there were always a certain number who returned even when the Southern economy was bad. Louis Armstrong was not the only one who felt that way when he sang his song about returning to the sunny South. In the 1930s, approximately one black returned to the South for every five who left. Since 1955, each five-year period saw one hundred thousand black Northerners returning to the land of their ancestors. Please note that this was during the heyday of the violence of the civil rights movement. By 1970, more were returning to rather than leaving the South. About two-thirds of those who moved between 1965 and 1970 were going back to the land of their birth, and from 1975 to 1980, 41 percent were return migrants.

There are other reasons for the why than simply economics; however, the economic improvement made other reasons more viable. One survey in 1973 listed kinship as the major reason for returning. The main one of these familial reasons was to care for an aging parent. Only 20 percent of these respondents gave economic reasons for their return though this was only the beginning of the economic reversal. Other reasons included nonfamily social issues, health, or climate. They may not have cited economic reasons as the main reason they returned, but if the economy had not improved, it may not have been possible for them to return. The crime that encouraged many white people to flee the Northern cities also influenced blacks. In 1971, Earnest Smith told one interviewer, "For the first twenty years, life in Chicago was real nice. But the last five years was when I come to gettin' scared. They killed King and the people started tearin' up the place. Crime got so bad that I got scared and started carryin' a gun."

There is also evidence that the blacks felt a bond to the land of their ancestors, just like whites. In 1971, Atlanta businessman Jesse B. Blayton explained the reason for his return. "Grandma is here . . . Most American blacks have roots in the South. The liberation thinking is here. Blacks are more together. With the doors opening wider, this area is the Mecca." Actor Morgan Freeman said it best. He was born in Tennessee and grew up in Mississippi before living North and then west. "This is our home. This is where my roots are. . . We built the South, and we know it. What I own in the South isn't because I went and bought it. What I own is my place here because my mother, my father, my grandmother, my grandfather, my great-grandmother . . . all the way back to my great-great-great-grandmother, who happened to be a Virginian—that's where they had the farms."

We must remember that this is their land too and that they have a say in what it is all about. Just as King convinced white Southerners that they should have a better life in the land that we share, we must convince blacks that we have pride in our heritage too. They have black history month; they must realize how important the sense of history is to a culture. I have a dream that someday black and white Southerners will be able to hold hands and respect the role that each has played in making the South the land that we all love. We have put black Southerners in the history books and respect the role they have played, and this is as it should be. Even blacks who supported the Confederacy are receiving their due honour. Now, we must convince black Southerners that we are proud of our ancestors too, even though times have changed for all, both black and white.

THE EVANGELICAL AND FUNDAMENTALIST RIGHT

Some discussion of the Christian Right is necessary since this is a part of the changes in the post–World War II South. I begin by making a distinction between evangelical and fundamentalist, then I will discuss the background of each. This will be followed by the Republican Southern strategy and then the discussion of the status of each today. Then and only then will I be prepared to discuss their role in the demise of our Southern heritage. As in the case of civil rights, I am not writing about the history of religion, and so I will discuss these topics only to the extent necessary to evaluate what I am interested in—the preservation of our Southern heritage.

I have often considered these two terms, fundamentalist and evangelical, to be synonymous, but there is a distinction. They are similar in that they are more conservative than many Christian denominations. By this, I mean that they tend to live by a theology in which the Bible is taken more in the literal sense than some other denominations. The best example is their view on evolution. There are Christians who have been able to retain their beliefs without having any difficulty accepting the theories of evolution since they see the Bible as a book of allegory. For some it does not really matter how many days it took God to create the heavens and the Earth, what matters most is the teachings of how to live and how to express their faith. Those who accept the literal interpretation of the good book cannot accept the notion that it took millions of years for life to evolve when Genesis says it took only six days for God to create the planet and all of the life on it. In addition, all the begats reveal that the age of the Earth as being measured in thousands of years, not billions of years as the theory of evolution states. Most important, it was God that created all life forms, human and animal, and that they did not simply pop up out of the mud and ooze of a primeval world.

The main distinction between evangelical and fundamentalist, as I understand it, is that the former has a tradition of political activity, and the later has been isolationist until recently. Fundamentalism is a form of Evangelical Protestantism and is thus, by definition, a minority representing about 15 percent of the Evangelicals. They appeared in the first decade of the twentieth century and started among the conservative Presbyterian academics and theologians at Princeton Theological Seminary, which is in the North, not the South. Generally speaking, the fundamentalists are more adamant in their literal interpretation of the Bible. Some will have a difficult time accepting the fact that this genre of Christianity is relatively new in the South. The stereotype that most Americans have, Northern as well as Southern, is that the South is the Bible Belt, and that is because it is and always has been the center of conservative Christianity. The fact is that at the time of the Scopes Monkey Trial, fundamentalism was a minority view in the South with less than 15 percent of total Evangelicals.

Fundamentalism was in its early stages from 1920 to 1960. The Churches of Christ was one of the first of the genre to appear in the South and has been around since shortly after the Civil War. It, in fact, was fundamentalist before the movement began. The Bob Jones tradition was the next major Southern fundamentalist which goes back to the 1920s. By the 1950s, their numbers in the South increased slightly. Prior to 1970, they remained separate from mainstream America. Except for a brief concern at the possible election of a Catholic president in 1960, they left politics to the world of Caesar. The change that I am most concerned about here began in the 1970s as fundamentalism spread to the Baptists, Presbyterians, and other larger denominations. They lack the isolationism of traditional Fundamentalism and have become politically active, which has fit in well with the Southern strategy of the Republican Party. It is hard to determine who influenced who.

The confusion that many of us have in making a distinction between fundamentalist and evangelicals is in part because of their political participation. The likes of Jerry Falwell, Tim LaHaye, and Pat Robertson have been labeled neo-fundamentalists as they abandoned the tradition of being isolationist. In the 1920s, H. L. Mencken and other modernist looked at the conservative Christians as being divisive, intolerant, anti-intellectual, and downright ignorant and foolish. When Clarence Darrow put William Jennings Bryan on the stand, the liberal press broadcast the event and made it clear to their public that Bryan looked foolish. For these reasons, those who in fact were fundamentalist began to refer to themselves as Evangelical in an attempt to avoid the label put on them by the liberal media and accepted by much of the American public.

THE REPUBLICAN SOUTHERN STRATEGY AND THE CHRISTIAN RIGHT

The seeds of the Southern strategy go back to the election of 1928. With the growth of Jim Crow, the influence of black Republicans declined. They simply could not vote. This left a void that the Republicans could fill with white Southerners. In the election of 1928, the Democrats ran a Catholic candidate, Al Smith, which enabled Herbert Hoover to win five of the former Confederate states which had been solid Democrat since Reconstruction. The Republican progress reversed itself with the Depression and the rise of Roosevelt. The elections of 1932 to 1944 were the only time in American history where all Southerners, black and white, voted for the same man. To this day, most of the Southern white conservative Christians who remain loyal to the Democrat Party are the elderly who remember the Roosevelt years. It is really remarkable when you realize that Roosevelt's Agricultural Adjustment Act put more of them out of their homes than the dust bowl, but regardless, many Southerners loved FDR.

The seeds of discontent for Southern Democrats actually began during the Roosevelt years as the Democrat Party became the party of civil rights. Franklin and Eleanor helped to lay the foundation for the changes that would come after the war with their rejection of the view that blacks were racially inferior. Americans were not much different from Germans in their belief in Aryan superiority. The National Origins Quota Act was designed to put an end to the growth of the non-Aryan population. The American army which invaded Nazi Germany was segregated. The Army Air Corps did not believe blacks to be smart enough to fly airplanes, and that was the historical significance of the Tuskegee Airmen. It may be that Hitler did most to change this way of thinking when he went to the next logical step of exterminating the inferior people. I am in agreement with the *Librevs* who think that this may have been a major reason that many Americans began to question their racial views. For whatever reason, after World War II, much of the western world began to reject their beliefs of racial superiority. The United States was among the last of the industrialized nations to make the change, and when change did come much had to do with peer pressure from the other more progressive western nations.

By the election of 1948, the Democrats had become so much a Party of racial equality that many of the more conservative Southern population formed the Dixiecrats. They were not prepared to follow the alternative party of Abraham Lincoln and Reconstruction, and besides, the Republicans did not have an anti–civil rights platform. Eisenhower, for example, was neither racist nor segregationist, he simply did not believe it to be the government's job to legislate morality. The Southern voters wanted someone who would stop any notion of racial equality. Most in the South did not like the growth of the federal government under FDR and the destruction of farm life. The Dixiecrats worked about as well as most other attempts at a third party, and so Southern conservative voters muddled through the fifties and for the most part remained Democrats. In 1960, they had to choose between the Democrats with another Catholic candidate or go with the party of Lincoln. Fifteen electoral votes went for Harry Byrd—Mississippi, six of Alabama's votes, and one electoral vote from Oklahoma. The rest of Oklahoma, Tennessee, Kentucky, Florida, and Virginia went Republican, but the remaining Southern states stayed with the Democrat Party.

The sixties offered too much controversy for the conservative Southern voters. By the end of the decade, segregation had all but ended. Hippies were smoking dope; war protestors were leading the way to defeat in Vietnam, and even gays were seeking acceptance as being simply an alternative lifestyle. The Republicans would not stop desegregation. In 1965, the Voting Rights Act guaranteed black voting in the South, and so the Southern population turned to other concerns. The Republicans convinced the new breed of fundamentalists that they best represented their value system. The plan worked so that with the help of the failed presidency of the Democrat from Georgia, Jimmy Carter, the South started voting Republican. The only exceptions in the election of 1980 were Carter's home state of Georgia, West Virginia, and Maryland. The born-again Christians had become known as the Christian Right, and they became major players from then into the twenty-first century.

There are many who dispute the success of the Southern Strategy by pointing out that the conversion to the Republican Party was not complete. In 1976, Oklahoma and Virginia were the only Southern states that went Republican after the development of the new Republican strategy. The South has continued to elect Democrat governors, senators, and congressmen, and a large percentage of the population remains registered Democrats. The counter to this is a reminder that the Southern Strategy was aimed at presidential elections only. Also, as the older generation dies out, younger Southerners are enrolling as Republicans at a higher rate than their parents. The trend is that more and more Southerners have become registered Republicans.

WHAT THIS MEANS TO SOUTHERN CULTURE

There are mixed signals about what this all means as it relates to the destruction of our Southern culture. That are numerous examples of the leaders of the Christian Right holding meetings at Confederate Memorials, speaking out in defense of Confederate icons that are being destroyed by political correctness, and of course many of the politically active are aware of their Confederate genealogy. It would be difficult to find examples of this political force promoting the cultural genocide that has been going on for many years now. Nonetheless, I am convinced that their emergence has been a detriment to those of us who give a high priority to the preservation of our heritage and especially to those of us who still consider ourselves to be unreconstructed. The recent actions by the Southern Baptist indicates that they are willing to abandon open defense of our heritage.

I find myself in agreement with a well-written article by Sam Hill, Professor Emeritus of the University of Florida. He wrote, "Despite its reputation, the advent of Fundamentalism into the South in recent decades has brought with it significant disruptions to the traditional religious order, and has challenged the established Southern culture as no other social movement this century." He went on to say later, "What the fundamentalist-minded Baptists and Presbyterians and their third force compatriots . . . have wrought is the supplanting of being true to the South. Now being the right sort of church person and citizen comes first." They may not even be aware themselves of the impact they are having, but as Hill says, "The old tribalism of Southern life, a product of its history and its heritage, has been dissipated by the recent developments in these central and stalwart denominational organizations." They are more concerned about social issues, such as abortion, same-sex marriage, and prayer in school. As summed up by Hill, "Briefly stated, the old base on which unity and identity rested that was social-cultural-historical has given way to a new base that is ideological, theological, and ethical."

CONCLUSIONS

Most of my life has been lived in the last half of the twentieth century. The America that exists today is not the same as that into which I was born. The South is probably the most changed region in all of the nation. We should be grateful for some of the change. Although many blacks complain of the continuation of racial injustice, things are much better today than they were at the end of World War II. The poverty, disease, and ignorance which ran rampant throughout the region have been replaced with prosperity, improved health, and thriving institutions of learning. It would be foolish to deny that these changes have marked an improvement for most of the population, black and white.

What I do resent about the America of today is the loss of our Southern culture and identity. The tragedy of the War and Reconstruction served to strengthen our resolve, so much so that the *Librevs* claim that this was actually the birth of our regional identity. They call the "Lost Cause myth." In many ways I can understand and even agree with much of what they are talking about. After the War and Reconstruction we had an identity as a region called the South in much the same ways that the various colonies which existed in 1775 developed a national identity by the end of the Revolution. The century of poverty and hard times after the war ended up driving many of our people from their homes and into the cities of the North and West, but they took our Southern culture with them. Rather than having a negative impact, they spread Southern culture throughout the land with the introduction of Southern music, some of our fine though unhealthy cuisine, and our folksy ways. During this period we did see an eroding of our regional identity.

There are a number of variables which have taken its toll on our heritage. With the growth of business combined with the invasion of foreigners into our land, from the North and other countries, merchants have been willing to sacrifice our heritage for their profits. The Christian Right has given priority to their social conservatism and are more interested in preventing gays from getting married, and from unwed mothers having abortions, and in reforming the education system that teaches evolution and at the same time bars religion. Those who have embraced racial equality are willing to submit to the forces of political correctness in denying the heritage of American racism by scapegoating the sins of our American past to the symbols of the Confederacy and claiming that America has always been a land of equality and freedom. They accept the Northern myth and blame the South for those things that were bad in American history.

The greatest change which has come about in the last half of the twentieth century is the near extinction of unreconstructed Southerners. Most of our people drive around with "United We Stand" bumper stickers and are willing to sacrifice our heritage for the good of the United States. As I have said before, you cannot serve two masters. It may work in the short term, but in the long term, it will fail. The crises comes when one master gives orders contrary to the other master. That time has come with our Southern heritage. The United States allowed us to keep our identity back in 1877, as long as we were willing to accept our military defeat. Now, more than a century later, they are telling us that we must give up the only thing we had left after they conquered us—our Southern identity. The *Librevs* do their part by claiming that our identity was never real in the first place, that it only came about in the years after the War. But *Librevs* have a distorted view of history. They give fuel to the fires consuming our culture by trashing our respected leaders and endorsing the idea that the war was a necessary evil in order to abolish slavery. Now they say that we should be willing to hide our Confederate heritage for the sake of racial harmony. At first the Southern businessmen, and now the Christian Right comply. I am sure that most would object to being called scalawag, but that is what they are. They are reconstructed. If we are to be united Americans, we must leave our Confederate past in the dust. This I am not willing to do, and this is why I call myself unreconstructed.

X: Conclusions

I AM AN UNRECONSTRUCTED SOUTHERNER. I define this as someone who is Southern first and American second. I do not accept what the United States has wanted us to accept since 1865, that they were right to invade our land; destroy our farms; burn our cities; rape our women; and kill our people because in doing so they saved the 'union' and freed the slaves. The reasons for secession are debatable, though the act itself is not; however, not the reasons for the war. It is a fact that the North did not invade our land to free the slaves. At the time of the invasion, Abraham Lincoln and his friends said they did not threaten the institution of slavery, and we know that neither Yankees nor politicians lie. If I accepted the distorted and convoluted arguments made today to show that the war was fought to free the slaves, even though the leaders said it wasn't when they started, then I am even more outraged. This is the only country in the world, of the very large number who had slavery in the past, which found in necessary to kill hundreds of thousands, and possibly as many as a million people in order to end slavery.

I do not apologize for the fact that some of my Southern ancestors owned slaves. Things have changed in many ways over the centuries. Catholic hierarchy no longer tortures, kills, or imprisons those who resist the authority of their church. Aztecs no longer make human sacrifices to their gods. Scandinavians no longer make goblets out of human skulls. Once cannibalistic tribes no longer eat human flesh. Southerners no longer own slaves, though slavery still exists in Africa. Of all of these cultural traditions which we now consider unacceptable, why is it that only those in the Southern United States cannot be forgiven for living by a different code in the past that we live by today?

The Catholic Church is a respected institution, and crowds number in thousands when the Pope visits. The cross is not barred, and Catholics are not expected to deny their heritage. The Aztecs are acceptable as the name for a college team at California State University in San Diego. They are not barred from using an Aztec warrior as their mascot, while the University of Mississippi or other such schools have been intimidated into banning their rebel soldier mascots. It is simply ignored that some people in Africa or various other countries around the world practiced eating human flesh. No one expects those in the Scandinavian countries to eliminate the symbols of their Viking ancestors just because some of their pagan customs are considered cruel and unacceptable by today's modern standards. No one objects to sports teams using Viking mascots. We discussed this in the first chapter. It is not considered proper to judge the past through the lens present values- EXCEPT when that past is Southern-Confederate. Why is it that everything Confederate and many other symbols of the Old South are targeted for removal? Is it because some of our people owned slaves? Why aren't all of the other previous slave-owning countries, including the United States, despised for their sinful past?

The way that I see it, the United States government endorses the attitude toward our Southern culture today just as they did toward our ancestors in 1865. They not only wanted us to accept defeat, but we must recognize that the United States was right for what they did. From the beginning of the war, there have been Southerners who did not agree with secession. After the surrender, some were proud to be American again and endorsed the occupation of our land by the United States. These people were called scallywags. With the Compromise of 1877, the majority of our population were allowed to maintain our Southern pride despite military defeat. The *Librevs* now call this the "Lost Cause mythology." They accept as proven that our people did not even have a separate identity until after the Compromise of 1877. As long as the United States government endorses the extermination of our culture, I cannot accept calling myself an American. I see myself as a Confederate living in occupied territory.

Today the majority of the Southern population are patriotic Americans. Many of them would resent being called scallywags, but that, in fact, is what they are. They complain about the political correctness that dooms our heritage to extinction, but they seem to be willing to make the sacrifice for the sake of a united America. I, as well as many of the unreconstructed, have a sympathy for the victims of American imperialism, as we realize that we are victims of that same imperialism. Ron and Donnie Kennedy illustrated this in their brilliant book, *Yankee Empire: Aggressive Abroad, Despotic at Home.* We have been conquered by the United States, and as is often the case, we are expected to be grateful for the fact that they have made us like them. I am not.

I am a realist and know that the Confederate States of America will never regain its independence. I think about the fact that Ireland was occupied for eight centuries when it finally won its freedom from the British Empire, and I fantasize that someday we too will be able to regain our independence. Then reality hits and I accept that there are some major differences between our situation and that of Ireland. The most critical is that we have finally achieved some prosperity. With that prosperity came a great number of new Southerners who have immigrated into our nation. Some come from India, some from Latin America, and some from New York. In cities like Atlanta, Miami, and Houston, the majority of the population are foreigners. They have no desire to be independent from the United States and have little interest in the preservation of our heritage.

What motivates me to write this book is that I hope to gain some recognition for the fact that our people did exist, that at one time we did have our independence, and that we are proud of our heritage just as most others are proud of theirs. I have a hope that our fellow Southerners, the black Southerners, will realize that this is all that we ask for. I not only accept their contributions to our Southern heritage but am proud of the influences they have had in making us different from those to the North, who insist that our uniqueness is a myth. It is not a myth. I feel more of a cultural bond with many of the islands in the Caribbean in comparison to those of New England. No doubt it is because of the shared plantation background complete with the African influences. I hope that when the black Southerners see the truth in what I am saying that they will stop leading the attacks on our shared heritage.

Their politicians appear to be leading the attacks under the name of political correctness. I do not believe that this accomplishes anything in bettering the life of African-Americans, but it does much for the black politicians. They fool many of the black people into thinking that they are doing something to better their lives and celebrating their culture, when in fact, they are only destroying our heritage. There is room for their culture and Southern culture, which includes African influences. One does not need to destroy another culture so that theirs can thrive. We can all have as much cultural pride as we want without depriving others. Cultural patriotism is not a limited resource.

Liberal whites possessed with white guilt are so worried about someone being offended. They either do not recognize that we are offended by the destruction of our heritage, or else they do not care. Many of us in the South have ancestors who fought to defend their homes when they were invaded. They gave their all and lost almost everything. Their widows and orphans scrimped and saved to build monuments to their bravery. Many of us are offended when these monuments are destroyed. We are offended when we are told our heritage is not real, that it is a "myth." Many blacks say they have no problem with Southern heritage, but that they are taught to hate and take offense by their so-called 'civil rights' leaders. This echoes the Booker T. Washington quote earlier, that there are always people who seek to make a buck, or gain a vote, by keeping black people agitated.

I have tried to give my fellow unreconstructed Southerners the weapons to defend the attacks against us. The liberal, Northern-dominated, academic historians seem to be on the side of political correctness. They like to think that they are objective and that only they can write the true history of the South. I am amazed. They know that the causes for the war are still debatable. I have covered the recent historiography in my Introduction chapter. Yet there are those who display an attitude that it is proven that it was all about slavery. I am most amazed that they not only stand by while the Orwellian dismantling of history takes place, but they have become active participants.

Many of these *Librevs* are anti-imperialist, yet do not seem to recognize that the Yankee history of the war is the product of US imperialism. This is typical of the arrogance that the United States has displayed toward those that they have invaded and occupied. Their attitude has been that the Indians, the Japanese, and the Germans should be grateful for the American way of life which has been given to them upon the conquest of their nations. The *Librevs* are convinced that it is only the conquest by the United States which could have ended slavery and the ways of the Southern civilization which they despise. I don't think most realize it was a far more advanced civilization than what they or their predecessors claim it was.

I do not believe this is true. I am not grateful for having been conquered by the United States. I do not feel that they have greatly improved our civilization. That is why I am unreconstructed. If an apology is owed to anyone for the past, then it is the United States who owes an apology to the people of the South. After hundreds of years, the United States government finally accepted that the conquered Indians had the right to preserve their tribal heritages. All that I ask for is the same respect for the South. Many cultures throughout the world honor and respect their ancestors. This is the foundation upon which cultures are built. Many of those who attack us today love diversity. I too love the diversity of cultures that abounds on our planet. This is why I have traveled and visited many nations on every inhabited continent. I love my Southern culture, too. I do not want to see it exterminated.

What I seek is the same goal that the Coexist Foundation hopes to find. The Coexist Foundation was founded in 2006 in London. Its goal is improving religious relationships between people of Islamic, Jewish, and Christian faiths, but I believe that their stated objectives can be expanded. On their web page they state "Coexist was created to address the crisis of understanding that tears at the social fabric of societies around the world. Globalization has outpaced our understanding of one another, creating divisions that plague communities with prejudice, hate and violence." They went on to say "Coexist is on a mission to advance social cohesion through education and innovation." Their method can work in ways even more basic than religious differences. "Coexist works at the faultlines of conflicting cultural identities to strengthen the bond that holds a society together through a sustainable model of people working and learning together." They do not seek to destroy the foundations of conflicting cultures but are looking to build. They say that working and learning together generates social cohesion that reduces prejudice, hate and violence and prevents conflict from emerging again."[48] Please end the cultural genocide which is being committed against those of us who are proud of our Southern heritage. Cultures can coexist.

---

48 "About," Viewed June 25, 2017, https://www.coexist.org

Bibliographical Essay

The following is not intended to be a complete bibliographic essay on the subject of Southern history but rather is aimed at the defenders of Southern heritage. I am covering the more essential books that we should be familiar with; some because they will help us defend ourselves, others so that we can better understand the *Librev* mind. The basic idea that I have employed is that we should be prepared to defend our culture by defending our history, and in order to do that, we need to know the enemy. Most of these are the books generally accepted by the academic, liberal, revisionist community of professional historians. Many of these historians at least appear to take the position that the symbols of our Confederate and Southern heritage are offensive. Many could be called "anti-Southern," but should be considered on their own merit as historians. I do not mean to imply that these historians are all wrong, and that they have evil intentions toward our heritage. Remember, these books were written by professional historians. Most of their work is simply historical research. Some of the revisionism is good. For example, I value learning more about the black population which had been all but ignored in earlier American history. Like all of human knowledge, present generations build on the foundation left to them by past historians, just as those in the future will improve on our efforts. However, historians have their interpretations and this means that they can be wrong. They have their bias just as we do. My only objection is against those biases which are being used to make the claim that our Southern culture is less noble than any other. Our people are no worse than any of the others who make up the population of the United States today, whether they be American Indian, of African descent, or even those from the North. Just like in that war so many years ago, my basic strategy is one of defense. It is the other side which is the aggressor. They are conducting another War of Northern Aggression.

Southern Identity

The basic issue related to what the *Librevs* call the lost cause myth revolves around the question of Southern distinctiveness. Those of us who object most to this myth are in agreement with Grady McWhiney and his book *Cracker Culture: Celtic Ways in the Old South*. His basic assumption is called the Celtic fringe theory. The idea is that the South is predominantly a Celtic culture while the

North, especially New England, is Anglo-Saxon, and thus, the conflict between the two cultures is older than the English colonies. He has been given support by some others in journal articles: Rowland Berthloff, *Journal of Southern History* (November 1986) and Forrest McDonald and Ellen Shapiro McDonald, *William and Mary Quarterly* (April 1980). This appeals to me personally and much of my interpretation of history is based on the acceptance of this assumption. I do not agree with the full extension of his thesis which is the basis for a book he wrote with Perry D. Jamieson, *Attack and Die: Civil War Military Tactics and Southern Heritage*. I do not believe the notion that the South is more militaristic because of their Celtic heritage. Academia in general accepts the reality that McWhiney is a professional and published historian, but they almost always preface any reference to him as a "controversial" historian. *Albion's Seed: Four British Folkways in America*, by David Hackett Fischer discusses the Celtic South and Anglo-Saxon New England, but includes a total of four differing points of cultural differences in the colonial past of America. Colin Woodard expands it to eleven in his book *American Nations: A History of Eleven Rival Regional Cultures in North America*. I favor this one over the others since he discusses the differences within the South, and expands to include parts of Canada and Mexico, as well as points west which had origins in the older regions of the country.

Very important to the question of Southern identity is the colonial background. This is important to the *Librevs* and those who reject our claims that Confederate symbols represent our heritage, not hate. This is why they want to deny that the South has a heritage separate from the United States in general. As stated above, I personally accept the assumption that the South is basically a Celtic culture, but even if one cannot accept this, I see that the South has differed from the North, especially New England, from the first days of the colonies. This is the main reason colonial history is so critical. One of the more widely accepted histories on the early South is Wesley Frank Craven, *The Southern Colonies in the Seventeenth Century, 1670–1689*. Though published in 1949, it is still widely acclaimed. Some other volumes include: T. H. Breen, ed., *Shaping Southern Society*, a collection of articles; Edmond S. Morgan, *American Slavery, American Freedom: The Ordeal of Colonial Virginia*, noted more for his thesis that the land of slavery gave birth to democracy. The theory is that with slavery, there emerged a feeling of equality among the white population. Carl Bridenbaugh, *Myths and Realities: Societies of the Colonial South* deal with those myths not related to the Confederate flag controversies since it was published in 1952 before this became a topic. See also Wesley Craven, *White, Red, and Black: The Seventeenth Century Virginian*, Gloria Main, *Tobacco Colony: Life in Early Maryland, 1650–1720*, and Rhys Isaac, *The Transformation of Virginia, 1740–1790*. The emphasis on Virginia and Maryland is justified by the fact that much of the population in the western states and even the Deep South states, including the Carolinas and Georgia, migrated there from the Chesapeake colonies.

Through the years, many have assumed that the South resisted modernity while the North spread the capitalist economy and ended slavery, and this is what justifies their actions. For this reason, the topic of the Southern economy is important. Some of the more widely accepted books related to the economy will be discussed later under the New South.

Many of those who love to hate the South see it as a land where the Anglo-Saxons dominate over all non-Anglos, especially those with darker skins. The reality is that before the War, the South was more diverse than the North, especially New England. Not only was it more diverse but most of these non-Anglos, or what should be called non-Celtics, helped to defend the Confederacy. There is no denying that they quite often had lower status than the white population, but they seemed to do as well or better than their counterparts in the North. This included the Indians. Though they are older books, two that are still good were written by Annie Heloise Abel; *The American Indian as Slaveholder and Secessionist*, 1915, and *The American Indian in the Civil War, 1862–1865*, 1919. Some others on Indians include Wiley Britton, *The Civil War On the Border*; Kenneth W. Porter, *The Black Seminoles*; W. Craig Gaines, *The Confederate Cherokees*; Angie Debo, *And Still The Waters Run*. Jeffrey Burton, *Indian Territory and the United States, 1866–1906*, covers the period after the war. See also *Africans and Creeks: From the Colonial Period to the Civil War* or *Africans and Seminoles: From Removal to Emancipation* and *The Cherokee Freedmen: From Reconstruction to American Citizenship* by Daniel F. Littlefield and *Slavery and the Evolution of Cherokee Society* by Theda Perdue. A good one on Jewish Southerners is *The Jewish Confederates*, by Robert N. Rosen. Some others are Leonard Dinnerstein and Mary Palsson, eds., *"Turn to the South": Essays on Southern History*, Eli Evans, *The Provincials: A Personal History of Jews in the South*. John O'Donnell-Rosales has compiled lists of *Hispanic Confederates*. Some other sources on Hispanics in the South include Silvia Pedraza-Bailey, *Political and Economic Migrants: Cubans in Florida*; and Alejandro Portes, *Latin Journey: Cuban and Mexican Immigrants*. There are some books on French and Spanish colonies; *The Spanish Frontier in North America* by David J. Weber; *Africans in Colonial Louisiana: The Development of Afro-Creole Culture in the Eighteenth Century*, by Gwendolyn M. Hall.

SLAVERY

There are many books on slavery; I will discuss only some of the more popular. On the slave trade, there is Philip D. Curtin *Atlantic Slave Trade*, and one that I find objective is *The Slave Trade*, by Hugh Thomas, an English historian. His book is well-researched, and I like it because he is not out to find someone to blame. Ulrich Phillips wrote one of the first books on the subject of slavery in 1918, *American Negro Slavery*, but the *Librevs* have their students read it so they can see the racism that was America at the time. Winthrop Jordan sums up the *Librev* view with *White Over Black*. For generations, Southerners have been guilty of justifying slavery by claiming that the slaves were happy. For this reason, many liberals like to discuss slave resistance. Since they know there were not many slave rebellions in what became the Confederate States of America, the *Librevs* like to show other ways of resistance Some books on rebellions and resistance include: Gerald W. Mullin with *Slave Resistance in Eighteenth-Century Virginia. From Rebellion to Revolution*; *Afro-American Slave Revolts in the Making of the Modern World* by Eugene Genovese and *Gabriel's Rebellion: The Virginia Slave Conspiracies of 1800 and 1802* by Douglas R. Egerton. Stanley Elkins is considered one of the more influential of *Librevs* because of his 1959 book *Slavery: A Problem in American Institutional and Intellectual Life*. Many of the *Librevs* like to study the preservation of African culture, which I also admire. Some of the better known works are Eugene D. Genovese, *Roll, Jordan, Roll: The World They Made Together*; Herbert G. Gutman, *The Black Family in Slavery and Freedom, 1750–1925*; Lawrence W. Levine, *Black Culture and Black Consciousness: Afro-American Folk Thought from Slavery to Freedom*; George P. Rawick, *From Sundown to Sunup: The Making of the Black Community*, and John Blassingame, *The Slave Community: Plantation Life in the Antebellum South*. Paul D. Escott compiled some interesting statistics from the *Slave Narratives* in his book *Slavery Remembered: A Record of Twentieth-Century Slave Narratives*. Some books on the economic aspects of slavery include Paul A. David with *Reckoning With Slavery: A Critical Study in the Quantitative History of American Negro Slavery* and Eugene Genovese, *The Political Economy of Slavery: Studies in the Economy and Society of the Slave South*. One which attracted a lot of criticism from the *Librev* community is *Time on the Cross*, by Robert W. Fogel and Stanley L. Engerman. I highly recommend this book. These men were from the liberal Mecca of Madison, Wisconsin. However, they compiled statistics and showed how the slaves were part of the Southern economy. David, mentioned above, was one of many who attacked them, so that they found it necessary to write a sequel in which they did not change their position but emphasized how slavery was still evil. I have always liked the book by Mechal Sobel, *The World They Made Together*, which stressed the impact that each culture has had on the other.

THE WAR OF SOUTHERN INDEPENDENCE

There are more books written about the war than any other topic in American history. I will make no attempt to identify the best, or even the ones I recommend, but rather only those that are most admired by the *Librevs*. When it comes to the causes of the war, they like to defend the position that it was over slavery. They know all the things that I and others have written, and they cannot deny the many quotes from Lincoln and Union military officers in which they said they were not fighting to free the slaves. Nonetheless, they still see slavery as the cause. I wish South Carolina had not backed down in the 1830s and then we could clearly state that secession was over tariffs, not slavery. One of the approaches they use is to try to show that the movement for secession was by the planters and was not supported by the poor. The middle class who did support the war, even those who were in the majority and did not own slaves, did so because they either wanted to profit from the system in the future or they wanted to keep blacks in a subservient role. Some of the books on the war and its causes also like to push the idea that Southern identity did not exist before the antebellum era. With this in mind, the following are on the *Librev* "must read list" relating to the causes of the war and those who supported secession: Daniel Crofts, *Reluctant Confederates: Upper South Unionists in the Secession Crisis*; Eric Walther, *The Fire-Eaters*; Eric Foner, *Free Soil, Free Labor, Free Men: The Ideology of the Republican Party before the Civil War*; David Potter, *The Impending Crises* and *Lincoln and His Party in the Secession Crisis*; James M. McPherson, *Battle Cry of Freedom: The Civil War Era*; Charles Royster, *The Destructive War: William Tecumseh Sherman, Stonewall Jackson, and the Americans*; E. Merton Coulter, *Confederate States of America, 1861–1865*; Emory M. Thomas, *Confederate Nation, 1861–1865*; Shelby Foote, *The Civil War*, Drew Faust, *The Creation of Confederate Nationalism*; Paul Escott, *After Secession: Jefferson Davis and the Failure of Confederate Nationalism*, Douglas B. Ball, *Financial Failure and Confederate Defeat*, and Frank Owsley, *State Rights in the Confederacy*. James McPherson did one that they all love, *What They Fought For, 1861–1865*, which is very interesting and suggests that Southerners did not fight simply to protect slavery. Again, I only suggest these books to gain an understanding of the more popular interpretations of the events among the academic community which I have labeled the *Librevs*.

When it comes to discussion of the war one must discuss Lincoln. I mentioned many times in the book how he is consistently picked as the best president in US history by academia, especially those I have labeled *Librevs*. *Lincoln Takes Command* by John Shipley Tilley covers how Lincoln used Fort Sumter to entice the South into firing the first shot. Perhaps the best known critic of Lincoln has been Thomas DiLorenzo. His book on Lincoln was *The Real Lincoln: A New Look at Abraham Lincoln, His Agenda and an Unnecessary War*. One description of his thesis is "Lincoln was a 'white supremacist' with no principled interest in abolishing slavery, believed in a strong central government, and imposed high tariffs and a nationalized banking system. He attributes the South's secession to Lincoln's economic policies rather than a desire to preserve slavery." His book *Lincoln Unmasked: What You're Not Supposed to Know About Honest Abe* expanded on this line of thinking. Despite his academic credentials he came under heavy criticism from academia, for both his research and objectivity. Not only is he considered a Neo-Confederate, but has been accused of being associated with the League of the South, which he has denied. John McKee Barr was among those critics, and in fact wrote a book about how this kind of thinking is nothing new in his *Loathing Lincoln: An American Tradition From the Civil War to the Present*. A good book on Lincoln's view on race is *Lincoln on Race & Slavery*, which is a book of quotes from Lincoln edited by Henry Lewis Gates, Jr. A recent book which offers some optimism in my faith toward academia is *Lincoln & the Politics of Slavery: The Other Thirteenth Amendment and the Struggle to Save the Union*, by Daniel W. Crofts. This not only offers a different view of Lincoln, but also covers the attempts to preserve the Union (and Southern tariff revenue) with a Northern attempt to preserve slavery.

RECONSTRUCTION

As stated in my essay, Reconstruction is one of the most critical areas of controversy between us unreconstructed and the *Librevs*. They use the work of William Dunning who wrote *Reconstruction, Political and Economic, 1865–1877* in 1907 as the benchmark for what they now call the "lost cause myth." Though Dunning was with Columbia University, he took the position that it was the North rather than the South which was wrong in Reconstruction. They even admit that Northerners were as accepting of this interpretation as Southerners were. The first ones to dispute this view were Kenneth M. Stamp in 1965 with *Era of Reconstruction, 1865–1877*. In 1982 came James M. McPherson's *Ordeal by Fire: The Civil War and Reconstruction*. I would say the most important book representing the *Librev* view today came in 1988, Eric Foner's *Reconstruction: America's Unfinished Revolution, 1863–1877*. Perhaps the most important aspect of this book is that he looks at Reconstruction as the end of slavery and thus saw its beginning as the emancipation proclamation in 1863. Richard N. Current defended the Northerners with his *Those Terrible Carpetbaggers: A Reinterpretation*, and Thomas Holt objected to the view of the black politicians as incompetent with his book *Black Over White: Negro Political Leadership in South Carolina during Reconstruction*. George R. Rable saw the violence of the time as an attempt to keep blacks in their place in his book *But There Was No Peace: The Role of Violence in the Politics of Reconstruction*. There are many others but these are the most important to the academic elite.

THE NEW SOUTH

The New South debate began in 1951 with C. Vann Woodward's *Origins of the New South, 1877–1913*. Woodward saw the Redeemers as "new men" who rejected the agricultural South in favor of economic diversity. Since then there have been numerous books defending or disputing this view. Some of the more popular have been Numan V. Bartley in an article in the *Georgia Historical Quarterly* titled "Another New South." Also important have been Jonathan Wiener, *Social Origins of the New South: Alabama, 1860–1880*; David L. Caroton, *Mill and Town in South Carolina, 1880–1920*; Edward Ayers, *The Promise of the New South: Life After Reconstruction*; Gavin Wright, *Old South, New South: Revolutions in the Southern Economy since the Civil War*; and Paul M. Gaston, *The New South Creed: A Study in Southern Mythmaking*. Related to this topic are Blaine A. Brownell and David R. Goldfield, eds., *The City in Southern History: The Growth of Urban Civilization in the South*; David Goldfield, *Urban Growth in the Age of Sectionalism: Virginia, 1847–1861*; Lawrence H. Larsen, *The Rise of the Urban South*. From discussion of the new South we can go into Populism and other economic topics. One book that connects the topics is Roger L. Hart, *Redeemers, Bourbons, and Populists: Tennessee, 1870–1896*. A good one on populism is Steven Hahn, *The Roots of Southern Populism: Yeoman Farmers and the Transformation of the Georgia Upcountry, 1850–1890*. More specifically on Populism, though it dates back to 1931, is John D. Hicks, *The Populist Revolt: A History of the Farmer's Alliance and the People's Party*. Getting into southern economics often leads to discussion of the Depression years. Some good books here are James C. Cobb and Michael V. Namorato, eds., *The New Deal and the South*. About the new South since 1945 see Bruce J. Schulman, *From Cotton Belt to Sunbelt: Federal Policy, Economic Development and the Transformation of the South, 1938–1980*; Peter Applebome, *Dixie Rising: How the South Is Shaping American Values, Politics and Culture*; Dan T. Carter, *From George Wallace to Newt Gingrich: Race in the Conservative Counterrevolution, 1963–1994*; John Egerton, *The Americanization of Dixie*.

RACE SINCE 1865

I cannot think of anything new to say. The South was segregated; Black Southerners were second-class citizens until recent times; and I see no reason for us to feel proud about the way our ancestors treated black folks. My only objection is to the attitude that this is a Southern thing. It was not much different up North. We cannot deny the way things used to be, and there is nothing the *Librevs* can add to make it worse. This is one of the main reasons that there are those who want to wipe out our heritage. The fact that many of our kinsmen used the Confederate flag as a symbol of resistance to the civil rights movement is why that banner is most despised. The only thing I can say is we should be as knowledgeable as possible on the subject. The defense of our heritage can only be based on the conviction that this is not the whole story of our heritage, and it is not what we are about today.

Many people think of the South as having always been segregated. However, if we think about it, we would realize that under slavery, blacks and whites lived together and worked together. The Jim Crow was brought South after the war by carpetbaggers. The foundation book on this topic would have to be C. Vann Woodward's *The Strange Career of Jim Crow*, a fourth revised edition was published in 1974. John Hope Franklin would be on the same level of respect. He wrote *From Slavery to Freedom: A History of American Negroes*. Some other related volumes include John W. Cell, *The Highest Stage of White Supremacy: The Origins of Segregation in South African and the American South*; J. Morgan Kousser, *The Shaping of Southern Politics: Suffrage Restrictions and the Establishment of the One-Party South, 1880–1910*; Joel Williamson, *The Crucible of Race: Black-White Relations in the American South since Emancipation*; Leon Litwack, *Trouble in Mind: Black Southerners in the Age of Jim Crow* and Howard N. Rabinowitz, *Race Relations in the Urban South, 1865–1890*.

Some books that cover a more general approach to the story of black Southerners in the twentieth century include John Hope Franklin, *From Slavery to Freedom*; August Meir and Elliott Rudwick, *From Plantation to Ghetto*, Herbert G. Gutman, *The Black Family in Slavery and Freedom*; Lawrence W. Levine, *Black Culture and Black Consciousness*; and, Gail Williams O'Brien, *The Color of the Law: Race, Violence and Justice in the Post–World War II South*. An interesting view is offered in Willard B. Gatewood's *Aristocrats of Color: The Black Elite, 1880–1920*. Some focusing on the violence toward blacks is Scott Ellsworth, *Death in the Promised Land: Tulsa Race Riot of 1921*; W. Fitzhugh Brundage, *Lynching in the New South: Georgia and Virginia, 1880–1930*; George C. Wright, *Racial Violence in Kentucky, 1865–1940: Lynchings, Mob Rule, and "Legal Lynchings"*; and, Stephen J. Whitfield, *A Death in the Delta: The Story of Emmett Till* tells the story of a 1955 lynching that probably played a key role in the changes that came in the next two decades.

There is no definitive general survey of the civil rights revolution that came after World War II though the books on the subject are quite numerous. Some of the more important include Adam Fairclough, *To Redeem the Soul of America: The Southern Christian Leadership Conference and Martin Luther King, Jr.*; David R. Goldfield, *Black, White, and Southern: Race Relations and Southern Culture, 1940 to the Present*; Hugh Davis Graham, *The Civil Rights Era: Origins and Development of National Policy*; Aldon D. Morris, *The Origins of the Civil Rights Movement: Black Communities Organizing for Change*; and, Juan Williams, *Eyes on the Prize: America's Civil Rights Years, 1854–1965*. Of course, Martin Luther King, Jr., has become synonymous with the movement; for more on him see David J. Garrow, *Bearing the Cross* or Taylor Branch, *Parting the Waters: America in the King Years, 1954–1963*. There were whites who helped create the change and they are covered in David L. Chappell, *Inside Agitators: White Southerners in the Civil Rights Movement*, and Elizabeth Jacoway and David R. Colburn were editors of a volume that discussed *Southern Businessmen and Desegregation*. A good one that shows that the civil rights movement was an American thing not just a Southern thing is Thomas J. Sugrue, *Sweet Land of Liberty: the Forgotten Struggle for Civil Rights in the North*. There are those who question the end of racial problems, see Michael V. Namorato, ed, *Have We Overcome? Race Relations since "Brown;"* William Julius Wilson, *The Declining Significance of Race: Blacks and Changing American Institutions*; and any book from John Hope Franklin should be given great credence, see his *Race and History: Selected Essays, 1938–1988*.

THE LOST CAUSE MYTH

My conclusion is that we have convinced the professional historians that we are not racist, that the interest we have in preserving our heritage has nothing to do with a desire to bring back slavery, etc. They cannot abandon the liberal cause, and so they have taken the position that things Confederate are not really symbols of Southern heritage but rather of what they call the "lost cause myth."

The books most related to this point of view are Charles R. Wilson, *Baptized in Blood: The Religion of the Lost Cause , 1865-1920*; Gaines Foster, *Ghosts of the Confederacy: Defeat, the Lost Cause and the Emergence of the New South, 1865 to 1913*; David W. Blight, *Race and Reunion: The Civil War in American Memory*; Karen L. Cox, *Dixie's Daughters: The United Daughters of the Confederacy and the Preservation of Confederate Culture*; Gary W. Gallagher and Alan T. Nolan, *The Myth of the Lost Cause and Civil War History*; and, Grace Elizabeth Hale, *Making Whiteness: The Culture of Segregation in the South, 1890-1940*. Of course they cannot go without attacking the greatest symbol of the Old South— Robert E. Lee. The latest to do this is Elizabeth Brown Pryor, *Reading The Man: A Portrait of Robert E. Lee Through His Private Letters*. It has gotten to the point where most graduate students and academic historians speak of the "lost cause myth" as if it were a proven fact.

RELIGION AND THE SOUTH

Religion has become even more important in the liberal interpretations of the South as the new Right, especially under George W. Bush, formed an alliance with the Republican Party. An overall history of religion in America is in Sydney E. Ahlstrom, *A Religious History of the American People*. Samuel S. Hill, Jr., is a good source on religion in the South with *Encyclopedia of Religion in the South; Religion and the Solid South*; and, *The South and the North in American Religion*. The role of religion and politics is covered in John C. Green, Mark J. Rosell, and Clyde Wilcox, eds., *The Christian Right in American Politics: Marching to the Millennium* and Samuel S. Hill and Dennis E. Owen, *The New Religious Right in America*.

AFTERWORD

What would society be like if Grace and Race ran together in the same circles? As Christians, it's unfortunate that our society reverses the order of these two giants by putting Race ahead of Grace. I'm convinced as a Christian that Grace trumps race. Our culture works counter intuitive to this biblical norm. White guilt and Black blame helps to produce a counterproductive Christian society. We not only live in a time when Christian virtues no longer set the pace for forgiveness, society now dictates the normative views of the masses. We live in a time that it is intolerable for Black folks and White folks to have independent thoughts. Thoughts perhaps, but nevertheless these thoughts must never be expressed in words.

I had a friend who asked me to explain why, "Black America is mad at me for what my ancestors did one hundred and fifty years ago by enslaving 4 million Blacks when today 300,000 Black babies are being killed annually?" I told him that first of all he misunderstands the Black man. He is not mad *about* slavery, he simply *blames* slavery. Blaming is different from being mad. Being mad is a byproduct of blaming just like White guilt is a byproduct of shaming. The beauty of grace is that it frees you from both vices. It is the crowning jewel of the Christian faith. When Blacks and Whites who are in Christ come to realize the power of this Grace, there is no mountain high enough, or valley wide enough to separate the love that comes between two foes that is greater than that which is produced by the manifestation of this one truth, there is no condemnation to those who are in Him. Yet, the primitive nature of our being fight against this with all will and effort. The spirit is wiling but the flesh is weak.

Blaming is freeing to a degree for Black folks. It allows you to focus the core of all of your frustrations on one people group. This blaming is not solely the tool of Blacks only. It's used throughout society. It's the original trickster for preventing deeper resolves and consequences within the soul of a person. We saw it first with the original man, Adam when he said, "It's that women you gave me," as his response to God when he was asked what he had done?

As a young Black man coming to maturation in the South, I was challenged by Black radical friends to see all White men through the same lens. He was framed as a blue eyed devil and that's just the way it was presented. I wasn't trained to see a divide among classes of people, even different cultural norms within a people group. This view of diversity within a specific sub group of people has been extracted from his narrative. A White man is a White man is a White man and that's how Black folks have come to see White men. They can barely make a distinction between a Yankee and a Confederate much less the difference between a poor White man and a rich one. Some of the conflicts in our society today are not because of race, but rather class. If classicism is ever to be recognized for the evil it plays on society, this shift will not only be required by Blacks but poor Whites as well.

One example of an event which may be more classism than racism recently occurred when a prominent White man in Mississippi took photos of two young Black women and posted them with the message that if the town doesn't clean up, the property values would plummet. Sometimes one person can speak up or speak out and the appeal in what they say is simply what most folks similar to them are already thinking. Property value is extremely important to upper class White folks in Mississippi, as it is in most States. Often upperclass Whites and Blacks want to keep poor folks out of their neighborhoods, regardless of the color of their skin, to protect their property values. What's sad is that the Black folks can't see that it would be no different if the man had posted pictures of undesirable White folks. This incident sent shock waves through this particular community as a race issue.

There are communities in Mississippi which are constantly on eggshells hoping that nothing racial will happen to remind people that this is Mississippi. For me, the problem is not as much a case of racism than it is classism, an even deeper symptom of sin. In my opinion this was just another example of where Race was placed in front of Grace. This is an example of where I would have applied Grace to an issue of Race. Is this gentleman a racist? Although the overwhelming message of this incident was filled with racial overtones and insensitivity to Black folks. Perhaps it may have been more a class issue than race? Yet, there is a deeper problem. Blindness to one's own sins. If you allow racism and race bating to control your cerebral cortex, the answer is a resounding yes, he is a racist. But if you allow grace to permeate your mind, then you would conclude, probably not. He is a human unfortunately expressing publicly the posture of most humans, looking down upon his fellow brother or in this case, sisters. Black folks who are quick to point out the speck in the White man's eyes but the plank of an unforgiving spirit creates the sane blindness. We, as a society, are too quick to use race when what people are really displaying is something worse, the human nature of sin. Unfortunately, sin has been closed up in the church in such a way that it is sinful to even mention it as a vice. Thus, a new standard has developed. A moral standard in which forgiveness, context, history or culture has no weight. I recently heard this new moral standard defined as, "Real Human Unity." Now, think about that. In what context does that happen or where can it exist? This is a false utopia created by a modern world view of humanism that is not only out of control but one that shatters the Cross of the one who died for people to have true peace of an inner spirit regardless of outward circumstances, words or deeds, accusations or past wrongs. Once we leave that place, the Cross, we are left to fight among ourselves across the many bridges that never meet.

Black folks can be guilty of classism too. Remember Bill Cosby when he lashed out at Black kids by telling them to pull their pants up? It may be that the White man previously mentioned was attempting to protect his property values, but Cosby was attempting to straighten what he saw as a weakness in the Black community. He was applauded by Whites and many Blacks. The actions of those White men who are labeled racist are consistent with many Blacks who have achieved some measure of success in their communities. They would never admit it, but even Blacks hate. They too can be guilty of classism, and object to the appearance of Black Trash and White Trash. Perhaps the primary problem is both examples is that the men didn't realize they couldn't say what they said publicly.

The idea that issues of class being greater that race has existed throughout modern history. I had one of my White friends say to me once, "Al, do you really think some poor white cracker is going to go around running in the jungle in Africa to find slaves?" His point was that it was wealthy rich men doing this and not the average poor White man. According to the historian Hugh Thomas, the slave trade was due to the ruling classes of both Europe and Africa. He said in his book *The Slave Trade*, "If one is looking for villains in this matter, and some are, one should certainly indeed look at royal families more severely than the Jewish ones." He went on to say, "I am partly thinking of the rulers of Benin; the kings of Ashanti, Congo, and Dahomey; and the Vili rulers of Loango, who sold great numbers of slaves over many generations." Then he went on to say, ". . . but also of monarchs in Europe, such as one of my own heroes, Ferdinand the Catholic, king of Aragon."

You see the problem? Black people have a hard time turning this circle because they are so used to running in squares. They can't see that these men are talking about poor White's also. Unfortunatly the square lines are not set by Blacks. It's transformative to turn a square into a circle by which people begin to see things without a default position of judgment based solely on race. It wasn't race when Cosby said it, or was it? Yes, it was race. He said what those of his status think about all poor folks. Pull your drawers up, educate yourself and stay in your own neighborhoods. The problem with the Cosby's of the world is that they don't see the wretched trash in themselves. Their money keeps them from smelling the filth. It's only when their words or deeds come to haunt them that they realize that they too are human and not above the fray our stinking wretchedness. In the end, every man will be laid bare and exposed for what he is. Why then should I hate my brother? Why should I blame him for my own filth and why should I not forgive him, if I have been forgiven? Is the narrative of Black and White so strong that Grace is muted for such men? I think not. Every man and woman fall short. I conclude that Black blame and white guilt is a byproduct of the inability to see the application of God's Grace. Both the poor Black man and the poor White man are in the same boat waddling in the cesspool of the those who pull the strings. They get there by walking two adjacent lanes of the same road. May the Holy Spirit reveal this to you as mysterious jars of clay and may you hold these jars with the grace in which he has given himself to you.

May this lead you beyond a theoretical Christianity and into the practical application of God's Grace. There is a difference. Mahatma Gandhi thought modern day Christians were Christians only in theory. Turning the other cheek was not just an expression for him. He thought teachings of Jesus were to be literal, if indeed, one was a disciple of Christ. Yet, he did not see this practical application of Jesus' teachings and concluded that Christianity was false based upon the apparent failure of its disciples in such practices. I cannot agree that Gandhi rightly applied the application of God's supernatural power to work in the lives of His believers. However, I do agree that his observation, does say a lot about where Christianity fails to serve as true Witness to the teachings of Christ. I think Apostle Paul and Christ puts forth the same charge. A mystery of the Gospel that is not embraced. That mystery being the great privilege of loving others who are not like you. Paul stated it this way, "This mystery is this, that the age rules are, fellow heirs, members of the same body, partakers of the promise of Christ Jesus through the Gospel.

I hold this same reality for my Confederate brothers, sisters, sons and daughters. They are partakers of the same Christ Jesus through the Gospel and I have been given the high privilege to love them. This is a mystery indeed. How God did it is up to Him. It's His story and I think all of history is such that it points toward Him. To be in a posture to receive this Grace is the challenge for us in our time looking backwards to the past or forward to the future. Christ left this same hope with his believers when he prayed, "For this reason, I bow my knees before the Father, from whom every family in heaven and the earth is name. That according to the riches of his glory he may grant you to be strengthened with power through his Spirit in your inner being, so that Christ may dwell in your hearts through faith-that you, being rooted and grounded in love, may have strength to comprehend with all the saints what is the breath and length and height and depth and to know the love of Christ that surpasses knowledge, that you may be filled with all the fullness of God (Eph 3:15- 19).

When you come to embrace this, there can be no escape from the reality that every family is included in this sphere pertaining to the mystery of the Gospel and its application. That is, the love that comes from its acceptance is toward all the saints and can't be relegated to the saints that we love. This is the challenge for Blacks and Whites, Jews and Gentiles, Slaves and Free, males and females. Polar opposites are faced with having to look into the height, length, depth of Christ's love and decide if they are comprehending its power to cause them to bow before the same Father, through faith, that it causes outsiders to be shocked and even confused as to the manner of love that lives in such a way.

And so, Les Tucker is not only my fellow Confederate Compatriot, he is much more. He is a brother in faith and through the love that surpasses understanding, I have the awesome privilege to love him with all of his differences and challenges that he brings to the table of diversity. It's a beautiful diversity if you could ever stop to see it as such. This is not forced inclusiveness based upon bullying, shaming or the degradation of one's culture or heritage. It is acceptance despite their culture or heritage through the one vein that overshadows all differences and causes one to embrace a newfound reality of Grace that extends far beyond the average boundaries commonly seen as rules of acceptance.

History is one of those things that doesn't change, and few change their minds about it. Thus, history often leave many on extreme opposite ends on issues that have ongoing implications in existing times. To use history to bridge gaps is an oxymoron in itself and I suggest it invites dangers to the souls of man without the proper application of God's Grace. Grace is a much more approachable, forgiving and reconciling tool by which the love of Christ affords us much room to live, coexist, grow and discover more about ourselves, our history and His-story of redeeming mankind.

I am on this journey with Les and many others. Each relationship on this journey is a wonderful start to a life of eternal brotherhood that started before our existence. Why can't we enjoy the fruits of God's Grace? Must this bond be denied because of history or should my love for him be so that it confuses the minds of unbelievers? And what of those who hold history as their God and see it as a triumph over such Grace that is afforded us in Christ? Does this Grace not apply to all of the saints? Simply put, it does. And so, for me to fully embrace this, God gave me a special thorn. A big gray one. And this thorn I have come to treasure as one of God's greatest gifts. To humble me and to keep me near His cross and to daily remind me of His marvelous grace. Not only am I too love my southern brothers, I am one with them. Oh, how I wanted to do away with this thorn. To hide it! To pull it out and say, it's not so! But the more I nurtured this reality, the more glorious the light of this Grace comes to me as a precious jewel to remind me of the height, depth and width of His love. I invite you to consider the riches that you lose without embracing your failure to love to the fullest those whom society would say that you should hate. Think of who that is for you and ask what glory does God receive when you lay down your own prejudices and extend such a Grace to the most unlikely people welcomed in your circles? This has been the greatest blessing of this journey. A freedom to live and love in a way that is truly free!

In Him,

Al Arnold, Author

Robert E. Lee's Orderly

A Modern Black Man's Confederate Journey

ABOUT THE AUTHOR

L ESLIE R. TUCKER was born in New Mexico, raised in California, but has lived most of his life in Oklahoma. He is a very proud 5th generation Okie!

Tucker has a BA in history and MBA from Cal-State East Bay, an MA in history from the University of Central Oklahoma, and Ph. D. from Oklahoma State.

Dr. Tucker was an accountant for many years but changed professions in 1994. He subsequently worked as an adjunct professor at Oklahoma City Community College, Langston University, and the University of Central Oklahoma. Although Dr. Tucker has retired from teaching, he continues with independent research.

He is proud to have many Confederate ancestors and has been active in the Sons of Confederate Veterans (SCV) since 1985. He has served in many capacities in the SCV including camp commander, Oklahoma Division Commander, and on the General Staff under several National Commanders. Dr. Tucker's other publications include *Brigadier General John Adams, CSA: A Biography* and *Major General Isaac Trimble: Biography of a Baltimore Confederate.*

Available From Shotwell Publishing

If you enjoyed this book, perhaps some of our other titles will pique your interest. The following titles are now available for your reading pleasure... Enjoy!

Joyce Bennett

Maryland, My Maryland: The Cultural Cleansing of a Small Southern State

Jerry Brewer

Dismantling the Republic

Andrew P. Calhoun, Jr.

My Own Darling Wife: Letters From a Confederate Volunteer [John Francis Calhoun]

John Chodes

Segregation: Federal Policy or Racism?

Washington's KKK: The Union League During Southern Reconstruction

Paul C. Graham

Confederaphobia: An American Epidemic

When the Yankees Come: Former South Carolina Slaves Remember Sherman's Invasion

Joseph Jay

Sacred Conviction: The South's Stand for Biblical Authority

Suzanne Parfitt Johnson

Maxcy Gregg's Sporting Journal 1842 - 1858

James R. Kennedy

Dixie Rising: Rules for Rebels

James R. & Walter D. Kennedy

Punished with Poverty: The Suffering South

Yankee Empire: Aggressive Abroad and Despotic At Home

Philip Leigh

The Devil's Town: Hot Spring During the Gangster Era

U.S. Grant's Failed Presidency

Michael Martin

Southern Grit: Sensing the Siege at Petersburg

Lewis Liberman

Snowflake Buddies: ABCs for Leftism for Kids!

Charles T. Pace

Lincoln As He Was

Southern Independence. Why War?

James Rutledge Roesch

From Founding Fathers to Fire Eaters: The Constitutional Doctrine of States' Rights in the Old South

Kirkpatrick Sale

Emancipation Hell: The Tragedy Wrought By Lincoln's Emancipation Proclamation

Karen Stokes

A Legion of Devils: Sherman in South Carolina

Carolina Love Letters

John Vinson

Southerner, Take Your Stand!

Howard Ray White

Understanding Creation and Evolution

Walter Kirk Wood

Beyond Slavery: The Northern Romantic Nationalist Origins of America's Civil War

Clyde N. Wilson

Annals of the Stupid Party: Republicans Before Trump (The Wilson Files 3)

Lies My Teacher Told Me: The True History of the War for Southern Independence

Nullification: Reclaiming Consent of the Governed (The Wilson Files 2)

The Old South: 50 Essential Books (Southern Reader's Guide I)

The War Between the States: 60 Essential Books (Southern Reader's Guide II)

Reconstruction and the New South (1865-1913): 50 Essential Books (Southern Reader's Guide III)

The Yankee Problem: An American Dilemma (The Wilson Files 1)

———————————

GREEN ALTAR BOOKS

Green Altar Books

(Literary Imprint)

Randall Ivey

A New England Romance & Other SOUTHERN Stories

James Everett Kibler

Tiller (Clay Bank County, IV)

Thomas Moore

A Fatal Mercy

Karen Stokes

Belles: A Carolina Romance

Honor in the Dust

The Immortals

The Soldier's Ghost: A Tale of Charleston

———————————

GOLD-BUG

(Mystery & Suspense Imprint)

Michael Andrew Grissom

Billie Jo

Brandi Perry

Splintered: A New Orleans Tale

Martin L. Wilson

To Jekyll and Hide

Free Book Offer

Sign-up for new release notifications and receive a **FREE** downloadable edition of *Lies My Teacher Told Me: The True History of the War for Southern Independence* by Dr. Clyde N. Wilson by visiting FreeLiesBook.com or by texting the word "Dixie" to 345345. You can always unsubscribe and keep the book, so you've got nothing to lose!

Southern Without Apology

Made in the USA
Monee, IL
11 September 2021

77820036R00144